TRAINS:

A Journey

of Remembrances

Irena M. Szpak

Published by

 GENERAL STORE
GSPH PUBLISHING HOUSE

499 O'Brien Road, Box 415
Renfrew, Ontario, Canada K7V 4A6
Telephone (613) 432-7697 or 1-800-465-6072

ISBN 1-897113-23-4
Printed and bound in Canada

Cover design, formatting and printing by Custom Printers of Renfrew Ltd.

General Store Publishing House
Renfrew, Ontario, Canada

Library and Archives Canada Cataloguing in Publication Data

Szpak, Irena Maria, 1926-
              Trains : a journey of remembrances / Irena Maria Szpak.

ISBN 1-897113-23-4

      1. Szpak, Irena Maria, 1926-. 2. World War, 1939-1945--
      Underground movements--Poland.
      3. World War, 1939-1945--Prisoners and prisons, German.
      4. World War, 1939-1945--Personal narratives, Polish.
      5. Translators--Canada--Biography. 6. Polish Canadians--
      Biography.   I. Title.

P306.92.S96A3 2005   418'.02'092   C2005-905160-4

Introduction

When my editor asked me to supply more personal information for eventual interested readers, I was just reading *Living to Tell the Tale*, an autobiography of Gabriel Garcia Marquez. One comment of his immediately came to mind:

"There are books that do not belong to the person who writes them, but to the one who suffers them . . ."

Although I, myself, was there to "suffer" as well, my book is definitely one of such books. You might say, following a tale of just one person's life, even, or especially, during global upheavals, is like describing a tsunami by observing just one drop of water--that is why personal information of "one drop of water" I did not consider important. True, I have written my own story, but only because I tried to bring to light the little-known hitherto sometimes wilfully obscured facts affecting thousands, even millions of people, on a more day-to-day existence level.

Please note that I have changed the names of people to protect their privacy.

ONE

Safe Haven

The snowbound Canadian winter stays safely outside the window. Black squirrels chase each other on high hickory trees. Tall pine trees maybe a hundred years old, maybe more, and the shorter spruce from the farm planted ten years ago, frame the sky, spreading protectively over the quiet neighbourhood with its attractive homes.

The little pile of letters on the kitchen table could be interesting. But we live in an era of proliferating organizations permanently short of ready cash, so when Ted picks them up one by one, they turn out to be mainly requests for money. Ted says in a tired voice, "Why can't the government take care of them; don't we pay enough taxes?"

Most people no longer bother to ask the question--a rhetorical one, at that, because nobody knows the answer for sure any more.

Though not exactly popular, bills are accepted as a necessary evil, a sign of belonging to that privileged group of consumers, the members of the affluent society, who are able to buy and pay! And then there are the advertising brochures--they have to be removed from the mailbox and brought home, only to add to the household garbage. Needless to say, these gaudily coloured forms that try to alert the world to the excellence of some product or other bring out the worst characteristics of business advertising. The latter is an exaggeration carried beyond the limits of credibility, and translates into a virtual contempt for truth and common sense. Well, it cannot be helped; we make room in the box, ever hopeful of receiving real mail someday.

As immigrants, we have become accustomed to expecting "important news from afar" for many years. We suffer the disappointment of junk mail with less patience, and display more selfish irritation, than would be typical in a "normal" response to such an everyday occurrence.

"Here's a letter for you."

"It's from the tennis club; it's time to pay the membership for this year."

I open the thick envelope.

"They've probably increased the rates again," I sigh inwardly, knowing I will continue to pay, like an addict, as long as I am able to play the game. So many of the other players, both good and bad, have had to stop because of all kinds of physical problems.

"Well, it's good exercise and a pleasant, social game." I continue with such remarks, as if trying to justify the expense. Ted voices no objections.

We are both retired now and our incomes have been drastically reduced. Nevertheless, we are reasonably comfortable, apparently much like other "regular" retirees.

It would be easier not to wake up the past, except that some wilful spirit keeps on tearing the cobwebs off the happily relaxing mind. It sneers at the camouflage of "quasi-conformity."

It is not a perfect camouflage, since people often ask me out of curiosity, or politeness, I guess, where I come from. I can be standing beside a beautifully groomed North American lady in the club locker room and the conversation begins:

"Irena, you're Czech, right?"

"No, I am Polish." Wave after wave of refugees have arrived in Canada, the most recent from Poland and Czechoslovakia. Although we don't all look the same, similarities exist, and I am not upset for being taken as one of those ladies, our close European neighbours. Like many other immigrants who have reached a comfortable level of financial security, they also have joined the recreational facilities that Canada has, and tennis clubs are a favourite.

The North American lady tells me she has recently read a book about Warsaw. It sounds like a special compliment to me, so I make a polite noise.

"How long have you been in Canada?" is usually the next question asked. The number of years in my reply increases every year. Soon it will be forty, almost fifty and more years, but the questions remain the same . . .

While most people would be quite happy to move on to another subject, some individuals, like this solidly preserved lady, are not so easily satisfied. Temporarily residing in Canada, maybe the wife of a Canadian company executive, she is keenly interested in the demographic evolution of her resident country.

"So you came from Poland?"

"Not directly. Before coming to Canada I lived in Germany and then in England."

My answers to questions that sometimes follow are:

"I came alone; I was separated from my mother and brother in 1944."

"I was in a prisoner-of-war camp in Germany."

And so it goes. I know by heart what will follow but I listen politely to the expression of surprise, wonder, and even commiseration, especially in view of my having had to suffer such miserable experiences at such a tender young age. However, the North American lady also asks this astonishing question:

"Were you able to bring out your money?"

What a question! What money?

When I left home for the last time, I took a few family photos, which were hurriedly plucked out from the family album, a change of underwear, and a sweater. These things became my entire inheritance, my share of family history and fortune. My dowry, perhaps?

I could be justifiably sad when I think about my past. In the list of reasons generally regarded as contributing to unhappiness, my experiences could be found there.

However, the past is no longer. I could be sad without an apparent reason, claiming as my excuse the capriciousness of human nature; however, I prefer to think of myself as generally happy and optimistic.

It is nice to get up in the morning from a comfortable bed, draw back the drapes, look through the large window at the frozen lake.

Outside, the neighbours walk their dogs; cars stand in front of large houses. We are all reasonably healthy. I ought to be happy. My brain tries to bring forth such hedonistic arguments, while deep inside I know that it is not a colour-coordinated living room, not brightly polished furniture, and not well-chosen carpets that will do away with occasional miserable feelings. Can aesthetic sensitivity to one's surroundings bring happiness?

I think of the family members who have devoted their life to the arts. If they did not know whether they had talent, perhaps it was just as well. My artistic ambitions are limited to matching the colour of Kleenex to the decor in various rooms; which, I secretly admit to myself, gives me a sense of visual pleasure. How trivial!

The question arises whether such trivialities are part of those minuscule elements necessary to live an agreeable life. Obviously, their importance is indeed microscopic in comparison with the things my mother taught me--faith, modesty, respect for others, the emotional treasures helping me to balance interest in myself against the interest one owes to the world outside. In many ways they are my "everyday" protection against depression. Thinking only of one's miserable "I" is bound to end in disenchantment. Life can be as interesting as a well-constructed novel--a good story populated with well-rounded personalities pursuing interesting action!

Many write memoirs, since some memories are so important that they cannot fade; they have to be preserved for the future even though posterity might ignore them. There is a compelling need to dutifully record, above all, the tragic loss of the people we loved, together with the denial of life as we knew it. Even the images of unflattering situations and pitiful omissions, of misunderstood people and bad encounters, depressing as they can be, clamour for attention. Still, the lingering reproaches should not entirely silence the gentle voice of cherished memories--they are needed to console those no longer young.

TWO

Different Times, Different Places

Not all my life has been spent in what you might call a "regular" way, just following a conventional path. I sometimes wonder what my conventional path would have been like. What would have been my prerequisite for a happy existence?

While ordinary individuals in this world seldom wish to object to an agreeable conformity, I and many other people were obliged to conform under conditions for which the circumstances of our birth did not consistently and adequately prepare us. Immediately after World War II, unprecedented numbers of people, including myself, had to function like actors cast in unsuitable roles; the operative word was "displaced." The "displaced" observed the world from a different perspective. Like a cracked mirror, our memories have sometimes played havoc with our perception of the surrounding world.

Memories of the Second World War are impossible to ignore. For the millions of viewers watching TV documentaries, World War II started when a bunch of burly German soldiers unceremoniously pushed aside the barrier marking the German-Polish border.

For me, World War II began when a burning plane trailing thick black smoke and turning somersaults in the air was suddenly in view from the veranda of our summer cottage. Not even a teenager then, I watched the plane with my father. His face expressed sad resignation-- but no surprise.

The veranda was a perfectly ordinary, slightly elevated wooden structure with a roof resting on solid beams, waist-high wooden walls, and a creaky gate at the top of four little steps to keep out dogs, chickens, or other animals straying away from the nearby farm. Such verandas are very common in parts of Europe.

"Did you see the German plane go down, Mister?" shouted a friendly farmer as he ran past. "It went down by the river--it's war!" He volunteered the information as he rushed ahead to attach himself to a group scurrying in the direction of the river.

Close to Father, I felt safe, even exuberant, on that perfect summer day--a Friday. The veranda, overgrown with vines, was not close to the river, which made it too far away for any danger. How could I know then that my father, left without proper medical care, would die exactly six months later, on the first of March? The urologist who treated him for cancer of the bladder was Jewish . . .

Only a few days before, kids from summer cottages in the neighbourhood had been playing a ball game late in the afternoon. Though some of the kids here were bigger, and there were boys, too, I was desperately trying to show off my skills that made me shine at primary school. Okay! Not one of the first picks, but eventually I was chosen to play--I was playing! The balls flew faster than back at school, the kids were stronger; one boy in particular had his eye on me. "I will show him!" Like a jockey flogging his mount, I strained and stretched my confidence to gallop ahead. Then, all of a sudden, wham! The ball came at me fast and big, right at my stomach! Got it--no use gasping for air--I could not get any, with my ribs locked together in a crushing spasm. Blue heavens! Blue heaven and treetops rotated gently above. Never mind, though it hurt, the air revived my lungs; finally, all was well.

"Where is the ball?" was the first thought in my head as I stood up slowly.

"Okay, kid?" asked The Boy; he alone seemed to have noticed!

Though struggling and in pain, I played on. Fortunately the hazy August sun soon disappeared behind the darkened woods, and dusk concealed the misery of my first encounter with panic. It was shameful to show pain or fear. I hated to be seen as smaller and weaker. And then there was the burning plane.

"Let's go and see the plane," said father.

Hoping to meet my playmates, I ran ahead and down the familiar sandy slope, jumping over scraggly grass while seeking passage through the wild brushwood. Then, suddenly, there they were--a group of people standing in awe around an unfamiliar monstrosity--a still-smouldering heap of metal marked with swastikas.

"Where is the pilot?" they wondered.

"They took him away." Surely, the pilot was dead. If only the six years of war could be squeezed into the few minutes it took to get to the river, the world would not sink in the mire of suffering; a multitude of deaths and all kinds of abomination would not have to be endured. The group of people looking at a twisted heap of smouldering metal by the bank of such an insignificant Polish river could not know they were being allowed a symbolic glimpse into the future--the final result of conflict--the smouldering ruins of the Third Reich.

Alas, to imagine the burning German plane as a final defeat of the bullies in this world had to be but a child's dream . . . If not for the war, the family would continue with its joys and its problems; Father perhaps would not die so soon, and Anna would not come into the family to break my mother's heart. Yes, poor mother loved her beautiful son so much! As often happens, it was the boy who was the pride and joy of mother.

I was my father's favourite. Unfortunately, Stan's looks, his athletic body, and, judging by his luck with the ladies, seductive charm would not translate into a very successful life.

The handsome teenager was often in trouble at school.

"Got in with bad company," explained Mother after every new calamity.

The mousy-haired young daughter was good at school; in fact, was judged to be very intelligent by the teachers, so the father transferred his hope of fulfilling parental ambitions to her.

If not for the war, presumably our life would have been more conventional. Nevertheless, no matter what transpires, the past tends to enslave people; it cannot be crossed out.

Warsaw, 1944--already the fifth year of brutal German occupation; here, the situation was growing desperate. Food was scarce and, such as was available, prohibitively expensive. The official food rations for the million and a half population of Warsaw were at starvation level; people who could afford it bought their food from farmers who risked their lives smuggling their products to the city by a slow train. Very often, all kinds of farm-produced goodies would be confiscated by German police raiding the trains. Worse still, the farmers could be arrested and sent to a slave labour or a concentration camp, depending on the whim of the German officer in charge.

When lucky enough to successfully deliver their wares to the clandestine markets, the farmers charged exorbitant prices that not many people could afford. Reduced to abject poverty and unable to feed themselves, some families had to enlist as labourers in German factories. Ironically, they helped to keep the war industry going. However, if they needed more workers, the Germans would simply catch people like stray dogs, right in the streets.

One spring night in 1944, my mother and I were awakened from a deep sleep to a frightening reality; it was three a.m.

"*Aufmachen!* [Open up!]" Hateful yelling disrupted the peaceful night; "*Aufmachen!*" The yelling and banging on the doors to the apartment steadily picked up in volume. What to do, what to do? Confused, we ran to the window; the blackout made it impossible to see anything.

Suddenly, as if prompted by some obscure instinct, I screamed through the open window: "*Polizei, Polizei, Banditen!* [Police! Police! Bandits!]"

The horrible noise of an axe hitting the door in the hallway announced that the door lock would soon yield to a few hard blows. Mother pulled me away from the window.

"We have to open it," she said; but I am sure she thought, *My daughter is right.*

A raving-mad German army officer blasted in through the broken door, a couple of underlings in tow; a split second later a resounding slap to my face sent my head flying to one side.

"How dare you call us bandits!" The officer appeared to be choking on his fury. He obviously missed the irony of the situation. Mother moved in front of me and bravely faced the brute. Poor Mother, she was shorter than I was then, but tried to shield her child! Was it the shock and shame, or helpless anger that suddenly emptied my bladder? I felt defiled, desperately humiliated, and, when one of the soldiers reached out to pat my hair--mumbling comfortingly, "Nah, nah"--close to vomiting with disgust.

Cupboards, drawers, and wardrobes were opened violently, as if demons had invaded our modest apartment. The sound of weeping, shouting, and heavy footsteps outside on the staircase added a heart-wrenching accompaniment to the macabre scenario. It was a shameless violation of human dignity easily perpetrated on people having no rights!

THREE

My School

When I reach deeper in the past I remember my school: one of the highly regarded private schools for girls--Marshal Pilsudski's daughters actually attended it for some time. Most pupils came from very prosperous families. Others, like me, were subsidized by the generous companies where their fathers were employed. It was apparently considered a desirable practice to send the female offspring to such establishments. Classes were small; for example, during one school year, there were only nine pupils in the class. Three of them were Jewish, daughters of parents belonging to the well-to-do Polish "intelligentsia."

One of the gentile girls, Basia, a bossy little character, apparently had the kind of parents who gave their eight-year-old daughter credit for a maturity far greater than she deserved. Basia was the only one in our little class to have her hair permed, and her small person seemed at first glance overpowered by the great, blonde mane. But her dominant feature was, actually, the penetrating gaze of a pair of eyes of nondescript colour. They were slightly slanted and elongated under too-well-defined, thin eyebrows--did she pluck them? Not only could she narrow her eyes in a very grown-up manner, which was intimidating to the more timid souls, but also, her permed hair gave her an aura of authority in the eyes of the unsophisticated company of Grade 3 students whom she met, when she first appeared at the school. Her father was a physician. His medical practice included the poor section of the Jewish population of Warsaw--this was his contribution to the state-run medical service.

Basia's father was a very witty, handsome man who royally entertained the little friends of his daughter at her birthday parties. I thought they were the best I had ever attended. Perhaps his daughter inherited his sense of humour, since she was always trying to entertain her classmates by exporting some of the possibly confidential exchanges she overheard at home.

"*Was tu te weh?* [Where does it hurt?]" she would say teasingly, repeating the phrase her father probably used while examining his Jewish patients.

Though shy, her Jewish classmates were offended enough to complain to their parents. The parents would then complain to the home teacher. Subsequently, the whole class had to endure what was generally known as a "homily" on the subject of human kindness, good citizenship, and other uplifting topics. The fact that the father of one of the Jewish girls had distinguished himself in the First World War fighting for the independence of Poland, and had received high military honours, was also mentioned on such occasions.

Like most teachers in the world, Mrs W., the home form teacher, looked really funny to her pupils. They secretly laughed at her somewhat wide behind that seemed to sway as she walked around wearing her perpetual grey dress. When about to deliver the homily, she would call the class to order, and with her pale blue eyes fixed in a very scary way on the squirming audience, she would dramatically spread her arms and take a couple of steps back. She personified shock and grief at what the little rascals had done.

"I am very disappointed in you," she would begin. "You call yourselves Christians?"

Throwing doubt on the class's capability of being Christian would be like questioning their belonging to the human race. The school was staunchly Roman Catholic and strived to nurture in its pupils religious and civic virtues of the highest order.

"You know Mr. C. (the father of one of the Jewish girls) fought for the freedom of Poland and was awarded the Virtuti Militari[1] . . ." The teacher's voice filled the room for a few minutes longer.

---

[1] The highest decoration awarded in the Polish Armed Forces (for Military Virtue).

But, since all that had already been repeated a few times, the minds of eight- and nine-year-olds moved to other things. The uplifting effect of the message was quickly dispelled in the gym afterwards, when impersonations of the home teacher acted out behind exercise equipment were greeted by squeals of laughter. At that age, they were ready to laugh at anything.

* * *

I enjoy travelling occasionally to Toronto, usually with one of our children, since Ted is not very fond of big cities. "I don't understand how these people can drive to work every day in this traffic and stay sane," he repeats every time we find ourselves stuck on Highway 401 anywhere near Toronto.

So shopping or attending a "cultural" event in the capital of Ontario does not happen terribly frequently--unless one of the kids volunteers to go with me. This time it was Roman. We are off to see the evening performance of an opera.

"We shall stop at the mall for lunch," I tell my son.

"Okay." There is not much conversation when Roman is driving.

Minutes later, carrying a plate of goodies in an eatery called The Baguette, I am looking for an empty place at one of the little round tables. They all seem to be taken by the lunchtime crowd. Roman has only had a drink and leaves to look for a book.

"I'll be back in half an hour," he says, and is gone.

Ah, there are two empty chairs at the wall. Sitting sort of squeezed against the wall is not very comfortable, but there is no time to await better prospects. The place is busy at this hour, and someone is bound to come soon to occupy the chairs, anyway. So I settle down, pressing my back against the hard, cool wall and begin to eat.

"The soup is not bad," I think. And today is developing quite pleasantly. The evening will start with dinner. A bottle of wine will surely add to the atmosphere--the delicious anticipation of the performance to follow . . . Roman is usually at his talkative best on such occasions, and I love listening to his stories and comments.

Outside, individuals of different shapes and colour break away from the multinational crowd and stray over to The Baguette in search of lunch. Dark people, but not black, seem to be in the majority. Blondes, once admired as preciously rare, and regarded as a symbol of goodness and purity, have chemically multiplied, thus diminishing the prestige of being blonde. Of course, other factors enter the equation. I remember reading somewhere about the "blond beasts."

"Hello," says a woman about my age only bigger, a suspiciously dark brunette.

"Oh yes, the place is free," I blurt out, awakened from reverie.

"I'm so tired," begins the woman, "I hate shopping nowadays--so many people--"

"I know."

My pleasant reverie must have left me in an agreeable frame of mind, for I feel an unexplained wave of sympathy towards her. She looks more European than North American--probably a "new" Canadian.

"I had to find a place to sit down first, and now I'm going to get something to eat." She definitely has an accent. "Is the soup good?"

"Yes, it's nice."

When the woman returns, we eat in silence for a while, while she observes me with growing interest. She then begins to tell the story of her family, which indeed comes from Europe. Gradually, the woman's story turns into a lament over lost relatives.

"Are you Jewish?"

"Yes," answers the woman, while I wish I could take back the question.

"And you, too?" She is not the first; I have been asked that question many times before.

"No, I'm not," I answer with an involuntary smile, because the question always makes me laugh, and I think that my nose must look rather "Jewish." I inform the Jewish woman I am from Poland. The friendly stranger suddenly changes into a quarrelsome old hag.

"They hate the Jews in Poland! My uncle and my aunt were chased away from their home with nothing . . ."

It would be so civil to return to a friendly conversation. I try to remain sympathetic, but it is so annoying to be arbitrarily singled out as a target for accusations.

"There are anti-Semitic people in every country," I just have to say.

"Yes," says the woman getting up from her seat, visibly irritated, "but the Poles are the worst!"

She is gone; she would not listen.

"Is the soup good?" the friendly question lingers on in my mind. The sour taste of uncompromising judgment will eventually fade. The noisy café, temporarily locked out of consciousness, recedes behind the memory of the old form teacher in her eternally grey dress, dramatically extending her arms, taking a few steps backwards . . .

"Do you call yourselves Christians...?"

Roman is coming, and it is time to leave. I wonder what the strange woman would think of old Mrs. W.? If she would only have let me speak . . .

Thoughts about the early days of my educational efforts popped into my mind one particular morning by the arrival of a letter from Zosia Kadlubek. Zosia, one of my best pals in the pre-war era, was the first and maybe the only genuine animal-rights activist I have ever met. Like the physician's daughter, Basia, she came to our school in Grade 3. Her father ran an experimental farm outside Warsaw, and every day Zosia brought to the class the latest news about life on the farm, which was eagerly absorbed by us city dwellers. She also possessed the adventurous life of a daily commuter, regularly transported to school in the family car, which gave her plenty of topics for numerous rather colourful stories as well. Even the car was endowed with human-like qualities--it was a creature weakened by a lifetime of hard work. Nicknamed "Pook-lot" for the strange noises it emitted, it figured frequently in the stories: feeble and failing but valiantly responding to the call of duty; enduring countless repairs and part changes; sometimes urgently required at the most inopportune moments.

Zosia's favourite topic, though, was the farm animals--pigs, chickens, dogs, horses, but primarily little piglets whom she favoured above all; she gave each one a nickname and watched their progress in the world with interest, perhaps not quite parental, but at least as that of a truly attached nanny. Inevitably, when the tragic moment arrived, and the little darlings met their destiny as an item on the dinner menu, Zosia vowed not to eat meat ever again. And she kept her word.

The steadfast resolve of this girl commanded my sincere admiration. It was particularly impressive during the annual "garden school" period, when our class spent two weeks in June in the country, at the villa owned by the school. Without companions my own age, I was bored at home. To spend all of twenty-four hours, every day for two weeks, in the company of my cherished classmates, seemed like paradise on earth. The class was assigned rooms accommodating four persons, and after assembling a group of initiated friends, we would plan crazy, exciting things to do after everyone--especially the teachers--was asleep.

But being on the go all day was enough to totally exhaust our young bodies, and alas, we would fall asleep, forfeiting all those fabulous plans.

Meals were served in a large sunroom, furnished with a long table and white wicker chairs; the walls on three sides of the room were all windows made pretty with white lace curtains and red geraniums. Trees and flowers growing around the spacious park beckoned from the outside. After a brief prayer, the plates placed in front of us would be slowly filled with food from platters circulated carefully from one end of the table to another.

"Don't kick under the table."

"Look at Ann; she takes such big mouthfuls."

Nobody could really whisper at this age. "Secret" conversations, carried on in piercing tones of theatrical whispers, would reach all ears, provoking giggles and guffaws.

"Don't talk while you're eating, please," admonished the teacher.

The teacher's smiles and persuasion were designed to promote generally decorous behaviour. But as a dignified silence finally began to reign, to be interrupted only by subdued chewing and swallowing sounds, Zosia Kadlubek would raise her voice, addressing whoever happened to be in charge at the table, and announce clearly:

"If you please, I don't eat meat, Miss X."

The teacher would then ring to summon the cook, who should already have been told about the presence of a little vegetarian. The cook would shuffle in from the kitchen wearing a funny-looking kerchief around her head, which again produced merriment among the young misses.

every time, exactly, when everyone was expected to
sed, it was so difficult not to laugh? Even the first
l, after months of pious preparation, developed into
h.

...when that one important day of confessions actually arrived,
everyone was a bit scared of what the priests were going to say to their
"sins"; the general consensus was to delay the procedure as long as
possible and to make it extremely short. Not too short--there had to be
something substantial to declare. Some went so far as to admit to some
bizarre, imaginary transgressions, producing laughter even in serious
clergymen.

Since the above strategy favoured long lines and long waiting, a
number of priests were virtually besieged by penitents, while others
remained idle in their confessionals. A sort of "cat and mouse" game
developed when, to restore a desirable equilibrium, the principal, aided by
the vice-principal, would chase the girls away from the overcrowded spots
and lead them towards the neglected confessors. To avoid being "taken," I
and a couple of others would hide behind the massive church columns.

"Here she comes!" Giggling, we dove inside the pews to avoid
Mademoiselle H., the vice-principal, whose pince-nez fixed on her thin
nose shone menacingly in the subdued lighting of the big church.
Finally, the game was up. There was no escape, and we were placed
firmly at the nearest confessional.

When you don't know the meaning of the word "irreverent,"
laughter is so innocent.

* * *

I rediscovered Zosia after almost fifty years, just after the collapse
of the communist government in Poland. I was staying in the Hotel
Forum in Warsaw. For a while, Forum, situated just a block away from
the busiest, most central crossing of two arteries, seemed like the only
place to stay in Warsaw. At the corner nearest to the hotel is a small
space covered with fresh flowers. An inscription on the red brick wall
marks it as a spot where hostages were executed during the German
occupation. The hostages, usually prominent Polish citizens, were kept
in prison. A number of them would be shot as punishment for acts of
sabotage or any transgression against the occupant. There are spots like
that all over Poland.

Inside the hotel room, I discovered for the first time a telephone directory placed in the usual spot on the shelf below the telephone. This improvement cheered me up. Leafing fondly through the precious book, I thought of the people I might like to call. As far as my relatives were concerned, I saw only the cousins on my mother's side frequently. Why? Partly out of respect for Mother, and because they have always belonged to the group of honest people who have tried to maintain contact, which has been very gratifying to me.

Classmates? It would be interesting to find out what exactly happened to the old school. Zosia Kadlubek, the great animal lover, could still be around Warsaw. I remembered with a silent chuckle how once Zosia inspired a great and lasting respect in our class of eight-year-olds--all standing on chairs in utter panic on that particular occasion--when she bravely picked up a huge, black, water beetle, and calmly returned it to its tank, from which it had temporarily escaped in a mysterious manner.

Zosia's family name and a telephone number were right there. I turned the numbers on the dial of the old-fashioned device with a somewhat unsteady hand, and then took a deep breath.

"Hello?" A woman's voice sounded a little too young.

"May I speak to Ms--?" I stopped all of a sudden, wondering whether my old classmate had married and changed her name. Trying to phone long unseen friends after many, many years is like trying to summon ghosts of the deceased during a séance. You can never be sure who will turn up.

Zosia was not a marrying kind--she cherished her freedom and her own way too much . . . I was momentarily lost in thought.

"Hello, hello," interrupted the voice a little impatiently. Carrying on a telephone conversation in the days of "stone age" telecommunications in Poland did not allow for unscheduled pauses. The person at the other end would immediately break into several nervous "hellos," thinking they had lost the connection--which, incidentally, was often the case. Fortunately, in this case the person at the other end responded readily to Zosia's maiden name.

"She is out at the moment. Who is calling, please?"

"We used to go to school together . . ." I began a lengthy explanation, not quite sure where it would lead. But the young voice of the hard-to-imagine speaker was friendly.

Finally, I gave the number of the hotel and hung up. Hardly a moving experience, but it took a walk around the room to quieten me down. Many years had passed since the last meeting with some of my good friends in Poland. Emotional stamina must have declined with age. Good God!

"I look the same as before," Zosia explained on the phone next day, responding to the question of how we would recognize each other, "only older."

Indeed, when Zosia entered the hotel lobby at the appointed time, I could see that she had hardly changed. True, she was an older lady, but the same confidence and cheerfulness she spread around half a century ago as a kid in primary school still radiated from her face.

She had not married. "Just could not find anyone suitable," she said simply.

Zosia told me how she helped her family; she lived with her niece, taking care of children and contributing to the family business. The family designed Tiffany lamps and other accessories.

"Now people are beginning to grow wealthy, so business is much better."

To my pleasant surprise, Zosia had not sworn off some fun in life. The contents of a bottle of my duty-free cognac were steadily going down as we talked about our present lives. But memories dominated the conversation--about schoolmates and what happened during the War.

Nearly sixty years have passed since the last year we were classmates. The old, established, and respected private school for girls eventually lost the unequal battle to the chaos of wartime calamities. Gone were the unsmiling caretakers, clad in black overalls, with their carefully groomed hair, who once constantly, or so it seemed to us, polished the gleaming parquet floors. I was tickled pink when on my first day at school--I was six years old--one of them addressed me as "Miss."

The elegant corridors lost their aura of pricey respectability and comfort. Everything began to look rundown and shabby, with too many people squeezed into a much smaller area. The best part of the school property was taken over by some German offices. Familiar faces disappeared, and new people arrived, as though brought up to the surface by unpredictable waves of wartime misery.

The Jewish girls were gone, of course; who knows what happened to them? Their families were well off and perhaps able to get out of harm's way; at least some of them did--but one family did stay maybe too long. Obeying the order issued by the Germans for the Jewish population, their daughter, Alina, my classmate, appeared at school with the Star of David on her sleeve . . .

The order covered the Jews who were Polish citizens and who historically had sought autonomy in Poland by maintaining their own political party, by choice living apart from the rest of society according to their own customs and culture. The order also covered the newly arrived Jewish people just expelled from Germany and other European countries already under German occupation. It was also directed to the members of the assimilated Jewish population who were, on the whole, closely engaged in the mainstream of Polish society.

Alina was a very shy girl, always looking somewhat out of place. Her pretty face and marvellous colouring, combined with clear blue eyes and thick, dark hair, qualified her many times over as a beautiful creature. But her ungainly posture, faraway gaze, and what appeared to be a consistent withdrawal from activities happening around her, rendered her inaccessible, inspiring in her classmates no sentiment other than bewilderment, often degenerating into derision.

Contrary to the generally known ability of Jewish people to master languages and other subjects, Alina had language and comprehension difficulties that reflected badly on her academic performance--especially math.

The math teacher, a woman in her forties, well qualified, as it were, was slightly unbalanced, maybe as a result of some upsetting episodes in her life, or simply because she was just peculiar. Her loud and emphatic voice had a peculiar timbre, like the voice of someone at the bottom of a deep well. It resonated all over--even outside the closed doors of the classroom--as she expounded on the mysteries of numbers and geometry, and terrorized her pupils into submission. Her pedagogical skills, as well as her patience, were directly proportional to the ability of each girl to absorb her teaching. Every time she was confronted with the allegedly lowly level of Alina's aptitude, she practically exploded.

"Can't you understand that you have to put a line in the middle under the numerator and write the denominator under it, so it will be a fraction--a *fraction*--remember, a *fraction!*" The voice was losing its explanatory tone and growing more and more angry.

Alina never showed any sign of being perturbed by the wrath threatening to discharge over her head, although the scene could be awkward enough for everyone in the room to feel sorry for her. Her body language remained absolutely unchanged. Alina's mother, however, was not ready to take her daughter's mathematical disasters lying down. She was heard one day expressing her opinion about the math teacher in a rather loud and irritated manner. The kids enjoyed listening, before she was discreetly shushed down by the form teacher, and led respectfully away to the principal's office.

Alina's father being a lawyer, the family could afford to reside in one of the most expensive areas of Warsaw. One year before the war, I was asked to help the unfortunate girl navigate the arcane maze of mathematics, and so visited the rather impressive apartment a few times, but I was never entertained as a guest, and never invited to visit anywhere but in Alina's room.

One day, maybe a month after the fall of Poland in September 1939, Alina's mother came to the classroom and excitedly announced: "We have all, the whole family, become Catholic!"

It was strange to hear, and difficult to absorb, such news. The form teacher congratulated the mother and the daughter, though, and so did the girls, not knowing exactly what to make of it.

FOUR

Avoidable Housework

I finish reading the letter from Zosia and contemplate the perfect view. The bright February sun is pouring through the patio door into the dining room. Two little islands, the Spectacles, and one large one, Wolfe Island, with trees and buildings scattered over them like in a children's storybook illustration, seem to hibernate on the frozen lake-- such a perfect view, framed by the neutrality of ivory drapes and softly gleaming hardwood floor. A new tablecloth, bought during a recent vacation on St. Martin Island, has been sitting folded on top of the dining room table for a week now, held up by the pending reorganization of sideboard drawers needed to accommodate the new acquisition.

Images and sounds of the distant ocean are still easily recalled by eyes and ears. I can almost imagine being there, and I see the sun-worshipping people on the beach. Bodies tanned to different shades of brown, red, or orange, spotted here and there with colourful bathing suits, are lying around like large dolls in an untidy toy store.

The ocean tries its best to discourage swimmers by sending huge waves loaded with sand picked up at the shallows. The powerful wall of water rushes at me as I try to reach the shallower area near the shore. Too late. I am overpowered by the weight of the salty deluge. Holding my breath, I feel my hair getting thoroughly wet inside my brand-new Speedo cap, "guaranteed" to keep hair dry. So much for Speedo!

It's hard to move forward against the pull of the ocean now in its offshore run. But the beautiful, sandy bottom quickly emerges underfoot. Best to run before the next wave unloads its watery charge. Too slow again, and hit hard, I fall on my knees, scratching them against the rough sand.

"I'm getting too old for this game," I have to admit regretfully, remembering the times when I loved swimming so much that any attractive body of water would tempt me.

A few years younger, I enjoyed entering lakes of different sizes and at different temperatures--like Cold Lake in Alberta, *brrrr*, or only slightly warmer Lake Tahoe.

I have also enjoyed the "heavy" Salt Lake in Utah, but most of all, the swaying motion of the ocean--the best ever was the Caribbean around the beaches of Aruba. Chlorinated water in swimming pools is not my favourite.

When I arrived in Dubrovnik, in former Yugoslavia, to meet my friend Elisabeth on Lopud Island for the first time in seventeen years, the Adriatic seemed to me the most gentle of all the seas. I thought Elisabeth was impressed by my swimming against the waves off the more rugged western shore of the island. The waves made her nervous, and she preferred the quieter waters at the beach inside the crescent of the island.

I put an end to daydreaming, get up from the easy chair, and with a deep sigh, I start busying myself with stacks of napkins, trying to figure out what to do with them all. They are hardly ever used anymore, what with the colourful paper napkins appropriate for any occasion, available in the stores nowadays.

"There has to be something more worthwhile to do; playing house is for self-satisfied housewives," an inner Voice sneers. "Isn't my life good!"

"Why is feeling self-satisfied such a bad thing?" I ask myself.

"Has it something to do with the heady days of idealistic youth?" the Voice gets sarcastic. "Who would be willing and able to shake out this old bag of memories?"

In my youth, I would have argued in earnest that excessive house pride is dangerous. One should be careful and wary of possessions casting their spell, of the charms of interior decorating dictating desire for perfection to the exclusion of other human desires.

There was a movie about a housewife who worked lovingly and incessantly, turning her home into a sublimely polished "Shangri-la" for her husband. Every morning as he was leaving for work, giving her a dutiful kiss, she was already descending on her knees to wax the stairs or scrub the kitchen floor grouting.

She made him pay the ultimate price for her years of slave-like devotion when she found out that throughout all that time he had had a mistress. Happiness derived from maintaining a spotless abode may be easily shattered by unforeseen events. Maybe because they seemed too fragile to relax and have a really interesting talk, very orderly people made me uncomfortable.

The first "real" home Ted and I lived in was in London--a room in a condemned house near Victoria Station that could not possibly awaken homemaking ambitions in anyone.

Totally preoccupied with our newborn son, we completely ignored the miserable furniture, and, as far as possible, the entire room. With its creaking floor running at an audacious angle to the horizontal, the walls and ceiling criss-crossed by cracks, and windows shaking in harmony with the heavy traffic outside, the room seemed to just barely hang onto the building, which had itself been rattled into a fitful collection of bricks and mortar by the merciless Blitz.

The fidgety windows in ill-fitting frames also let in cold air and allowed the passage of street noises at full volume. Almost heart wrenching were the voices of homeless British cats, which enjoyed the status of sacred cows in this country. They roamed the streets at night in search of food and romance. They sounded sometimes so much like a crying baby that if we were awakened, we would rush to the cot of our first-born, only to see him sleeping sweetly.

The mice stranded in the vicinity of the fireplace--another kind of noisemaker--were being hunted down and caught in Ted's camouflage net (a relic from his army days) deftly thrown over the hollow rail of the fireguard. The hapless creatures sought refuge there, and were duly dispatched through the window to feed the meowing hordes downstairs.

Enter Eva, my one-time colleague in a nursing course, a paragon of orderliness, cleanliness, and neatness. She was small and shapely and had lots of brown hair and a coquettish smile showing pretty, white teeth. A suspicious--even somewhat frightened--grimace on her pretty face was not due to cunning, decent soul that she was, but to slow thinking.

It was often hard for her to react quickly to what was being said. The interest she inspired in the opposite sex with her looks generally waned once she began to speak and indulge her passion for using--not always appropriately--some old, tired cliché she happily paraded as witty repartee.

As usual, she looked scrumptiously fresh and lovely.

"There he is," I whispered, leading Eva to the baby's crib.

"Ah." The visitor directed a hurried look at the baby she came to see; the baby could not appeal to her sense of orderliness--he had a wide nose, squashed by the labour of birth, and was bald, the poor thing. Eva preferred to look at herself, and turned her head left and right trying to locate a mirror. Then she moved energetically towards the miserable and hideous dresser where she found one. She suddenly started to laugh:

"Irena, I cannot see myself in this mirror; see the dust?" She moved her finger over the mirror's surface, tracing lines in the dust, and then grabbed a kerchief from her purse.

During the few weeks we had inhabited the place, I had never felt a compelling desire to clean the surface of the wretched mirror. Eva wiped it carefully, and I had to humbly acknowledge my lack of attention to housekeeping chores.

* * *

My lack of interest in normal domesticity was probably due to the fact that my life as a young girl growing up in occupied Poland allowed no such luxury. It was difficult to enjoy any normality when the only permissible ambition was a successful survival. It was more like a desperate clinging to life rather than a real life; we were enduring an existence severely limited and made difficult every step of the way.

Wars bear different names and happen in a variety of places, but the results are always death, hunger, cold, and disease. And suffering inflicted wilfully on men by fellow men.

Long winter evenings were spent huddling close to a source of precious heat in a room illuminated by a sputtering carbide lamp, when frequent power cuts extinguished our electric bulbs. Our sparsely nourished bodies could not spare too many calories to warm us up when necessary, especially in wintertime.

"Mama, the thick socks look terrible with these shoes," I complained one frosty morning while dressing to go to school.

"You have to keep your feet warm or you'll get chilblains, and they are a lot of trouble!" cautioned Mother.

But I got chilblains anyway, once my mother's shoes got too small and started cutting painfully into my heels and toes. To keep me warmly and respectably dressed, Mother had her own clothes altered to fit me. Taking care of my growing feet was the most difficult task. There was no money to buy winter boots. Even a pair of decent, sturdy shoes was beyond our means, since prices were exorbitant.

So off I went every snowy morning, up to my ankles in wet sludge on the pavement. If there was enough coal to keep the furnace hot, we could quickly dry our shoes and socks at school, but most of the time it was barely lukewarm. We had to sit in class in our coats; only the bravest teachers, especially the male math and Polish teachers, gave lessons in the chilly classrooms wearing only their suits.

I think there should be a monument built in Warsaw to commemorate the bravery and sacrifices of the Polish high school and university teachers during the German occupation. The education of Polish youth, according to the Nazis, was not to exceed elementary level. The seven years of primary education could be followed only by the learning of a trade. People who organized academic secondary and post-secondary education exposed themselves to a great danger.

University professors in particular were a favourite target for persecution--many of the faculty of the ancient Jagiellonian University in Cracow were murdered or imprisoned by the Nazis.

Only single pages from textbooks, disguised and hidden among the paraphernalia connected with the trade we were supposed to be learning, could be brought to school. The notes we were taking during lessons also had to be limited to one page. Any moment, an inspection could descend on the school--none were exempt from playing their part.

However, these were only minor inconveniences in comparison with what was going on in the grim shadows of prisons and concentration camps. Our teachers and families were trying to shield us as much as possible from the overwhelming horrors of war. Their faces were always ready to welcome us with a wan smile for our little successes and childish explosions of joy. Still, we got an unmistakable inkling of the trauma around us, when one of the students would appear in school after a few days' absence, her eyes red from crying, her mother deadly pale in the corridor, telling the teacher a horrible story of the sort happening so frequently now.

I remember Magda P.; she was my classmate from the very first year at school. She appeared so different that day in 1943. Her charming young teenaged face wore the stamp of a grown-up tragedy. She looked at us in a strange way.

"What happened? Are you ill?" we asked, staying at a respectful distance from this new Magda.

"I am all right," she said, turning her sad eyes towards the floor as if preserving a secret.

We left her alone.

"Magda's father has been arrested by the Gestapo," the principal informed us later.

It meant her father could become one of the hostages to be executed at one of the spots marked by the commemorative plaques to be seen at the present time in different locations in Warsaw, and all over Poland. Or he could meet with an even worse fate before being murdered. I felt miserable for Magda, and almost relieved that my father was already dead and out of harm's way.

The 9:00 curfew imposed by the occupant prevented any social get-togethers or any other kind of gatherings in the evening. In the summer, hanging around parks or at the no longer attractive, rundown beaches by the river was to risk being picked up and sent away, God knows where.

The quality of my existence was elevated at the age of thirteen when I joined the clandestine organization of quasi Girl Guides to try and help the Resistance movement. Apart from the aura of nobility, it allowed me a little personal independence as well. My mother, a great patriot, tolerated these activities with painful resignation.

In due course, I started to train as a nurse, but our first "practice" in the hospital with real patients made me almost faint, and I had to agree with my Girl Guide leader, who said: "Let the older girls train as nurses; the younger ones can be messengers or telephone operators."

Although, at my age, being called "younger" was an insult, I gladly embraced the communication service from then on. Apart from the practice with field telephones and a switchboard, the training included long runs around the city so that the budding messengers could familiarize themselves with the city's streets and secret passages, and generally learn to choose the best route from point A to point B under difficult conditions. The most thrilling and dangerous part of the training was using a real army rifle. We learned how to handle it and how to take it apart and put it back together again.

One day I came home struggling with a fairly heavy package.

"What's that?" asked Mother.

"A rifle."

"What? Child, do you know what would happen, if--" She was afraid to say it.

"Mom, I am only to keep it overnight; tomorrow I have to take it to Wlochy."[2]

"Where are we going to hide it?" In her true manner, Mother had already abandoned contemplating a disaster, and turned her mind to practical matters.

The rifle had been taken apart and wrapped to form a square-shaped package. We decided to put the package inside the coal box in the kitchen, disguising it, as best we could, among the few pieces of coal.

I missed school the next day, so as to promptly remove the menace from the coal box and our home. My brother, who appeared especially for the occasion, carried the wretched thing almost the entire time. We had to take a commuter train, exposing ourselves to the presence of German and--sometimes almost as dangerous--Polish police officers. They had a bad reputation because of their obsequiousness towards the German bosses; the police were always snooping around the stations and other public places.

We tried to act "cool." Actually, I would have been safer by myself. As a young man of twenty-one, Stan was always suspicious in the eyes of the occupants, and could be accosted as a matter of principle.

---

[2] A suburb of Warsaw.

Although the affair ended successfully, we were taking an unnecessary risk. During the two months of the Uprising in 1944, so few weapons were at our disposal that not even all the men in the fighting units had a rifle, let alone a skinny little messenger like me.

Understandably, the pages of our national history, glowing with tales of passionate struggles for independence, fostered a literature steeped in romantic ideas of love for one's country, nurturing in the young minds ample patriotic energy. The ideals of God, Honour, and Fatherland have been implanted in our brains from early on. The impressionable young teenager, I was ready, or so I thought, to die a heroic death for my country. People were saying: "Whether you are engaged in some activities of the Resistance movement or not, you could be killed or carted off to a concentration camp anyway."

Even people too careful to harbour any subversive intentions towards the occupant were likely to be caught in the street to be sent as slave labourers to Germany, or to a concentration camp, or be held hostage in the notorious Pawiak prison, only to be shot in a morbid ceremony staged at one of the busy crossings in Warsaw in retaliation for any act of resistance. Although recognized leaders and cultural icons were, so to speak, in the first line of fire, just being Polish was enough to be in danger. Obviously, our generation was not going to escape the cycle of gory disasters that have periodically beset our country.

Young schoolgirls with pretty hair and fresh, angelic faces, instead of dreaming of beautiful gowns and festive balls, were cowering in icy cold classrooms secretly acquiring knowledge forbidden by the occupant, because Mr. Hitler had decided that the Slavic nations were destined to be slaves and not permitted to raise themselves up with any cultural or intellectual ambitions. However, our devoted teachers, risking their lives, carried on doing their jobs, employing an endless variety of tricks to confuse the Nazi bloodhounds. One year of secondary education was disguised as a course for seamstresses, another as learning the art of making hats. Luckily the war ended before our educators ran out of ideas!

Instead of gossiping about romantic encounters, young girls were asking each other nervously: "What would you do if you were captured by the Gestapo and tortured?"

We swore to keep the secrets; how did the oath go? "No matter what happens to me . . ."

FIVE
Decision and Action

Nineteen forty-four was the year of decision. The war was going badly for the Germans. The Soviet army, aided generously by the Western Allies, continued to push the Nazis west, and in the spring, the eastern front line was running across pre-war Polish territory. The leaders of the Resistance laboured under growing pressure from all sides. The people of Poland were desperate to put an end to the ruthless occupation; the Resistance leaders themselves yearned to find a way of stopping the constant horror of continued atrocities. Outside of this immediate orbit, the exiled Polish Government in London was exerting its own brand of speculative pressure about the political repercussions should Poland, and especially Warsaw, be liberated by the Soviet army unaided by the active and overt participation of the Polish Resistance forces. By a cruel twist of fate, all that pressure played into the hands of Stalin, who also called on the Poles to join the Red Army in the battle against the Nazis.

In midsummer of 1944, when the Soviets were practically outside the gates of Warsaw, the Germans unexpectedly announced the decision to defend the city. They called for "volunteers" to build the necessary fortifications. The inhabitants of Warsaw ignored the order, and then nervously awaited repercussions; but nothing happened. In such a desperate limbo, the Polish Resistance leaders forced the hand and decided the Uprising would start August 1st at the "W" hour.

Sensing unrest, heavily armed German patrols, with their automatic pistols at the ready and hand grenades tucked into their belts, took to the busy streets of Warsaw on July 31, walking like harbingers of the impending disaster among the gingerly stepping pedestrians.

That night, for the very first time in my life, I was going it alone, attending to my own responsibilities away from my family. I left home in the evening after my mother blessed me with her rosary, crying very quietly. I and four other young girls slept on the floor in a friend's apartment.

Call it blatant nonchalance in the face of approaching battle or an irony of fate, the owners of the apartment had just had it fumigated for bedbugs. The offensive chemical smell, acting like some weird anaesthetic, nearly succeeded in overpowering our senses, partially wrestling down our insane excitement, which was almost too much to bear. And who could blame us, considering that we had spent months, years, preparing for this--the morning of the first day of August, 1944!

And, we had to wait again until the afternoon, when it would be safer to set out. As it happened, we were on the verge of leaving the house in pairs in the morning, when a message came through: Apparently, isolated unplanned skirmishes had already begun at several points in the city. A group of insurgents, hurrying to an appointed outpost, were carrying weapons and hand grenades in the folds of their coats; they happened upon an armoured car carrying German soldiers. Apparently, the Germans decided that a bunch of young men dressed in coats on a warm August day had to be up to no good. The Germans opened fire--the insurgents did likewise. This premature engagement robbed the insurgents of the advantage that a simultaneously planned action would have had, of surprising the enemy all over Warsaw. Having been warned, the Germans immediately fortified all the strategic points in the city, considerably diminishing the insurgents' chances of success.

I, together with another girl, finally left the house and hailed a "rickshaw"--a peculiar contraption created in answer to wartime gasoline restrictions; or rather, as far as civilians were concerned, in answer to an absolute lack of it. The vehicle consisted of the backseat of a car mounted and propelled on a modified bicycle. It ran on manpower and needed no gasoline.

"Where do you want to go?" asked the driver.

"Take us as far as you can, towards Dabrowski Square."

The "driver" started pedalling like mad. He was "in the know."

A sudden burst of machine-gun fire cut through the tension around us, sending us in sudden panic on the sidewalk against the wall; so this was real danger!

"Sorry, I have to run, good luck!" And the rickshaw was gone.

More shots were fired, and people scattered away leaving the street unpleasantly empty. My companion and I huddled against the wall, both clutching our little bags with prescribed "necessities" for what was to be a few days of the triumphant liberation of Warsaw. There was nothing we could do but run into the next apartment building entrance. Most apartment houses in the centre of Warsaw, built at the turn of the century, had entrances with vaulted ceilings large enough to accommodate a horse-drawn carriage. They usually led into a spacious yard surrounded by the wings of the building. Several people were already seeking refuge within the massive walls of the entry; the heavy gates were securely locked behind them, offering the comfort of at least temporary safety.

"Come on!" We heard a voice urging us to advance. It was Maria, a member of our unit; we knew her from the meetings. She emerged from one of the staircases leading up to the apartments. "Come on upstairs to my uncle's place," she insisted.

Well! Here we were, all sitting in a comfortable living room sipping a tasty drink offered by the host as a toast to the insurgents. What a turn of events, what a change from last night! The friendliness and enthusiasm of the people around us was so heartwarming, and yet, I was not sure things were going right.

"We have to get to our unit," I interjected lamely, especially since Alika, my companion, did not seem worried in the slightest.

"Wait till it gets dark," suggested somebody. "Then you can run over there safely."

So much for the exciting adventure--I felt we were stuck and would miss everything.

Maria was having a great time: "We'll get there, don't worry."

Food and more drinks appeared. The Uprising was going to be over very soon--an unqualified success; and why not? The Soviet troops were just on the other side of the Vistula River. The Germans would run for their lives, and we, the inhabitants of Warsaw, would actually welcome the Soviet warriors entering our city. Such was the plan of the Polish Resistance. Besides, they were encouraged by the Red "friends" who were urging them not to sit idly by, waiting for liberation, but to show courage and help the Soviets avenge Nazi crimes everywhere.

That summer afternoon, everyone was too happy to think of the dirty business of politics. Unbeknownst to these affable people, their fate was already sealed.

The last London message from the Polish government-in-exile, advising the Resistance to postpone the August 1st date, came too late. The die was cast; the shackles were broken; the masked knights of the Resistance revealed their faces to the hateful foe. Warsaw's flamboyant youth had sung the triumphant hymns too early, and managed only to betray themselves.

Was it necessary?

Fifty years later, I am in this venerated Warsaw cemetery. I am standing spellbound by the sight of row upon row of simple birch crosses, sorrowful testimonials to the sacrifice of those whose names figure white on row upon row of black plates, attached like signs of mourning to the white bark of the trees. I stare through tears at the digits under the names: "21 years old, 22 . . . 24 . . . 18 years old . . ." So young. May God almighty punish the murderers--but which ones? Those who set the trap, and waited, watching? Those who carried out the slaughter? Or maybe those who gambled and lost?

Today, the Communist government installed by the Soviets is gone, and the Polish people are free to celebrate the anniversary of the event that happened half a century ago.

Drops of perspiration flow like tears down the nose and lips of the motionless young sentry at the "Gloria Victis" (Glory to the Vanquished) Memorial. The summer of 1994 is exceptionally hot in Warsaw. Maybe the temperature is typical after all, and I have forgotten. Finally, the official ceremony is over, and people tired out by the heat and having to stand uncomfortably close together start to disperse among the trees and the graves.

I start walking very slowly along a peaceful alley; here, time is of no consequence.

Another woman walks beside me. She is also from the Canadian "delegation." We both wear the "veteran's" uniform: dark grey woollen skirts, white shirts and ties, and navy blazers sporting the crest of the Polish Home Army. We both feel very hot.

"Did we have to dress like this?" The president of our veterans' association was a little too ambitious . . . putting so much emphasis on military dress.

The woman walking beside me is a stranger. We have just met and I would rather be by myself. I excuse myself, and turn into an alley to find the grave of a young girl from my school who was killed during the first few days of the Uprising, shot by a sniper as she was running with messages across a wide boulevard.

Janka was a pretty girl with delicate features and wavy dark blonde hair. She could have been a little older than I, since she was one grade ahead. When we started with the Girl Guides who were secretly organized under German occupation, Janka was my leader. A well-brought-up daughter of a lawyer, she was the example of a perfect young lady. She had a gentle way about her and a sweet, quiet way of speaking. We met almost every week at different houses to plan and organize various "affairs"--most often such tasks as distributing the underground press copy, affixing posters on the walls after dark, etc. "She" is now the stone marked with her name.

I am walking, taking in the quietness, when someone speaks to me rapidly:

"Please could you stop for a minute?" says a youngish woman. "My aunt came here from Chicago . . . she cannot walk very fast. She saw you back there and she thinks she knows you."

I wait. It would be wonderful to meet an old friend here. Well, with such crowds around as far the eye can see, it could happen. But the Polish woman inside an American exterior is a stranger. We stop for a brief conversation in the midst of the passing multitude.

And then I hear that voice--a lusty voice coming from a deep throat of a woman from another epoch. I know it's a cemetery and ghosts may appear, but . . .

Is it Anna--after all these years? Anna? Somebody wrote to me about how she was supposed to have died. She was old enough; older than Stan, who died two years ago in his late sixties. They divorced shortly after the war; Stan remarried and had a son. I remember when Anna and Stan got married during the war; my mother was devastated and did not attend her beloved son's wedding. Anna had a reputation of being allegedly too friendly with the Germans. And so, when Stan was arrested by the Gestapo on suspicion of being responsible for the shooting of a young woman with whom he was romantically linked, and who turned out to be a collaborator, it was owing to Anna's intervention that he was set free. She claimed later she bribed somebody.

Anna sounds fine. I am overcome by sudden nervousness and can hardly look at her face, which is partially hidden by the brim of a large hat . . . how long has it been? As a young bride in 1943, in her late twenties or maybe even her thirties--people said Stan, who was only 22, married her out of gratitude--she was always carefully made up and stylishly dressed. She also smoked.

A young teenager, I could not help being impressed by this sophisticated creature, so unlike all the women in our family and so different from the mothers of friends at school--all shabbily dressed, since dispensing with make-up and fashionable clothes was considered patriotic. Most people could not afford either, anyway. Tempted by curiosity, when Stan invited me to visit, I came wide-eyed and open-mouthed, and even tried to smoke their hand-rolled cigarettes. However, to remain loyal to Mother, I avoided becoming too friendly. Their apartment in one of the better sections of Warsaw was very comfortable for war standards. It had a certain aura of forbidden excitement and suited Stan's budding artistic aspirations to a tee.

They even had good tea and some cookies to offer as refreshments . . .

"Ira! Is it you?" Anna's voice is as throaty as before.

A rapid deluge of split-second fractions of memories, mostly troublesome, invade my brain like droplets of poison, temporarily preventing me from speaking.

I last saw Anna in the middle of the ruins of Warsaw, almost exactly fifty years ago to the day, and now we are standing in the middle of a cemetery; a beautiful cemetery, but still, undeniably, a sad place. Startled, I can hardly look at this proverbial "ghost from the past." People come by in groups, couples and singles. Trees offer a rest for the eyes with their gentle colours so characteristic for an early Polish autumn. Finally, I say: "I recognized your voice . . . er . . . where do you live now?"

"Oh, in . . ." The name of the place is hard to hear. I think I heard "Florida." Is it possible?

" . . . You have to visit; oh yes: here, let me introduce my husband . . ."

I find the prospect of facing some character, whom Anna married after separating from my brother Stan, quite unpleasant, but I strive to appear polite. The approaching short, balding gentleman is not anybody I know and looks harmless.

"Dulciu, darling," intones the Voice, "this is Ira, my friend. We were close in the past . . ."

The newly introduced husband kisses my hand and murmurs appropriate words of enchantment.

"I see you came home," Anna continues.

Fortunately, not quite, I think and heave a secret sigh of relief. "My home is now on the other side of the globe," I say aloud.

Not wanting to continue the uncomfortable situation, I excuse myself clumsily and leave, silent and ashamed of the silly, noncommittal smile I know appears on my face, when in reality I suffer from intense embarrassment.

I cannot perform in the old role; I have been cast in a new piece. The Future did arrive--alas, in another country. I had to learn everything anew: the language, different customs, the rationale behind strange opinions. It always seemed to be such humble pie: straining to know, to understand, and to appreciate, often without being understood and appreciated myself.

SIX

Elusive Triumph

Ted and I are sitting in the kitchen having lunch. The kitchen window offers a generous view of the lake, or, technically speaking, the St. Lawrence River. It is one of those occasions when something clicks, and our minds go into "memory mode."

"The last time I was home, it was perhaps the fourth or fifth week of the Uprising," I begin, "but things were not going well at all . . ."

The first few days of the Uprising, people were out in the streets singing patriotic songs that had been forbidden by the occupant for the past five years. Polish flags, hidden away in various dark places, made their appearance at the entrances of many buildings; it was like a long-awaited national holiday. In the downtown area, free of the occupant, we already had our own administration. The newly organized militia rounded up hated collaborators and the infamous *Volksdeutsche*," the predominantly despised breed of people who had improved their lot during the lean war years by coming up with documents testifying to German ancestry. They obtained better food rations, reasonable peace of mind, and generally decent treatment.

Some of them also served the occupant, by spying on the very people who used to be their neighbours and unsuspecting friends. Too bad--in many cases even *their* menfolk were eventually called up and sent to the front to pay for the privileges. But as long as it lasted, the *Volksdeutsche* lived well, occupying, just like the "real" Germans, the best housing in Warsaw, enjoying the comforts of properties belonging to Polish families who had been expelled and frequently imprisoned.

Initially, at the beginning of the Uprising, we were billeted in an elegant apartment vacated by Germans who were running away from the approaching showdown, not only with the Red Army but with the natives, whom they might have feared even more. We even found sausages drying out in the beautiful modern bathroom. Wow! Everyone was ecstatic, triumphant. Ordered to build barricades to mark out the lines of defence, we ran out in the street, jubilant.

"Let's use the sidewalk slabs," announced an energetic voice.

And we all started grabbing the uprooted, cement slabs and dragging them to the growing mountain that barred the passage along the street.

"Be careful, they must weigh a ton each," admonished our leader, Kora. Poor, decent Kora was still trying to mother us, while at that very moment we were undergoing a metamorphosis--from polite young daughters of respectable families into beasts of burden, slaves to a cause! Surging adrenaline carried me past the pain in my arms and my straining stomach. I looked upon the growing barricade as the most glorious and necessary achievement of my life!

Having never lifted anything heavier than a few schoolbooks, I was half dead from such unaccustomed effort. Fortunately, there was still lots of food and there were peaceful places to rest. We took turns to operate the switchboard. Everyone was cheerful, expecting the Soviet army to arrive soon, and, together with some Polish units formed under its wing, finish off the Germans. Everyone around was young, and if not young, at least smiling and full of enthusiasm. During brief breaks in our activities, we talked and sang patriotic songs.

A very strict routine was joyfully followed during those few wonderful days. In the morning we gathered in the yard for a daily briefing. We got our orders for the day. The sad news of people being killed and wounded did not diminish our eagerness to do our part no matter what price would have to be paid. Hala was wounded first, and we all crowded around her. She was so brave! A pretty girl with a bandaged head.

The tragic reality would begin to stare us in the face later. As minutes and hours ticked away into days and weeks, and the expected aid failed to materialize, the battle against the well-armed and trained foe grew more difficult. The insurgents, who were by this time suffering terrible casualties, desperately tried to hold the many positions they occupied in the early victorious surge, and eventually had to withdraw.

At first, we did not realize what was happening in other areas of the city being taken over by the insurgents, and then regained by the enemy. But soon enough the people miraculously escaping from such locations informed us about the carnage and the bestiality unleashed on the defenceless. People unable to escape--the wounded, the old, the sick, mothers with young children, medical personnel--were ruthlessly butchered.

An orderly from a hospital full of the wounded told us this story:

"First, they asked who the chief surgeon was; they went to his office and shot him on the spot. Then they put us all in a very small room and started shooting."

Bodies falling over each other covered him up. He lay motionless. The Germans listened for moans, and fired some more to silence them.

"When all was quiet they left; a couple of us who were still alive climbed out from under the bloody pile and escaped."

When the Germans returned a little later, they set the whole place on fire.

"I was very lucky I had a chance to escape, otherwise, you know . . . even if not yet dead . . ." His voice shook with the horror of it.

Our "ring of safety" gave us space and security for some time-- enough to create an illusion of success. As the uprising continued for longer than just "a few days," I was growing up fast. By the second week I had received my first real kiss on the lips.

I was just running out of the entrance into the street. Conscious of leaving the safety of the building, and keeping my eyes wide open, my body suddenly stiffened in response to perceived danger--I was stopped in my tracks by a young boy carrying a rifle.

Probably scared out of his wits, he was trying to resurrect his "manly" courage by grabbing my arm and holding fast.

"Please, kiss me," he whispered through tightly clenched teeth.

"I . . . I don't know how," I protested.

"Please, we are going out to fight. Please . . ." he pleaded, and holding me in a clumsy embrace, he pressed his lips against mine.

The wetness of this desperate contact was cold and unpleasant. Millions of men going into battle have extracted from women all kinds of semblance of passion in their need for comfort. No more passion could be extracted from me, as people wanting to enter put an end to this little drama.

"Good luck," I managed to whisper to the boy, as he was disappearing into the darkening street.

Then the reason for my being out in the empty street, frequently illuminated by explosions, jolted me out of a bewildered state, and made me follow the boy out into the growing blackness of the evening. The messages I was carrying were to be delivered to the other side of the large park. The place, so familiar in normal times and in daylight, loomed menacing and dangerous, scarcely visible at the end of the boulevard. To proceed into this abyss was the last thing I wanted to do.

The street seemed totally strange, like in a horror movie. I ran close to the walls of the buildings, all silent and dark. I arrived at a wide avenue that had to be crossed to reach the park. Hesitating and listening for any sounds, any possible cue, I thought about Danka, another messenger, who was wounded the day before crossing an avenue like this one.

"Well, here goes." Trying to make myself as small as I possibly could, by bending down and hiding my head between my shoulders, I threw myself toward the park on the other side. I was a good runner. It was safer on the other side among the trees.

I heard voices in the distance. It was impossible to make out who the people were; as far as I was concerned, they were not far enough. I ran into the thick bushes further inside the park. Rapid noise like a machine gun volley seemed to pass just over my head, and deafened me temporarily. Within a matter of seconds, I was lying flat on the ground; I tried to paw my way inside Mother Earth.

The voices moved farther away. With my breathing almost stopped, my extremities refused to obey; it was difficult to move. Chattering teeth made a strange noise in my head. Finally, after what seemed like eternity, I realized that I could move my arms and legs, and I slowly got up to a crouching position. I waited again. Nothing happened, so I darted deeper into the wooded area. Searchlights swept the dark area of the park I had already left behind. Running and stopping to listen, I lost count of time and distance. My shortness of breath, due to sheer fright combined with fast running, made me slow down. The other side of the park was now near.

"Please, God, let me get there safely," my lips repeated automatically.

It had to be the right side of the park or else I would be back in German-held territory. It was difficult to tell in the darkness. Before emerging from the shadow of the trees, I stopped and listened again.

"What the heck are you doing here, and who are you?" I heard a loud whisper in Polish.

Startled, I just managed to spell out the password.

"Give the girl a shot of vodka," ordered the commanding officer after receiving the messages. "Well done, kid!" he said loudly, but I saw more pity than admiration in his eyes.

Drinking carefully, and determined not to choke on the unfamiliar, strong liquor, I felt courageous enough to look at him more searchingly. He looked vaguely familiar.

Have I seen him somewhere before . . . ?

The other girls and guys were mostly older, but the normality of all our lives had been suspended first by the war and now by this. It was difficult to know how to behave in different situations; after all, how many times in one's life does one participate in an uprising? During the subsequent two months before the total collapse of the insurgents' capacity to fight, I would be forced to witness and deal with many peculiarities of war. Any morning, we could be shocked out of our wits by encountering heaps of body parts, assembled out in the street after a night of bombardment in the vicinity.

On the other hand, powerful instincts to preserve life could not be denied, and forced people to seek romance--perhaps to assuage their desire for feeling human, to assert their right to happiness, or maybe just out of mischief.

This blond and rather stocky fellow in his pseudo, haphazardly chosen uniform, had a laughing face and kissed me in a friendly way when we met by chance after duty. We went for a walk and had a pleasant talk.

"I'll see you tomorrow," he said, smiling.

"He runs after everything in a skirt," warned our patrol leader, Kora; she was four years older. Maybe she knew him or maybe she knew something about life.

My new "friend" was wounded. I ran to visit him in the hospital. Happy to find him, I rushed to one of the beds in a dimly lit basement hospital ward. The shadowy figure of a woman rose before me.

"Look at her, the bitch! Came to his bed, the little whore, the whore!"

His wife! His wife was standing right there shouting. Fortunately my brain was functioning well; my legs carried me quickly out of the wretched place, but I felt suddenly dead within myself, and as if dispossessed. A whore? I thought of myself as friendly, good-humoured, intelligent; well, perhaps a little flighty now and then . . . but a whore? The shock of this word directed at me swept away the protective cover of ignorance disguised as innocence--yet undiscovered paths suddenly opened before me in a threatening way. Bewildered, I even forgot to blame the cheat for forgetting to tell me he was married! However, there was no time to feel sad and hurt longer than maybe for one half of a weepy night.

Far more harrowing than such personal problems was the rapidly deteriorating situation around us. The general euphoria lasted precisely until the Germans retreated clear out of their isolated positions, to consolidate their forces on the outskirts, and switched from heavy machine guns, hand grenades, and other hand weapons to some heavier hardware--dramatically evidenced on the third day of the Uprising. That day, Bogda and I finished our switchboard duties early.

With the furious activity of incoming calls, interruptions on the line, and wildly competing messages, Kora would not let us work the switchboard any longer; she and another experienced woman took control. We were used to handling slower communications activity.

"Let's go up on the roof and see what's going on," I suggested. We had a little time before being called to stand by for carrying written commands. We quickly climbed the elegant staircase of the apartment building and emerged at the threshold of the sky. It was a beautiful summer day, sunny with a refreshing breeze.

"We could go to the beach . . ." sighed Bogda, smiling and conjuring up sudden visions of clear water and green bushes around the river.

"Look out, there! Hide behind the chimney!" yelled Sergeant Bodo behind us.

And, seemingly berserk, the normally likable and witty man, whose company was enjoyed by the whole unit, pushed us roughly behind the bulky structure of the chimney. A deafening roar of engines and an onslaught from a plane's machine gun just swished past us.

"The SOBs are using the *Luftwaffe*," cursed the sergeant under his breath. "They mean business."

Later the same day, we were ordered to leave the upstairs flats because the wailing sirens announced an air raid. I saw an officer of the Resistance army getting panicky, and hiding fearfully under a table-- with everyone pretending not to see. Eventually, the sirens were dispensed with as an unnecessary formality, since the insurgents had no anti-aircraft at their disposal. The air raids continued with only short breaks and became practically constant. We could still sleep upstairs; they could not bomb us in the dark. Not for long, though, since we started to get hit with enormous artillery projectiles from the railway guns, which the Germans had just installed on the outskirts of Warsaw. They were even worse than the planes--they came without warning, except for the terrifying swishing sound they made, when it was already too late to hide.

Though the technicians worked tirelessly repairing the lines under fire, the constant bombardment kept throwing our communications network out of whack. The heroic efforts of the Warsaw power station staff maintained the supply of electricity--the lifeline of the city's hospitals. Electricity was also essential to maintain the primitive manufacture of ammunition and weapons. It was also a necessary element in providing cooked meals, which, within some sections of the city, was becoming more and more a joint venture.

And still there was no sign of the Red Army. Tired after running across the city, carrying more and more messages, since the telephone connections were no longer reliable, the messenger girls were glad to sleep on mattresses spread around on the cement floor in the basements of partially destroyed buildings.

Even during the first days of the Uprising, crossing the wide streets was extremely dangerous. Timing and good running were absolutely necessary. Usually, a guard would be on the lookout at the point of departure at each side of the road. He would calculate the time between the shots from whatever weapon was being used. One had to jump on the road a split second after the detonation and run like the devil to the other side. It was like playing Russian roulette, because, like the game, it did not always work out. Later a network of barricades and underground passages was developed to give some protection.

We already had two girls wounded by snipers. The casualties and deaths were rising incessantly, though life, what was left of it, went on. When settling down for the night, dead tired, we pretended that everything was normal no matter how wretched the conditions.

"Look at Alika," someone remarked. "She still puts curlers in her hair."

"Are you in love with Sergeant Bodo?" came the question from a dark corner, where Alina was already reclining comfortably. Such silly remarks tried to, but could not, drown out the dangerous sounds from outside.

Accustomed as we gradually became to all kinds of hellish noises, we suddenly all stopped to listen to a strange new sound like a ping-pong ball bouncing off a table.

"Pick, pick, pick," it went.

In the morning, the temperature in our basement went up considerably.

"We'll have to move," announced the lieutenant in charge of the unit. "Our building is on fire; they dropped incendiary bombs on us last night."

Bad news kept on coming. The insurgents and civilians alike were dying in battles, buried under the rubble, bombed by planes and by artillery, murdered by the enemy troops. And still no help arrived. The commander of the Uprising, General Bor-Komorowski, sent out desperate messages demanding ammunition and other supplies, to maintain resistance against the increasingly deadlier weapons the Germans were using to fight the stubborn Warsaw insurgents.

The Germans' losses were high as well. Many of their soldiers were killed, and some, taken prisoner, were put to work repairing the damage inflicted by their comrades. They could be seen in the streets shovelling debris--a thankless job under the circumstances--or carrying large containers of water to hospitals and field kitchens.

Eventually, the German High Command decided to concentrate on an offensive strategy based on driving a wedge between the various regions of the city held by the Poles. The Old Town, the historical section of Warsaw, preserved for posterity in its original style, was attacked so furiously that the insurgents were forced gradually to retreat. Every house, even every room was stubbornly defended, but to no avail, and hope was waning. The British promised to drop ammunition and supplies, but Stalin refused to grant permission for the Allied planes to land and refuel on Soviet territory. The drops were coming few and far between.

We were trying to keep up our spirits. The night our burning building grew too hot and threatened to collapse, we carried our mattresses to another house a few blocks down the street, illuminated by houses burning on both sides. There was no water to put out the fires. Scarlett's escape from burning Atlanta in *Gone With the Wind* looked about the same. But we were still singing.

There were some successes. The insurgents managed to make headway at certain important points in the city. They liberated a group of Jewish prisoners. They continued to repel the attacks of superior German forces at sensitive sections of the "front." But everyone knew that the murderous pace of the unequal struggle would lead to a colossal tragedy unless help from outside arrived soon. Still, apart from the aerial drops delivered by Allied pilots under unbelievably difficult conditions, where some of them lost their lives, no outside help was forthcoming. Frequently, due to danger and confusion, the precious cargo was dropped on German-held territory.

There was no shortage of bad news.

"The situation in the Riverside district and at the power station is not good. We are trying to hang on . . ." announced our commanding officer.

My father used to work at the power station and we lived in the Riverside district. As far as I knew, my mother would still be there in our apartment. It was then that I decided to try and bring my mother over to a safer place, closer to where I was, so we could see each other more often; no one knew how much we had to endure yet. Mother was very strong during the occupation; I admired her so much. The bank accounts were frozen right at the beginning of the war. Polish citizens were allowed to make a small withdrawal only once a year. Needless to say, any Polish government bonds were useless. Mother juggled our meagre finances to pay a little for my school each year; she had her clothes altered so I could have something to wear when I grew out of my coats and dresses. She sold every piece of her jewellery, father's collection of Russian gold coins, and everything in the house of any value, just to keep us fed. And then, to make a little money, every day she made sausage, using our traditional Easter recipe. It was delicious, and more and more people wanted to buy it.

Under normal conditions, her enterprise could have developed into a successful business venture. As things were then, just getting the meat was a major challenge--it meant risking her freedom or even her life, if she happened to be caught at the clandestine marketplace during a German police raid. After that, the work itself, although time-consuming and boring, seemed almost pleasant.

It may sound ridiculous, but as I was going to get her to leave her home and come with me to embrace God knows what kinds of experiences, I felt guilty and responsible for all the disasters, and very protective toward her. I thought she was old and helpless, and didn't deserve to have to suffer so much at her age; she was fifty-six, so much younger than I am now! It seemed entirely appropriate for the younger generation to feel responsible for exposing the population to the horrible consequences of apparently foolhardy actions.

The memories of the Warsaw Uprising will be forever saddled by the query: "Was the Uprising necessary?"

To go to a different sector of Warsaw, especially one under heavy German attack, I remember, I had to have a special pass from the commanding officer of our unit. How ironic! After all, I was a messenger; it was my job to run around even in dangerous places. I also had to have permission to bring over my mother.

It must have been the fourth week of the Uprising, and as if by evil magic, the constant artillery and aircraft bombardment transformed the reality of familiar streets and buildings into a horrible nightmare. The sidewalks were dug up and piled up as barricades, tramway carriages lay on their sides like dead beasts; useless power lines created a tangled chaos on the ground. Whole apartment blocks or office buildings and shops stood here and there, though some displayed horrific gaping holes. Numerous buildings were partially or totally reduced to shapeless heaps of bricks and mortar. Windowpanes were gone. Windows in what was left of some walls were cavities resembling the empty eye sockets of dead monsters.

Thick wires that used to support business signs, twisted as if by violent convulsions, protruded from walls. Billions of glass particles from broken windows coated the pavement. When raised by sudden gusts of summer breeze, and mixed with the blinding dust from the ruins, the particles danced around in the air, hurting eyes and making breathing painful.

It was surprisingly quiet. People in the streets went about their business in a seemingly normal way. Apparently ignoring the nightmarish scene, they jumped over the horrible obstacles barring the way, climbed the dreadful heaps that used to be buildings, and almost jauntily descended into craters left by exploding bombs. They all carried packages or even bags--probably scraps of food or cherished belongings. I can still see the shabbily dressed and unwashed people, their pale faces disfigured by the strain of the fight to survive against overwhelming odds. Was there still a glimmer of hope?

Hurrying on with the others, I tried to keep my mind just on the task at hand. On reaching the apartment building that had been my home for as far back as I could remember, I told myself not to get weepy about one more damaged building, while so many others were now in ruins. Most people were in the cellars. Mother was there, too, pale and strange, not like mother at all.

I was anxious to leave as soon as possible; while mother readied herself, I ran quickly upstairs to the apartment. Well, it looked . . . different. The windowpanes were broken, and the curtains, still clumsily flapping around the gaping windows, did nothing to muffle the noise of the not-too-distant machine-gun fire and explosions.

Holding a photo album in both hands, I crawled under the solid dining room table. There seemed nothing suitable to take as a souvenir of this now destroyed existence. I grabbed a few family photos. It was pretty clear that there would be no coming back here.

Violent explosions outside appeared to be coming closer, as if urging us to go. Mother and I set out on our laborious trek back. The past was left behind.

SEVEN
The Screw Tightens

By the end of August 1944, in attempting to break down the desperate defence of the oldest section of Warsaw, the Old Town, the Germans introduced every method of destruction at their disposal. Air raids were carried out with impunity by low-flying aircraft supplemented by railway guns. The tanks got new companions, the so-called "Goliaths" --huge robot tanks that exploded on contact.

The latest piece of arsenal was a new kind of gun firing a sequence of four powerful incendiary projectiles. The fired projectiles announced themselves by a corresponding number of terrifying howls that somebody compared to the roar of a mad monster cow, and so the diabolical weapon was nicknamed "the roaring cow."

Ingenious insurgents invented "Little David"--a device shaped like a low wall, which, when put in the path of "Goliath," made the killer machine explode prematurely, hopefully minimizing damage. There was no defence against the stealthy "roaring cow," and no hope for people hit by it; they became living torches.

The Old Town, with its 400 years of history, was gradually reduced to one huge ruin. Heaps of rubble replaced the old churches that had been full of art treasures. With an ever greater number of casualties under continued bombardment, and deprived of reinforcements, the insurgent troops, prevailing for so long, were about to be forced to withdraw. Any penetration of the circle of surrounding enemy forces was impossible. By then, the only route connecting the Old Town to the Centrum was through the city sewers. Using the sewers, some of them as low as ninety centimetres, was the only way to evacuate the remaining fighters with their commandants--a couple of them over sixty years old--as well as the wounded and the sick.

The intensified destruction of the city, amplified by the violent battle skirmishes, in which the Germans were apt to use civilians to shield their tanks, resulted in a horrendous loss of life and overcrowding at the hospitals, where wounded occupied every inch of available space. The hospitals, gradually deprived of the means to offer care while continually tormented by air raids, were becoming a replica of hell on earth for patients and caregivers alike. The enemy played dirty.

The difficulties of going through low sewers made it necessary to find more roomy passages under the main arteries of the city. Although they were more spacious, the water in these passages was running high and fast, causing people to fall and sometimes faint from the sickening odour. To prevent oneself from drowning, one had to hold onto a rope, which was also used to drag smaller persons out of and through the water. The higher sewers were also more dangerous. People who were passing through the sewers located under the boulevards were liable to be hit by enemy grenades thrown into the manholes and drainage openings.

My friend Elisabeth had been through the sewers a few times, carrying ammunition to the Old Town. She told us what it was like the first time.

"Imagine walls running with slime dripping on your head. Still, it's better than a grenade. Then you have to bend in two and stay that way for as long as it takes. And the stink! Shit sticking to your bare legs. You don't want to ruin your shoes--you carry them around your neck along with the hand grenades you wear like a necklace."

The hand grenades, known as "philipines," produced for the insurgents in a nearby primitive munitions factory, were quite small but very effective. Bottles filled with gasoline were also good. During the Uprising, many young boys specialized in throwing such bottles under approaching German tanks.

I met Elisabeth during the last year we both attended high school in Warsaw. It was a surprise to see her one day delivering messages to our unit--the glamorous Elisabeth with hair tangled untidily at the back of her head, smudges on her face. She was enveloped in a man's camouflage jacket--a gift from an admirer, no doubt. Both taken aback at seeing one another enslaved in this tragic enterprise, we spoke in clichés.

"Elisabeth! What are you doing here?"

"Irka! And what are YOU doing here?"

"What do you mean? Most of our whole school is here."

"Well, Rita and Maggie are with me."

We were in the same grade, but I hardly knew her; she ran with a different crowd. We got to be close friends later. People became more approachable during the Uprising. They forgot their usual reserve in the midst of common misery and the superhuman effort to believe in success. Major B., the father of one of my schoolmates, was a parachutist just "dropped over" from England, who walked around smiling at us, a familiar figure in army fatigues. He was one of those incredible people trained to parachute behind the enemy lines on secret missions, armed with false documents and extraordinary courage; they knew how to disappear in the crowd in any occupied country. After the war, he was accused of being a spy by the communist regime in Poland, and executed.

People of all nationalities who lived through the Second World War and fought against the tyrants share the understanding of how these frequently horrid memories could be mixed with nostalgia and even some romance. Unfortunately, what some of them had to share was the disappointment of being left out of the winner's circle, abandoned behind the "Iron Curtain." I remember my friend's father was one of the many victims of this political arrangement.

As the destruction continued, people escaping from ruined houses had to live together in cellars. They obtained meals from communal kitchens, since food and drinking water were now scarce. Once, in such a gathering, I spotted our high school principal. She used to petrify us with her cool demeanour. She embraced me, crying, her thin neck shaking with sobs.

"We are so proud of you girls," she whispered in my ear.

Sometimes during a lull in the bombardment, the distant roar of Soviet army artillery, reaching the ears of the doomed inhabitants of Warsaw, seemed powerfully close, temporarily lifting spirits and reviving hope. But that and an occasional airdrop, which usually missed its target, was all the help we were getting.

By the end of August 1944, the bestiality of the Germans in dealing with the insurgents, the civilian population, and the wounded in crowded hospitals, had aroused indignation in the civilized world. The feeling of complete isolation and hopelessness in Warsaw was relieved somewhat by the news of the intervention of the British government trying to mitigate the barbaric behaviour of the Germans. The British government conferred the status of "combatant" on the Home Army, of which the Warsaw insurgents were an integral part. The British demanded that the insurgents should be treated in accordance with international law. With this statute in place, the mistreatment of the insurgents, as well as the populace, would be regarded as a war crime. Accordingly, the perpetrators would be punished after the end of hostilities.

"Now that we are recognized as combatants," announced a local wit, "maybe they will send us more ammunition!"

Unfortunately, ammunition alone could not stop the carnage. Defending against air raids, railway guns, "roaring cows," and giant robot tanks required equally formidable hardware. As it was, it finally became impossible for the dwindling insurgent forces to hold on to the Old Town. The high command came up with a plan for evacuating the civilian population, as well as the wounded and the fighting units, by opening and maintaining a corridor connecting the Old Town with the downtown. During the night of the 31st of August, the strongest capable units were to advance from opposite ends, in order to meet in the middle area and defend the corridor, keeping it safe for the passage of the evacuees. The element of surprise was to play an important role in the successful execution of the plan. Unfortunately, the plan was leaked to the Germans, who met the attacking Poles with a murderous fire. The huge holes in the half-standing walls of buildings, blown out by explosives to facilitate passage, became a target for German machine guns, killing one hundred fighters and wounding many more as they attempted to cross to the other side.

In the meantime, bombs kept falling on the remaining churches and hospitals of the Old Town, bringing death to crowds of people who had been seeking safety there. In the parts already taken by the enemy, old people, the wounded, and the sick were shot.

This desperate news reached us in the still relatively quiet downtown area but did not succeed in robbing us entirely of optimism. As if to lessen the shock of the terrifying details, rumours of a breakthrough at the Soviet front and a new offensive action sprang up, fortifying the will to persevere and make sense of survival under the appalling conditions.

With power gone and the city waterworks destroyed, the water supply was reduced to what could be obtained from the wells, wherever access to subterranean water was possible. Long lines of people with buckets and other containers formed around the wells, usually located at the base of bomb craters. Considering that you had to risk your life trying to get a little water, washing became a rare luxury.

Chased by the roar of the "mad cows" and unstoppable air raids, we kept changing our quarters almost every other night. During the day, we still ran messages, but the places to go to grew less distant and fewer. The enemy was slowly tightening the ring around us. For the third time in one week, we lugged our miserable belongings and what was left of our "beds" into a quiet cul-de-sac yet untouched by the wrath of the foe. The buildings were large and looked solid. One of them, at the very end of the short street, was the school building. My brother used to go to that school. Our family went there on different occasions: celebrations, I recall. I adored the place. A few years younger than Stan, I had to wait, very impatiently, to start going to my own school.

"Hey, that's my brother's school," I could not resist telling my companions. It was hard to believe how undisturbed and safe it looked.

Everyone was responsible for his or her own safety. On hearing an approaching plane or the "roaring cow," we would hide under any still-standing solid doorway or wall; or run into a cellar; or, if nothing like that was near, simply throw ourselves flat on the ground, as was recommended. Resting was another luxury. Luckily, I was allowed a brief rest shortly after arriving to the new quarters. Not for long, though. The droning sound of low-flying planes sent us to the cellar. There were about twenty or so people we could count in the candlelight.

"My feet are killing me," complained Danka, taking off her shoes.

"Good idea." I did the same.

The composure of even the most stable and courageous individuals can crumble if they allow themselves to be terrorized by the repeated whining of bombs dropped from low-flying planes, unchallenged by anti-aircraft, or any other weapon, for that matter.

"One, two, three . . ." we counted the explosions, hoping they would go away, and the deceptively gentle swaying of the earth underneath our bodies would cease.

The next one must have been a direct hit. Before we could count "four," the ground positively heaved up and down, a vicious sudden draft blew out the candles, and as a cloud of dust descended on us in the darkness, our breath, instead of being a life-sustaining blessing, became a suffocating menace.

"We're buried," somebody said quietly. Refusing to contemplate the practical consequences of that statement, my brain desperately pursued trivial concerns of the living. Finding my shoes became very important. As I began desperately groping around the floor, somebody was striking matches revealing the thick, grey air enveloping us in a confusing blanket.

"Stop lighting the matches," someone advised. "You're using up good air!"

Not wanting to contemplate how long the air would last, I was groping without thinking, when we heard faint voices, as though coming from a great distance.

"Sh, sh . . . they are trying to dig us out--yes, we are here," we tried to reply. Not loud enough.

"Thank God! Yes, we are here!" we all screamed.

Digging went on and on. We were alive but buried. We could hardly wait. Finally, scratching out the last bits of dirt and rubble, the rescuer's spade made a small opening shining brightly in the sea of darkness like a window of hope. There was more anxious waiting on the inside, and hard digging on the outside, before the opening was large enough to let us squeeze through one after another. Fortunately, we were all safe and sound, but now we better understood the horror suffered by those who perished by being buried alive; being buried under tons of rubble of a bombed house can be described by only a few people--those who were rescued. A large percentage of all who lost their lives during the Warsaw Uprising were the buried victims of vicious bombardment by low-flying planes and heavy artillery.

Emerging from our temporary grave, we found ourselves in a different world. Within half an hour or so, everything was turned upside down beyond recognition. At one point the road surface had been violently disturbed by the falling bombs, and lifted up to the second-floor level of what used to be houses, now shapeless mountains of rubble--an eerie picture seen through the suspension of dust floating in the air. People were digging out the buried.

The southern side of the city centre was next on the German list of annihilation projects. The Uprising was at a critical stage. Throwing at the insurgents everything they had in their arsenal, the Germans finally broke down the defences and took over the Riverside. Neither the inadequately armed insurgents, nor the workers turned soldiers at the power station, nor the ordinary people throwing all they could in the unequal battle, could defend against and withstand the destruction let loose over their heads.

At the time, I had congratulated myself for having brought my mother to the Centrum. But then, the Centrum itself became exposed to the fury of the enemy, intent on finishing the burdensome struggle that was costing them so many lives. News of deaths of young messenger girls, our schoolmates, in many cases, arrived daily. We had three wounded so far in our group.

At night, a new place to settle had to be found once again. Any shelter was difficult to find, as we marched past partially destroyed, partially burning buildings. Our order was to occupy a house close to the main train station, a German stronghold. Abhorrent as we found the idea, at this stage we had to silently admit the possibility of total defeat. There was no power, no water, not much food left.

"Spitting soup for supper!" was the cheerless announcement at the end of the day.

The soup, consisting of boiled ears of oats, was full of mostly inedible fragments. The spitting made a meal noisy but it was occasionally improved by a generous helping of red wine. A huge quantity of bottles had been found in some magazine and distributed among the population as, incidentally, a good remedy for a by now fairly widespread diarrhea. The oats were donated by a local brewery.

The commandant of the Uprising was sending desperate messages to London for help.

"Although the spirit of the fighters is excellent, they are running out of ammunition and have no means to defend themselves against the powerful forces of the enemy. . . . The civilian population of Warsaw is now at the limits of human endurance . . ."

And so, carefully construed investigations regarding armistice began to enter as a subject for consideration at the highest command of the Resistance in the second week of September 1944. These considerations were quickly abandoned, however, when the flagging will to persevere received new encouragement.

"Hey, Vanyas [Russians] are coming at last!" Wretchedly exhausted and hungry, people lifted themselves from the edge of the abyss to a new plateau of optimism and hope.

"The Red Army has reached the right side of the river and now occupies the eastern outskirts of the city," announced the official news report, still miraculously published from maybe the sixth hiding place.

"Please, let them come soon," we prayed in the privacy of our most secret thoughts.

Expressions of despair and hopelessness were to be avoided at all cost. When I heard Bogda crying during the night, I went into my dark corner and cried, too. But in the daylight, my wan face had to mirror determination and poise. It was a little easier now, since the Soviet artillery could be clearly heard, booming in the distance. We did our best not to dwell on the terrifying news about the suffering population. It was very easy to surrender to crushing despair, contemplating what the sick, the mothers with young children, and the old people were going through. Every little ray of hope had to be clutched at like the proverbial straw.

Indeed, whether at the urging of the Allies or due to some diabolical mischief aimed at prolonging the agony, our "friends" from the east dropped supplies limited mostly to biscuits and ammunition, as well as encouraging leaflets. They visibly engaged the German forces.

Warsaw was now predominantly in ruins, and burning constantly; an enormous cloud of dirty smoke hung over it like a funeral shroud for the whole world to see. Under the cover of darkness, and avoiding the heavy German fire at the approaches to the river, two messenger girls succeeded in crossing the Vistula, and reached the command of the Polish contingent under the Red Army forces.

Only Bogda, Chris, Basia, and I were left with Kora to perform messenger duties. Hala was hit by shrapnel in the forehead and stayed around with her bandaged head, but she was too weak to run anywhere. Our domain had shrunk so much that there seemed to be no need for elaborate communications protocol at this point. The Germans were just across the street from us, and could not harass us with heavy bombardment anymore.

More and more, we were busy in making life easier for people needing help. Getting water was one of my tasks. One of the messenger girls who came to us from the Old Town was ill and could hardly walk.

"Bring me some water, darling," she asked quietly. "I haven't washed in a week."

I would set out at about three in the morning with two buckets. The artesian well was only about a couple of hundred metres away and the heavy bombardment was not a problem, especially after dark. The greatest danger now was the snipers, hiding at elevated vantage points, who picked out unsuspecting victims with high-powered rifles.

Setting out well before sunrise was necessary for another reason as well--there would be a lineup.

Trying to help more people that morning, I carried two buckets. Walking the distance proved difficult even with empty buckets--it was more like a cross-country run over extremely rugged terrain. The buckets jiggling at my sides, I at last climbed one really high mountain of rubble and arrived at the end of a queue. The pump was at the bottom of a particularly deep bomb crater. People in a variety of attire, ranging from dirty blankets to expensive coats, depending on what happened to be saved or found in partially destroyed, abandoned apartments, were wearily awaiting their turn at the pump. They passed all kinds of containers forward, to capture the precious, cheerfully bubbling water.

The only one wearing a semblance of an insurgent uniform, the most consistent feature of which was a white and red band on the right arm stamped with the official seal of the Resistance Army, I stood in the lineup awaiting my turn.

"Well, what are we going to do now?" asked a woman, grey with exhaustion and dirt from living in subterranean quarters.

She was looking at me, but I had no answer, and kept my eyes glued to the pump.

"Well? What are your generals going to do? They will leave us so the Germans will shoot us all!"

I looked around at the strange people; there was nothing I could say to them--maybe only that they, or all of us, just happened to be in the wrong place at the wrong time. My white and red band, always a source of pride, branded me as a culprit in the eyes of this group.

"Now, now, what do you want from the girl? These youngsters wanted to save us all. They try and fight; they are so brave. Where do you live, Miss?" asked another woman with a kind smile. "My daughter is a messenger, too; I have no idea where she is . . ." She looked at the ground, then noisily wiped her nose with a dirty handkerchief.

Machine gun fire exploded close above. Though it was fairly safe to be standing in a deep crater, we instinctively cowered against the slopes of the formidable mountain of rubble.

"Getting water is dangerous these days, ha, ha." There was always someone trying to make you laugh. The man was smiling but not everyone appreciated his effort.

Getting back was a real trial. Carrying buckets full of water on a "cross country" run is not easy. Bending double to make myself smaller, the water heaving inside the buckets, I made my way close to the remnants of walls. While climbing through holes in some still-standing walls, I had to lift the buckets one at a time, trying hard not to spill too much when pushing and pulling at impossible angles, painfully knocking my legs against treacherous obstacles. In the end, I made a sick person very happy for a little while, though the buckets were only about three-quarters full. Getting water that way was far from efficient, you might say. I guess it was symbolic of our whole situation, where desperate efforts were made to little or no avail.

In the face of such colossal tragedy, faith in tomorrow was hard to justify; personal life and feelings were robbed of any consequence. Still, people experienced feelings, even fell in love, eyed the future, and, taking advantage of an odd quiet period and the presence of a priest, some actually got married. Life had to go on.

Even the horrible devastation after six weeks of battle affected my consciousness less strongly--it became almost acceptable to be living among ruins. Until one morning when I went to see my mother.

When we left home in Riverside and arrived in the relatively safer centre of the city, she joined a group of ladies who stayed in the basement of a school building. The ladies made themselves useful in a variety of ways, especially in helping to look after the wounded.

"How is your mother?" Kora asked; we were all worried about our families.

"She is fine except for an upset stomach." What I really meant was "diarrhea," but it sounded so harsh.

"You mean she has diarrhea like almost everybody now. We don't exactly enjoy a healthy diet. Give her a bottle of red wine."

And indeed a bottle of wine materialized the next day. I felt a lot happier. The second time I ventured to visit Mother, I was sorry I had nothing to bring her. Thinking hard to prepare a little "cheering up" speech, I turned the corner and . . .what? All the buildings, so solid and even imposing yesterday, were gone. Only shapeless fragments of walls and chimneys were sticking up as though reaching to the heavens in desperate prayer. There was nobody around--at least no one alive was around.

EIGHT

Wavering Assistance
from the Allies

Beginning on September 16, 1944, aid from the eastern front became increasingly noticeable. Soviet planes were actually spotted engaging the German anti-aircraft guns, which at times they managed to silence completely, allowing for substantial drops of food, ammunition, and weapons, as well as medical supplies. The decreased pressure from fewer air raids, some relief from bombardment, and especially the sounds of battle outside Warsaw, planted seeds of new hope in the hearts of the insurgents and the population at large.

Despite the efforts of the information agency, the true situation of the outside world remained unknown to us. The political activities of the Polish government-in-exile were revealed, probably to a limited extent, only to the highest level of command in Warsaw. The demands and entreaties for help, directed to the leaders of the Allied Powers, were meeting with an inexplicably weak response. All was obscured by a heavy veil of speculation and wishful thinking. Frankly, there was very little time for listening to rumours and analytical rhetoric. Apart from our continuing messenger duties, life without water and electricity became quite difficult. Existence had to be reduced to very basic elements. Moreover, we were hungry most of the time, and repeatedly disappointed by false good news to care anymore. However, some rumours about help coming were too hard to ignore.

"The American planes are coming!" was one of those fantastic announcements carried from mouth to mouth, from one cellar to another.

Where it originated was anybody's guess.

"They are coming in two days from now." There was no information as to what they were going to do or how, but somehow the date was firmly established.

The whole city, close to total exhaustion after six weeks of excruciating efforts simply to carry on, came back to life. The martyrdom of the innocents, the courage of the fighters, and the fortitude of the commanders were finally to be addressed, and found deserving of assistance. Warsaw was going to be rescued. But then:

"They could not come; the weather was so bad over Western Europe, they had to go back to the base." That was the explanation offered to heal a devastating heartbreak.

"Here we are standing up to the might of the German war machine, and they are afraid of a little bad weather?"

"They are coming tomorrow!" stated the new announcement.

The distant drone of a multitude of engines was heard about noon. They really were coming! Though still slightly skeptical, people emerged from the cellars and hiding places and stood with faces turned upward as if to witness a miracle. A formation of American Flying Fortresses, a bunch of dots at a high altitude, moved across the sky. Soon minuscule bright points disengaged themselves from the powerful planes, swarming around them, reflecting sunlight like jewels. The crowd looking up with joyful solemnity--they might as well have been expecting diamonds from heaven.

"Paratroopers!" shouted a man, as the German anti-aircraft guns went crazy. "They will all get killed, God!" he despaired in the name of all of us.

"No, they are just dropping stuff," declared our Sergeant Bodo, who happened to be standing nearby. "That will help a little." He smiled broadly.

As a matter of fact, the help proved to be mainly psychological. It managed to give a boost to sagging spirits, but since the drops were made from a very high altitude, the wind carried most of the packets beyond the areas occupied by the insurgents. Some were hit by the anti-aircraft and scattered as they fell.

"They should have come when we controlled two-thirds of the city. Now it's too late," was the verdict. Not much to cheer about.

Not much was accomplished on the ground, either. Efforts were made to establish communication with the Soviet army on the other side of the river. A few parties of couriers from the besieged city crossed over to meet with the command of the advancing Allies. However, any communication on a larger scale was made extremely dangerous by the Germans, who were constantly keeping the riverbank under intensive fire. Two parties of Polish troops, newly established under Soviet patronage, volunteered to cross to the city but were apparently insufficiently prepared for such a sortie. They went the wrong way, were decimated by heavy German fire, and only a few managed to return to base safely.

Still hoping for a miracle despite all the disasters, the insurgents desperately tried to maintain control over different areas of Warsaw. House-to-house, even room-to-room battles were raging at the outer limits of the insurgents' domain. Some strategically important buildings changed hands repeatedly from day to day, from hour to hour. Tragic loss of life occurred every time a piece of Warsaw had to be abandoned to the enemy. Invariably, the captured fighters were shot, the civilians and the wounded murdered. Therefore, it was essential to try and evacuate as many people as possible, especially the hospital patients, from the territories. Unfortunately, by the seventh week of the Uprising, when a position became untenable, no safe evacuation route, except the city sewers, remained. How safe were they?

The route through the sewers was neither safe nor easy, but as it was the only option, people fought their way to take it. The smell, the water, the awful, filthy closeness could make people sick, but far more dangerous were the Germans, waiting at the open manholes, to throw down hand grenades on hearing the slightest noise.

At some points they also erected barricades right inside the sewers to completely close up the passage. However, before undertaking each evacuation process, the insurgents would send ahead a reconnaissance party, in order to ensure passage was possible. Openings were made in the barricades, so that one person at a time could slide through. Even for healthy individuals, it was quite a feat to squeeze through the small opening; it was close to impossible for somebody who was wounded. The harrowing procedure took time, holding up the evacuation's progress, and straining nerves to the limits of sanity. Incredible discipline on the part of the helpers and those waiting to pass through was required to maintain absolute silence in the face of mortal danger from above; there was no margin for error.

At some points of the centre of Warsaw, the Germans were too close to drop bombs or harass us with heavy artillery. We had to be careful, though, of machine guns, hand grenades, and, most of all, snipers lurking across the street or on a roof, picking out their victims with high-powered rifles.

Barely surviving, we were just going through the motions. At this point, the question was, what kind of a life was it that was to go on? What kind of a person had I become? Externally, I must have been permanently grey with dirt and dust. To eliminate the need for combing and arranging my hair, I wore it swept up "*à la Pompadour.*" There was no time or opportunity to have it cut. My friends were saying I looked like an onion from behind. Emotionally, after accepting the painful fact that my mother had probably perished under the tons of rubble of the ill-fated buildings, I felt increasingly dependent on the group of insurgents, the men and the women, who were my companions during those wonderful days presently turning more and more dreadful. They were not only friends--they were my family. I could not imagine myself ever leaving them, no matter what the future held in store for us. Indeed, the people of Warsaw, civilians and insurgents alike, were like a big family trying to support each other in the hour of extreme need. Together, we were ready to endure Armageddon, dying to the last, or perhaps be saved by a miracle.

Incredible courage was incessantly demonstrated by the fighters and, hardly to any lesser extent, by the nurses striving to assist the wounded under the deadly barrage of enemy fire. The doctors in absurdly ill-equipped hospitals; the priests saying Mass within visibly crumbling walls and administering to the dying; even those looking after the distribution of the rapidly shrinking supply of food and water-- they all performed with superhuman patience and determination, all like members of a family, never neglecting one, never giving up. The difficulty of surviving and helping others to survive left no time for speculations about the future. A tiny spark of hope prevented us from dropping into a tenebrous abyss. Being with others, and knowing that they cared, kept the tiny flame from being snuffed out.

The exception to the rule of this energy amazingly harmonized for one single purpose was an occasional manifestation of human greed reaching for easy spoils. Food hoarded in secret places by unscrupulous individuals was being offered at exorbitant prices to the starving population. They were aptly called human hyenas, and were marked for future action against them after the war. Ironically, the incoming communist government used this pretext to accuse perfectly innocent people of, among other things, criminal profiteering, to persecute and get rid of its opponents.

We helped each other in different ways, even weird ways.

"Are you hungry?" a now pretty well unemployable telephone line repairman asked me. He was carrying a small box.

"Of course I am hungry."

"I mean, are you very, very hungry?" he persisted.

I just shrugged my shoulders impatiently. He opened a box displaying a neat row of cigarettes.

"You know, smoking one of these babies could make you feel less hungry. Want to try?"

Once during the last school year, it seemed ages ago now, a girl I was tutoring in math gave me a cigarette. Her father ran a funeral parlour--a very lucrative business in time of war, when good food and medical care are scarce and stress is plentiful. The cigarette was smuggled from a more fortunate country; it had a mild, slightly heady flavour, gentle enough even for my inexperienced palate. I breathed in the smoke and enjoyed a mild sense of intoxication; it was fun.

"All right," I said, reaching for the box. The man quickly produced matches, and a little fire started smouldering in front of my nose. A foul smoke reached my lungs; I exploded with a nasty cough.

"Heavens, what kind of cigarettes are these?" red in the face and choking, I managed to spew out with difficulty.

"'Junaki.' Most people can afford only those--we were lucky to get them. What did you expect?" he argued.

The irony of the brand name, "Junaki," which in Polish means "plucky fellows," was not lost on me--indeed, plucky you had to be, to smoke them. Gradually, almost everyone learned to pacify a growling stomach with a few puffs of the vile weed.

* * *

There is a lot of talk nowadays about the effect of wartime action on soldiers. Several court cases have been fought on the premise that a murderer could have been irrevocably destined to commit his crime, as a result of shocking wartime experiences. Would people who have witnessed, or even have been forced to participate in the indignities that war inflicts on human life, be more likely to kill? Would people hate their neighbours for having seemingly too much of anything--food, clothes, living space, even happiness--because they themselves once suffered the misery of hunger, loss of friends, terror of brutality, and danger of death?

People living in North America, or in any wealthy country for that matter, have heard many times how lucky they are to be living in prosperity. I have heard those clichés, too. Every Thanksgiving, every time there is news of some major calamity in the world, the call for being cognizant of one's good fortune is addressed to the masses, basking in the sunshine of their frivolity. My experiences are reflected in the way I react to such appeals: "Don't bother! They will never understand!"

But, since past generations have paid their dues in misery and back-breaking effort, why should the heirs to accumulated wealth be blamed for their good luck, and be denied credit for the way they build up the inheritance? Examples of what can be done with a lot of money are plentiful--for example, the models of planning and superb maintenance that are the highways in the United States.

* * *

The car travels smoothly away from the frozen Canadian landscape towards the more benign weather of Florida. Lucky to organize time off work, I accompany Ted, who will attend a symposium in Orlando. We will take a few extra days, maybe a week, after the symposium to have a rest in the sun.

This was not the first time we were setting off like that. In the seventies and eighties, before the arrival of advanced technology and the fear of terrorism, business travel had been regarded both as an activity necessary for conducting business, as well as a prestigious privilege for valued employees. No one had seen anything wrong with travelling on company business as an occasion for taking a side trip to an interesting location.

On one occasion, Ted had to attend a conference in San Diego. For some good reason, we flew to Los Angeles first. Our flight landed late and by the time we collected our luggage, rented a car, and emerged from the maze of highways around the airport, it was well after midnight. However, there was no reason to worry--until we were still driving at half past two in the morning. Worse, we could not say whether we were in San Diego, Santa Barbara, something-something Mission, or La Jolla.

"It's a new conference centre and nobody knew exactly how to get there," confessed Ted.

We kept on driving, and the place where a nice bed was waiting for us, in a pleasant hotel room, could not be found. Ted was getting exasperated.

"I have to ask someone," he declared.

But whom to ask--the streets are empty and the stores are closed. I kept these statements to myself, not wanting to add to the tension we were experiencing. Rolling along in the empty streets of an unknown city late at night can be unnerving, so when after a while we saw an open store, its bright lights lifted our spirits.

"It's a liquor store," Ted said, not quite so joyously anymore, especially on seeing a couple of black men standing in front of it.

"Don't go there," I said quickly, but he was already closing the car door behind him.

Ted acted at that moment not as an American, not as a Canadian, but as a European. We had hardly ever seen black people, even in the streets of Warsaw. When one appeared, he was regarded as a curiosity. In contrast to the European countries, where black people are few, on the North American continent, they represent, if not yet a power, at least a large section of the population. And the colour issues still rankle.

From the very beginning of our life in North America, we have witnessed the kind of fear and prejudice one would never expect in countries so proud of their devotion to liberty and the pursuit of happiness!

Ted went up to one of the men, and they talked for a while, with both of them using their arms like guideposts. Having the same sense of unease as local attitudes might dictate, I breathed easier when Ted was back inside the car driving.

"Now I know where to go; there is a side road which is very easily missed," he said. "You have to watch out for it . . ."

"I can hardly keep my eyes open . . ."

A vociferous group of people who were also arriving late played out a lively scene in the hotel lobby. Elegantly dressed women were escorted by their husbands, who tried to out-talk and out-laugh each other, apparently refusing to surrender to fatigue at this late hour. A lifetime of covering distances in thousands of kilometres has taught North Americans to draw energy from the excitement of travel, instead of being overwhelmed by it.

Our Canadian friends suggested a late dinner.

Some people can eat all the time, my mind grumbled because my body was tired. I actually begrudged these people their capacity for enjoyment! One couple there was particularly entertaining as dinner companions. The man had the habit of collecting information on the best restaurants in any spot in the world where he happened to find himself. He possibly even avoided going to a place unless it had a good entry or two in the *World Encyclopaedia of Restaurants*.

His wife's blue eyes lighting up her attractive round face signalled that the lady was ready for a drink--which we always welcomed, and we kept her company with pleasure. Smartly turned out, with a cigarette elegantly held in manicured fingers, she presented an image of glamorous sophistication of a "certain age."

Both of them and Ted indulged their good appetites for food and drink with appropriate sounds and lots of laughter, while I, the youngest of the foursome, sitting silent and miserably tired, was unable to appreciate neither the elegant surroundings nor the excellent service, and least of all the food. Feeling simply too sour to properly enjoy this chirpy, jolly feast, I consoled myself, thinking maliciously: *America is a paradise for gluttons.*

I really appreciate and admire the dry and sunny beauty of Arizona, the awesome mystery of the Grand Canyon, the expanse of the beaches on all three sides of the continent, the majesty of the "big reds" and so much more of America's marvellous scenery. Nevertheless, when we enjoy a fabulous meal in an interesting American restaurant, mean thoughts about the barely edible concoctions put in front of the captive customers along the routes from Ontario to Florida surreptitiously enter my mind.

Deliciously overdressed ladies in shiny outfits make me think of the poor black women I'd seen sitting forlornly in front of battered old houses in Alabama. Maybe I'm just envious.

NINE

The Beginning of the End

The fifty-seventh day of the Uprising marked the beginning of the end. Despite the ongoing battle against the ever so slowly advancing Soviet army somewhere on the east side of the Vistula River, the Germans were able to stage devastating attacks on the southern and northern suburbs of Warsaw. Continuous efforts to persuade the Soviet army command to undertake effective steps towards helping the insurgents were hampered by the frustratingly slow communication exchange, largely due to the political ill will demonstrated by Stalin, as well as a perplexing lack of interest displayed by the Americans and the British. The arguments pointing out the advantages the Red Army was enjoying, since the Uprising engaged a significant portion of German forces, fell on deaf ears. Even brotherly understanding between the Polish and Russian generals in the face of a common enemy could not prevail against the cruelty of Stalin and the Allied indifference to the critical situation; it could not blossom into a sincerely desired cooperation. Warsaw was to be brought to its knees not by one, but by the two cruellest enemies, right before the eyes and with the tacit agreement of the city's former friends.

Just barely armed with a haphazard selection of weapons, sporting an occasional machine gun or howitzer, backed by a meagre supply of ammunition, the insurgents faced a mammoth power of three times the troops, who had at their disposal the whole inventory of modern war hardware. Trying to work out a proportion between the resources of the two adversaries was just mind-boggling. A German armoured division overpowered the defenders of the northern suburb, Zoliborz, while

Goering's tank battalion, using civilians as human shields, eliminated resistance in Mokotow, the southern suburb. The battle in each case lasted just four days.

It was time to take to the sewers. Evacuation of the wounded began at four in the morning. The wounded were followed by a group of insurgents belonging to the communist sympathizers' section of the Resistance, who were particularly vulnerable if captured by the Germans. That group had to retrace its steps, after laboriously covering a length of the sewer, only to find it completely blocked farther down.

While another route had to be found, time was rapidly running out. The unit remaining above ground to cover the entry to the sewers in Mokotow was squeezed into a stubbornly defended territory just two city blocks in area. To make the evacuation practically impossible, the Germans raised the water level within the sewer system, and threw carbide and other noxious substances down the manholes to poison the air. Incredibly, nothing could stop the wretched procession in the bowels of the city. The evacuees crawled along, some in agonizing exhaustion, foul air ravaging their lungs. Scores fell dying, defeated in this desperate bid to reach safety, their bodies sinking into the mire under the feet of other relentlessly advancing marchers. Finally, recognizing the attempt to evacuate through sewers as disastrously futile, the insurgents decided to surrender.

The only part of Warsaw still in the hands of the Polish fighters was the Centrum. As one of the last surviving units of insurgents, we were holed up in a narrow street just a couple of blocks away from the main railway station, occupied by German troops. The news of catastrophic defeat advancing to engulf us soon in its deadly chaos all but disengaged our connection with the living world. The robotic action of preparing was conducted in total ignorance of its purpose. We were trying to hide behind an unsteady wall of hope, erected on a shaky base of rumours--the only news that reached us.

"We are going to POW camps," announced Kora at the morning briefing.

"Where?" was the anxious question.

"In Germany, of course. Where else?" Her voice trailed off sadly.

The next day, the news was not quite so good.

"We cannot be absolutely sure of anything. We only know that our delegation is meeting with the German command," Lieutenant Kazik informed us.

He might have wanted to add: "I hope everything will go well," but there was no such option. Whatever was going to happen would be the consequence of the unqualified catastrophe to which we fell victim, and nothing could make it any better. The political turbulence started to make itself known on top of every other calamity. Kora, silent and morose these few days, suddenly approached us obviously agitated:

"I have heard that our Home Army IDs are at a premium. Beware of the AL insurgents ["AL" stood for the communist Army of the People] trying to get them. The AL people are in particular danger. Germans hate communists even more than us."

One more problem was thus added to our already crowded agenda. Imagine, a Pole, until moments ago a comrade at arms, now suddenly turned into a deadly foe? No food, no water, scarcely a hope for survival, and now this!

For better or worse, usually better, enough people managed to keep their heads in the midst of the avalanche of disasters. While negotiations regarding the terms of armistice were being conducted with the Germans by representatives of the Resistance and the Polish Red Cross to ensure humane treatment of the insurgents as well as the civilian population of the city, somebody in our group made preparations at a much lower level. Bales of charcoal-coloured cloth, suitable for outer garments, were found somewhere in the ruins, and a tailor, who happened to be in a nearby cellar, was given the job of making ski-type outfits for the girls. Trivial as it seemed at the time, the idea worked out very well. In addition to giving us renewed hope, the new outfits served us well throughout our POW time, until we gave them up after liberation, to don the latest styles in men's uniforms specially altered for girls!

The uprising ended initially with a so-called armistice, which everybody knew was just a euphemism. How could an army, almost weaponless, literally standing up to its neck in ruins, presume to negotiate with a powerful and ruthless war machine?

The negotiators signed the paper, whatever the surrender document was called, in the presence of Red Cross officials, desperately hoping for humane treatment of what was left of the vanquished army and civilian population. What comes blatantly to mind is that we, in Warsaw in 1944, did not have exposure and publicity. Nobody was making consolatory speeches; nobody condemned our enemies; nobody promised vengeance: there was no "unequivocal support of allies."

And yet, the pain suffered by the wounded, burnt, buried under rubble; the despair of children suddenly orphaned, wives suddenly widowed, the pain of everyone mourning a loved one was just as unbearable then as it is now.

When we were finally told that we were to be treated as POWs, nobody was really sure that it would turn out that way. However, there was nothing else left to do but to "roll with the punches." The Uprising could not continue. Almost two hundred thousand civilians had perished. There was no food; horses and dogs, some said even the cats and pigeons, had been consumed. The environment was ripe for dysentery and a host of other diseases without any possibility of medical care.

We were given a choice to leave the city as part of the insurgent army or to join the civilians--the way chosen by some of the highest-ranking insurgent officers, who hoped to continue their activities by going "underground." I think two of our messenger girls chose to join the civilians for various personal reasons. Their lot was to be as uncertain as ours, since all the population of Warsaw was to be interned somewhere. Most of the people lost their homes anyway, and could only hope eventually to be allowed to find relatives or friends, if they had any, outside of Warsaw.

A vast majority chose the POW option. My closest friends from school, Kora and some women teachers we knew, were in the same group. It was to be hardly a school excursion, but if I closed my eyes and just listened to their voices, I felt greatly comforted and was able to fend off the feeling of being completely alone in the world, as if left adrift rowing a tiny boat in the middle of the ocean.

Amazingly, my communications unit had behaved as though it was time to take a long journey, not necessarily dangerous and unpleasant, as it was bound to be, but somewhat interesting in its unpredictability. The last evening before we were to leave Warsaw, we ate the rest of the meagre food rations, and sang nostalgic songs while drinking the rest of the red wine. Now that we were leaving, there was no point in preserving the wine for medicinal purposes; it was enjoyed as it normally ought to be. The commanding officer stood up and spoke briefly:

"I am sure we will meet again in happier times, in a free Poland," he began.

He looked around at the young people, some of them really children, now grown older than their years during the last two months. They had been severely tried, and passed the test of courage, loyalty to the cause, comradeship, and physical endurance. That was the gist of the CO's speech.

"Take care of yourselves, and God bless you all," he finished, and sat down quickly, lowering his face as if ashamed, not knowing where to direct his eyes.

We learnt to look to him as a father, and he was like a father--not at all like an army officer; but then, we were not a REAL army . . .

The next day, I remembered that my shoes were buried in the cellar of the building, which had collapsed on top of us all after that direct hit. Luckily, the rescuers managed to dig us out, but though the people were all out, the shoes were not. I had a pair of donated sneakers full of holes.

"Here, these are the only shoes I could find." I looked up at the handsome corporal dressed in motley attire, whose only military insignia was his field cap with the white and red ribbon.

The shoes were burgundy suede with at least a four-inch heel and open toes! They might have been obtained from one of the ladies of the night, who normally worked in the vicinity and perhaps wanted to contribute to the "war effort." Though the prospect of marching several kilometres in such contraptions was depressing, I had to laugh.

"Thank you, thank you!" I grabbed the shoes and showed them to whoever wanted to see. They shook their heads.

"Too bad you don't have nice walking shoes to go with your outfit," commented the patrol leader.

Only a few days before the armistice, the local tailor finished making the charcoal grey, very presentable "ski" outfits for the messenger girls in the unit. As it turned out, I stood quite a bit taller with the fancy shoes on, and took my place in the column, which was readying itself to begin the march.

During the Uprising, our presence in the streets was limited to harried running and jumping from one spot to another. We avoided being shot or wounded by not staying too long in unprotected places; now, we could walk at a slower pace and acquaint ourselves freely with the incredible devastation of the city. For more than two months, we had been exposed to almost incessant mortal danger, under systematic bombardment by every weapon known to man.

Normal feelings in response to traumatic experiences are hard to define; normal feelings of fear and distress have to be suppressed, or controlled, if only to preserve sanity. In the end, a profound despair could have a numbing effect, manifesting itself as an inability to react in a predictable manner. We were going through the motions, anaesthetized by the overwhelming grief of losing our freedom again after a brief triumph, childishly surprised at being able to move without a single shot being fired in our direction when we emerged out in the streets. Here and there German soldiers stood watching the progress of what must have been a pretty dismal sight to behold. At some points, the young insurgents were giving up their weapons. The German guards watched in disbelief, wondering how such a large contingent of the powerful Nazi army had to struggle so long to subdue these youngsters with old-fashioned rifles, outdated hand weapons, and homemade howitzers.

The girls marching beside me tried to maintain a decent pace. Each carried a little bundle of clothes and maybe some precious memorabilia of the life that was not to return soon--maybe never. My incredible shoes kept me drifting to the back of the line with every step. It was obvious that I wouldn't be able to walk the distance of fourteen kilometres at a decent pace. We were to assemble in a small town south of Warsaw to await further developments. It was growing darker on that early October day; and an almost imperceptible drizzle deposited refreshing moisture on tired faces. A horse-drawn cart appeared out of nowhere, slowing down close to the marchers.

"Irka, go on, get on," urged Kora, the patrol leader. "You only slow us down."

"But, but . . ." I protested.

I, known to be so strong and healthy, will now ride in a cart, while the others continue walking! How pathetic! For a few metres we walked side by side, still undecided; finally I gave up. The crude peasant cart moved on.

"Wait, we'll put our stuff on it, too." I sat down beside other people on the rough boards already covered with all manner of stuff, and found myself surrounded by all kinds of bundles, eagerly deposited by the women who were passing me by.

"Take care of this box; it's the first aid kit." Kora pushed a fairly large carton onto the cart beside me; she was still saying something when the cart accelerated rapidly on the urging of a guard, and continued at a good clip, leaving the marching people farther and farther behind. How far did we travel? Two kilometres? Perhaps ten? Darkness fell and I might have dozed off.

Cries of "*Halt!*" and "*Raus!* [Get off!]" made me jump. A German solder, screaming uncontrollably and brandishing a rifle made us get off the cart. I jumped down on the ground, instinctively grabbing my bundle. Ignoring the shouting momentarily, I deposited as many of the other bundles on the ground as I could, half hoping to somehow preserve them for my friends. The driver cracked the whip--the horse and the cart disappeared in darkness.

"Have you ever . . .?" I stood by the roadside next to a pile of miserable packages, getting more wet in the light rain. I was determined to wait until the rest of the convoy caught up. The highway reflected dim lights in its watery surface. People continued on in a grim parade, but no sight of my group. I was determined to wait as long as it took.

"*Los! Los!* [Get going! Get going!]" Another guard was approaching. He did not want to wait, and wanted me to move on. I indicated the pile and tried to explain. Well, there was no discussion. "*Los!*" was repeated several times at an increasing volume.

Once more I suffered the horrible humiliation and frustration of a person without rights. Nothing I could do would remedy the loss of the meagre belongings entrusted to me by my friends. They paid dearly for trying to make my life easier.

God! Shall I ever forgive myself? There should have been a way . . .

Some encouraging news brought a measure of relief and lifted me from utter misery; rumours of the German army retreating hastily on the Russian front could mean the near and infamous end of the Third Reich. It was also confirmed that the Allied Command recognized the Polish Resistance fighters as combatants, and General Bor-Komorowski, the commander in chief of the Warsaw Uprising, was named the commander of all the Polish forces fighting side by side with the Allies.

"So we are women solders and we will insist on our rights!" It is hard to remember who said it, but everyone was thinking it!

Meanwhile, by this time we were reclining on our bed for the night: a cement floor strewn with a thin layer of straw in one of the abandoned barracks designated as our "hotel." Hunger and fatigue kept us from going mad with despair and anxiety; sometimes physical factors, even negative ones, help to maintain a life-preserving balance. We were about to leave our country; no one knew where we were going or for how long; but in the back of our minds, we were hoping to be given something to eat.

The night was spent in endless talk and dozing on and off. The colonel, commandant of the division, hastily signed the IDs of the messenger girls, promoting us to the rank of sergeant in order to improve our lot in the POW camp. Germans always cherished rank.

"You will get more respect as *Unteroffiziere*,"[3] he said, smiling. There was no guarantee the ruse would work, but the sergeant's insignia brought me a lot of attention after the war for as long as I was proudly wearing my very unflattering uniform.

I think we were given some hot liquid, the kind that came to be known as our daily "coffee." Though trying as hard as I can to remember how we went about our needs to go to the bathroom, to wash, or how we got ready for the journey, I am aghast to realize that I have forgotten. A pity, because it is impossible for anybody to visualize such a situation; now, it is even very difficult for me! How on earth could it happen?

Nevertheless, when we were ushered into the presence of a cattle train on the sidetracks of the local railway station in the morning, it all seemed so logical. We knew from the "war stories" that prisoners of

---

[3] Non-commissioned officers.

war travelled in cattle trains. About thirty girls and women were told to climb aboard each car. The cars were empty except for a little straw spread around by some unlikely caretakers. In this instance, I have found it hard to forget that our "toilet" was to be a not so very large metal can, which had to be emptied through a small hole in the floor. There was an opening like a window in one of the sides. Even though it was not large enough for a human being to squeeze through, it was criss-crossed with wire.

We crouched or stood around, everyone trying to pick a spot to settle down, when the noisy slide of the still open doors of the car left us in semi-darkness as the doors were pushed closed. Like moths, we all rushed to the little "window." There were some people out in the station. Kora stood in the suddenly crowded space, her eyes streaming with tears.

"My mother! I see my mother over there! Oh, God, it's too late now!" She scribbled something on a little piece of paper and threw it through the opening onto the railway tracks.

"Maybe some kind person will give it to her." We were all close to tears. A sudden jerk and the train started forward.

* * *

It is heavenly, being carried forward in a comfortable seat of the train, passing the trees painted fiery colours by the sun and the approaching cold season--the colours of fall. Most of the terrain in this part of Ontario could be described as waste. A rocky, uneven base barely covered with soil, growing miserable thickets and scratchy bush on the carpet of rough grass and lichen.

It makes you wonder why nature lavishes so much colour and artistry on the waste. The best those fields can do is maybe feed cattle.

"Has anyone ever noticed the colour of cornfields in late October?" I amuse myself with utilitarian thoughts. "A famous movie star ought to dye her hair this colour and start a new fad."

But then the colours of humble but noble nature should not be exploited in such a pecuniary way. There are very few people on the train speeding to Montreal. It is the way I like it best because it provides peace and silence for the mind to roam over fascinating expanses of time and distances. I have already seen very similar post-glacial scenery, with soil scraped down to bare rock by sliding glaciers, and trees fighting to survive by desperately sending their roots down the tightest crevices in search of nourishment. Untold ages have passed and spread a modest cover of soil over the stony nudity. Little shrubs and low vegetation of the mind-boggling variety quickly took advantage of the offering, creating a living carpet that boasts of indescribable hues.

* * *

The giggling girls would rather wander down the long corridor of the express speeding from Warsaw to Vilna. They poke their heads into the different compartments, making faces and inspiring other gigglers. Soon, the noise will alert one of the teachers and the fun will be over.

"Please return to your seats," sounds a firm command. The girls have to comply and go sit inside the compartment, with nothing but boring scenery rushing past to entertain them. To be allowed participation in the excursion to another city, at their tender age of ten to twelve, they had to solemnly promise to behave--Heavens, not like grown-ups, but at least like mature teenagers.

"Look at those huge rocks!" sighs Magda, reluctantly coming to terms with her enforced quietness.

"And the lake." I strain my neck to see the fast disappearing vistas. "I have never seen such a large lake before."

"Bet you anything there will be an essay to write: "Describe what you have seen on the way to Vilna," adds a voice from the depth of a cushioned seat.

Just then the compartment door opens briskly, and Miss Borowska, the geography teacher, drops in for a visit.

"You will do well to pay attention to the scenery," she announces in her competent teacher's voice, "You will see classic post-glacial formations, moraines . . ."

It was the spring of 1939. We were on our way to Vilna to celebrate some national anniversary; we were to take part in an enormous patriotic demonstration in a city lauded by the greatest poet of the land. But neither the poetry nor patriotic love would be able to keep Vilna in Poland. During the agonizing days of the Warsaw Uprising, Poland's Allies were arbitrarily giving away former Polish territories to placate yet another monstrous dictator second only to, or maybe even worse than, Hitler. One more treasure irrevocably lost in the fray, though perhaps a well-deserved prize for the Lithuanians. They've got the moraines now. I have the memories of a quaint city, so different from Warsaw: people speaking with a funny accent, the charming theatre on a hill overlooking the outskirts of the city and beyond. And stores with different cheeses and bread. There were so many things I saw for the first time in my life.

Part of the magic of my childhood is no longer there for me to admire. Not without difficulties. But there will be more and more journeys by train.

Trains were not so much fun when travelling with the family. My parents were well into middle age when I was born; Father was old enough to be my grandfather. They espoused the conservative values of their generation. When all of us were dressed in our fine clothes for the journey, lady-like behaviour was expected of me. I would be sitting bored, while my brother would go off somewhere with Father, who would soon find and be talking to old or new acquaintances. Left to his own devices, my brother would then be running along the train from one car to another, opening and closing the heavy doors, and getting a kick out of watching the tracks racing noisily under his feet, until the conductor would chase him back into the compartment. I knew because once or twice I managed to take part in such explorations, only to be reprimanded afterwards. Naturally, I would try to defend myself:

"But Stan was there, too . . ."

Then I would be reminded once more: "Stan is a boy. You should not try to imitate him!"

The trip by train with my family that was really more than just exciting happened in September 1939. We were returning to Warsaw from holidaying in the country.

Whether or not to stay in the country where the risk of heavy fighting might be less, or go home to the capital city, which may be exposed to the hardships of a long siege--our parents agonized over the decision. But, eventually, we were on a train going back.

We did not take the electric commuter train, newly introduced in Poland in the late thirties, probably in preparation for the 1940 Olympic Games, which were to take place in Warsaw. The old stations in its path were rebuilt to provide a same-level entry to the train. I never cease to wonder why in different countries the passengers, sometimes laden with one or two suitcases, have to laboriously climb steps to reach the interior of a railway car.

No, on that sunny but grim day, because sections of the railway track were already damaged by the efficient *Luftwaffe*,[4] we had to take a little, narrow track train, a thing so trivial that the Germans forgot to bomb it. The locomotive was a living picture of the "little engine that could." It really needed all its strength on that occasion, what with an unusually large number of passengers crowded into its grotesque little cars.

Most people were, like us, vacationers returning home. In addition to suitcases, they were carrying preserves in large glass containers. The pace of travel was erratic. With the unreasonable demands on the mechanically limited locomotive, it frequently slowed down, or sometimes stopped abruptly, to let the passengers take cover in roadside ditches, when enemy planes were in sight.

The fighter planes, throwing no bombs, but noisily directing a stream of bullets from their machine guns at the people running for cover, were equally deadly in the final analysis.

All this coming and going provided a thrill of adventure for kids: a lively interruption of the slow progress and the present punishment of the uncomfortable pressure of the crowd, accompanied by mournful predictions for future, much worse calamities, which, unfortunately, did come to pass rather soon after. The danger of losing one's life overshadowed the possibility of being suddenly covered from head to toe with raspberry jam or cherry juice, from one of the voluminous glass containers collapsing under pressure.

I can imagine what this eventful trip must have been to our parents! Of course, worse was still to come: The journeys in cattle cars to the prisoner-of-war camp after the fall of the Uprising and, subsequently, to the slave workplace in Hanover, were still in the future . . .

* * *

The motion of the train stopped. Where were we? Apparently it is possible to fall asleep on the floor of a cattle car sparingly spread with straw. Nightfall had taken us by surprise. Suddenly, the sounds of

[4] Air force.

voices shouting in German were broken by the door opening noisily.

We were invited to go behind the tracks and do our "thing." Was it tempting us to make us run away? Human shadows scurrying around in the dark--who would know?

"We are fenced in with barbed wire," a man's voice sounded in the dark, as if answering the question.

"Where are we?"

"In Konin, the boundary of the Gubernia Generalna[5]; it will be the Reich from now on."

"We are supposed to be disinfected to get rid of our lice!" Somebody else in the dark obviously knew what was going on.

And so, at the threshold to the Reich, there stood a big barrel full of some disinfectant fluid, or so we were told. Although I hadn't heard of anyone having lice at this stage, we were ordered to drench our clothes in the fluid; even the guards perceived the nonsense of it all. One by one we approached with just a piece of clothing, preferably something that could be readily thrown out, and submerged it in the fluid, shining milky white in the meagre illumination of the railway tracks. Long lines of people in semi-darkness, each person dipping a piece of cloth in the barrel--we might have been performing a ritual in some bizarre cult, or acting as extras in a horror movie. Even so, it was a relief to take a little walk away from the stuffy boxcar.

When the train started moving again, one of the "older" women said: "My husband heard we're going to a *Stalag*[6] in Fallingbostel."

What we did not know at the time was, that there were more than fifteen thousand of us POWs, including almost two thousand women. General Bor-Komorowski had also chosen to go to a POW camp, perceiving it as his responsibility.

"We're leaving," whispered Kora. "Let's hope we'll be back in Poland soon!"

---

[5] The central part of pre-war Polish territory as distinct from the regions annexed to the German Reich in 1939.

[6] POW camp for non-officers.

The rest of us kept quiet, privately marking the moment in our hearts. Nobody in that miserable wagon, nor on that train carrying us away from everything we understood and loved, suspected how miserable would be Poland's spoils in the victory over the Nazis.

Such was the Future, with a capital "F," mercifully unknown to us in October 1944, when we arrived at *Stalag* 4 in Fallingbostel, which is situated in Lower Saxony, the central part of Northern Germany.

The Germans decided to divide us into groups, which were then sent to different camps. Most likely, they were not prepared to accommodate close to two thousand women in one location. Our group of about one hundred and eighty included Major Yaga, the commandant of the entire female section of the Home Army in Warsaw, and her two lieutenants-adjuncts.

By then I was ready to march. I was given a pair of comfortable, even elegant, walking shoes by a glamorous older sister of my classmate, who found herself in our boxcar.

"I happen to have an extra pair." She spelled out slowly the wonderful news, articulating the words carefully with her pretty lips.

Thank heaven for women who love clothes, I thought, thanking her profusely.

"That's all right," she was saying with a quiet assurance of a person who knows she can acquire a new pair of shoes, or anything else for that matter, any time she desires. Well, she might have had to wait a while this time!

A couple of days inside stuffy cattle boxes must have made our group look, if at all possible, even more miserable, but our commanding officers--all ladies in their thirties and forties--wanted to whip us into some sort of orderly ex-military unit. After all, we were to march into the very centre of the POW camp, with crowds of prisoners hailing from different countries lining the road to our two barracks, watching us.

We not only marched, we sang, too. We gave the loudest possible rendition of one of our resistance songs that had sustained us throughout the Uprising. Somewhere in that camp, we were sure to find the Polish POWs from the 1939 invasion of Poland; we wanted them to hear our singing! The gloom of the barrack we entered could not extinguish the sudden influx of fiery enthusiasm and hope in our hearts. We felt good in the presence of the fellow prisoners; they were our kind of people!

When we first arrived in Fallingbostel, which was to be only the first stop in our prisoners' odyssey, we encountered the typical German heavy-footed spontaneity. The appearance of a group of women prisoners threw the German orderliness into disarray. The invasion of POW camps by females was more than could be handled in an orderly, Teutonic fashion. Nevertheless, to quash any budding friendships with the men, a heavy barbed-wire fence was already erected around the two barracks destined to be the living quarters for the female population of the camp. The German guards were models of propriety--they could not enter the women's barracks. There were two civilian German women, and they alone were allowed to enter and count the sick females who could not appear outside at the morning roll call.

Perhaps because of insufficient briefing, the male guards slipped badly the first day the women arrived, as they took advantage of their "duty" to guard the prisoners and accompanied the ladies to the showers, where they stood around in the steamy atmosphere of the bath house fully dressed and armed like so many evil spirits.

Sticking to the rules sometimes yielded absurd results. The prisoners were required to present any photographs in their possession to be "approved." All photographs of men were confiscated so that they could not be used in falsifying documentation for the purpose of escape. Enforcement of this rule resulted in my losing the photographs of my father and my brother.

The area around Fallingbostel was nicely wooded and uneven. We were assigned two huge barracks, each accommodating close to a hundred people on three-tiered bunk beds. The barrack to which my group was assigned had one pleasant surprise--a hedgehog marching noisily during the night. Too bad both barracks were also infested with bedbugs.

"We have to organize a cleaning raid," announced our lady CO. "We'll get the Germans to give us some cleaning stuff, and we'll do a job on these bunks."

Were our "hosts" embarrassed about spotty housekeeping? Perhaps, because a stinking disinfectant was soon made available.

"Let's get to work," commanded Kora. "Each one of us will scrub just one bed and the floor around it."

The cleaning would not be excessively strenuous, especially since the smaller people, like me, were sharing one bunk with another girl. Unfortunately, my partner, Anita, had been shot in the arm during the Uprising, and had the entire length of her right arm in a cast; hefty and hard as a rock, it made her a most uncomfortable companion in any kind of sleeping arrangement, and completely useless as a cleaner.

All the fit people worked their hearts out, trying to ignore the horrible odour of the cleaning fluid provided. We enjoyed more restful nights afterwards.

After a while, life began to pulse to a rhythm reminiscent of a quasi-boot-camp routine. The day in the camp began at 6:30 a.m. The October weather continued on the pleasant side and it was not at all mortifying to appear for the morning roll call. Standing in line, we fidgeted outside the barracks each morning, feeling like sheep being counted before being sold at the market. A young corporal was obviously embarrassed trying to come up with a correct number of bodies. Arriving at the right number was complicated by absentees--the sick remaining indoors; the work party getting the hot liquid called "coffee"; others absent on some false pretext, etc. But the weather was still pleasant, and we did enjoy the embarrassment of the apparently inept Kraut, even though it meant standing outside longer.

And why not? The nature of the camp made for having lots of time with nothing to do. The presence of some interesting personalities--a Polish movie star, a veteran actress from a family of legendary performers, and a couple of university professors proved to be a source of welcome variety in the dull routine. Very soon, lectures and entertainment were organized to try and elevate our minds, frequently forced to contemplate on an empty stomach, to a higher level of consciousness and prevent it all from becoming a colossal waste of time filled with self-pity. Most importantly, it was a great opportunity to learn about people.

We kept to the same groups of people we knew during the Uprising. At least working out new relationships would not be added to other difficulties. Loneliness could never be a problem. Owing to the kind of accommodation and facilities, intimate contact with a whole crowd of women, mostly total strangers, could not be avoided. The accidental intimacy was rich in revelations.

Bogda, always one to favour a bit of sensationalism, returning from our common washing facility one evening, surprised us with an announcement:

"Bloody luck! I went to wash myself and there was that woman, you know--I could not undress with her in there!"

"What? Why?" I was soon to be terribly embarrassed under the scrutiny of condescending gazes and then ignored with a shrug. I think I was the only one to ask. Bogda came up close to me: "You know the dark Helen?" She was called "dark" to distinguish her from the blonde Helen; I nodded.

"Well, you know she is--you know what."

"What?" I was growing impatient with her reticence.

"A lesbian!" She finally spat out the word like an expletive. I had no idea what Bogda meant. I was still watching her, clueless.

"You are a baby," she laughed. "It means she is like a man, you know."

I did not know, but not to show a contemptible ignorance, I decided to figure it out by myself.

Sometimes it was possible to sit outside in the waning October sun and talk. Ever since the incident with Bogda, I began to notice couples, more women than girls, treating each other with more than usual consideration and their obvious delight to be in each other's company. It was hard to put a finger on it, but it was there, something completely new to me--something that made two women a couple. I did not understand the full implications of such friendship but I suspected that these women found a convenient way of excluding lots of complications from an emotional life, such as would arise from the involvement with a man.

* * *

Although friendship has always been important in my life, lately I have become rather introverted. In my youth I made friends easily. I had one very "serious" girlfriend during almost the entire time I attended school. Ever since I can remember, and particularly during the war, Danusia and I met after lessons and discussed arts, politics, our families--any topic worthy of the attention of "budding intellectuals." I liked Danusia very much, even though she shared only the most ponderous of my interests. She had no time for sports and was totally free of any inclination to the kind of frivolities generally considered second nature to young teenagers. We were together during the Uprising and later in the POW camp. We were separated only for a short time, when she was wounded by a sniper while carrying messages and had to be hospitalized.

However, demands of a romantic nature caught up with her, too, and after our liberation, still in Germany, true to her young heart and body, she fell deeply in love with a very handsome man. He personified everything that impressed her. She was intensely patriotic--he had spent some time in a concentration camp, arrested for his resistance work. She loved the arts, especially, literature--he was a young writer, and later became rather well known for his books describing wartime experiences. One thing he was not--he was not prepared to be faithful to Danusia. A man in his late twenties, very attractive, he was far too sophisticated and open to new experiences to exclude them from his life for the sake of a simple young girl, no matter how intelligent and gifted she was.

Shortly after the war, she was accepted at the University of Louvain on a modest scholarship. We only got together a couple of times, when I came to visit her. I saw my first opera, *Aida*, at the opera house in Brussels--it was every bit as opulent as the opera house in Paris, or so it seemed to my eyes, completely overwhelmed by the splendour of the occasion. Danusia herself bought the tickets out of her quite miserable scholarship.

We could not know that this would be our last meeting. A year later, I was about to leave the continent for England. I'd had no news from her. The answer to my inquiries was: "Danusia decided to return to Poland and has joined the other repatriates at the point of departure." It was to be expected.

Still, the news hurt me keenly; I felt abandoned. I brooded over the loss of this friend and despaired over never again being able to repay her kindness. Finally, I accepted Danusia's decision. I realized that it was dictated by her lofty patriotism and idealistic nature, and understanding this was my consolation. She could not stay abroad for good.

A couple of years later in London, I saw her one-time love at a reading of his book.

"Do you remember Danusia?" I asked with a vague intention of embarrassing him.

"Danusia is a very nice young girl," he shrugged as if nothing else could be said.

Danusia's life ended in tragedy. Like many young Polish patriots, she first embraced the communist government's lies with enthusiasm, and then, when the truth came out, she lost her will to persevere and committed suicide. Idealists have always been an endangered species.

Elisabeth, who had carried hand grenades through the sewers during the Uprising, was also at the camp. She was different. Back in Warsaw we were not close. She and I moved in different circles. I was inclined to be more serious and preferred rather "cerebral" company (like Danusia) to the more boys-oriented bunch of adolescent charmers. Elisabeth was exceptionally attractive and lively and professed to be engaged already at sixteen. Her face was cute rather than beautiful, but her brown eyes, overhung by long eyelashes, charmed and disarmed with their golden sparks. Her willowy figure, set off by a pair of long, slim legs, was outstanding.

"With such great legs, you don't need a high school diploma," joked male classmates, on seeing her studying for the matriculation exams.

But when the time came to study, she did, although she did not achieve success consistently. Despite the fact that after the war was over, school and our friendship were bound to occupy some space in her mind and some time in her daily schedule, her imagination and a boisterous spirit, frequently setting the stage to lure Elisabeth into a treacherous ambush, distracting her just as much as the procession of admirers. Following the instinct for self-preservation, Elisabeth sought a steadying influence, and, considering me a safe and reliable friend, she was certainly capable of feeling a genuine attachment towards me. However, because following a straight path was horribly boring at times when we got back to school, occasions to run amok were not always avoided; my steadying hand was occasionally quite shaky.

In a couple of weeks after our arrival in Fallingbostel, we and our existence became subjected to the dynamics of a well-oiled process. We were governed by rules imposed by unseen robots without consulting us, and without our agreement. Since the necessary routine for handling POWs had been worked out and perfected during more than five years of war, the *Stalags*--the camps for lower ranks in captivity--and *Offlags*--the camps for officers--might as well have been run by machines.

I saw the commandant of the camp only once during the roll call, as he deigned to accept the report from an underling. He seemed very important and very far away; well, he was at the far end of the field sitting on a horse. It seemed inconceivable that this stranger could suddenly get involved in my life.

The bizarre novelty of the experience had a pacifying effect and affirmed that life was going on. French conversations were carried on across the thick barbed wire fence by some of the older girls with predominantly French POWs. Friendships flourished. More chocolates and American cigarettes from the Red Cross parcels regularly received by the long-term POWs were soon arriving in the female quarters and shared by all.

Not only chocolates and cigarettes. We began to receive information about the progress of the war from our well-organized fellow prisoners, who were quite capable of hiding a radio receiver under the noses of the guards.

Good news from the front, particularly from the Russian front, produced a mood of high expectations. Even a half-empty stomach could not dispel the feeling of hope. A third of an American Camel cigarette carefully dissected with the aid of a borrowed safety razor (I think there were four of those in our barrack) and stuck into a longish cigarette holder went a long way towards making life almost bearable, if one could only forget for a moment where we were.

Our "chain of command" was perfectly preserved, and Kora had us regularly informed about news from the top. One morning, we gathered to hear her announce the latest:

"Rumours have it that we are going somewhere else, to another camp."

"Where to?"

"Which camp?"

"Why?"

"Do I have to leave Maurice?" interjected Bogda, only half jokingly.

"Have we made ourselves too comfortable?" continued Kora, waving away the questions. "I don't know why or where; it seems we shall be moved further west." The move would be further away from Poland. Suddenly it seemed our return would have to wait longer.

Our new friends were sorry to see us go. By now, practically everyone had a "guardian angel" from among the Polish POWs, who were helping us in any way they could. I had one, too. Even now I can see his face--dark, laughing eyes, dark hair--though I cannot remember his name . . .

We were moved further west to Bergen-Belsen.

Although the atrocities committed in concentration camps were not generally known at that time, as they are now known, the sinister sight of human figures in striped overalls covered with blankets, moving slowly, just barely visible in the distance, made everyone uncomfortable. Our leaders, mature women, who were trying to take charge of our existence, probably knew more, but not much more. Nevertheless, furtive glances followed by a grim silence was the only reaction possible under the circumstances. Unbeknownst to us, that reaction was inexplicably shared by the rest of the world. During that time, the holocaust raging in German-occupied Europe was completely ignored by the nations enjoying relatively more freedom and prosperity.

The proximity of the Belsen concentration camp worried our superiors. The younger girls, true to the indomitable spirit and energy of youth, were eagerly looking forward to the end of the war, anticipating exciting adventures; the thoughts of older and newer romances begun during the Uprising seemed to sustain them now under these miserable conditions. Even the older generation participated in these romantic goings-on. One of the commanders of the fighting units in Warsaw, Colonel P., suddenly made an appearance in our new location.

We were overjoyed to see him, though maybe some eyebrows were raised when he spent a few moments seated on a bunk below and to the left of mine, right beside Ania, the prettiest girl in our group. Taking advantage of his high military rank, and maybe bribing some guards, he was able to enter our barrack in Bergen-Belsen. Kora was sitting at a table nearby and we just exchanged glances. She lifted her shoulders momentarily as if to say: "The old guy has had a bad time of it. Let him have a little fun."

So what happened next was not entirely due to the "old guy's" interest in Ania's welfare, for he was actually doing his duty as a good leader, considering we all served in his division. He must have sized up the situation well, and discussed it with our intermediate leaders, more mature ladies, who kept a cheerful countenance, but who worried about the proximity of the notorious concentration camp. Maybe he had something to do with what was accepted as a stroke of good luck, when the Germans suddenly demanded people to work at repairing railway tracks that had been badly damaged by Allied bombing.

A list was prepared. It included about twenty of us belonging to the same closely knit group, including Ania. In the tense atmosphere of an extraordinary, late evening meeting, we fixed our wide opened eyes on "Nika," our commanding officer.

She was one of the three mature ladies who were to lead us into the unknown.

"The Germans want us to work," Nika said firmly, and with such emphasis that the news seemed almost joyous. "The first group will go to Hanover."

"Well," it occurred to me and probably to the majority of those present, "anything is better than being stuck in this place."

"Now, we are going to be separated into small groups, and perhaps exposed to some pressure. We have to present ourselves as worthy members of our army . . ." She went on about the obligations and rights of POWs who are put to work.

My thoughts strayed as I suddenly imagined a sports coach trying to persuade a bunch of average players that they can be world champions. I felt ashamed of feeling so inadequate; it was necessary to rise above oneself and feel proud, no matter how difficult it was to shake off the inherited, somewhat cynical approach so typical of my father. Survivor of family calamities and national disasters, he faced life without illusions. I remembered how, ignoring air raids during the siege of Warsaw in 1939, Father went to bed in our apartment with only a heavy, mahogany wardrobe in front of the window as a shield against shrapnel. "No use protecting yourself against a direct hit," he would say, while Mother and I spent many nights in the cellar together with other inhabitants of the building. I considered my father absolutely fearless, but his courage became overshadowed by failing health, and the pessimism engendered in him by hardship grew to destroy his ability to sustain hope. The Second World War was for him one more ruthless blow that he would not survive.

So, here I was in the dimly lit barrack, a daughter of my father, trying to rise to the occasion by conjuring up improbable claims to perfection to fend off fear and danger. Like my father, I'd had my enthusiastic vision of the world darkened by experiences during the Uprising.

"There's not much to pack," we would be saying to each other in the morning. The volume of shabby belongings was diminishing constantly, due to the opportunities to supplement the paltry rations of bread by barter. Some girls were particularly lucky; they had bottles of eau de cologne to exchange for bread from Red Army prisoners, lurking on the other side of the triple barbed wire fence, who were only too happy to assuage their need for alcohol any way they could.

"Fancy prisoners of war with bottles of cologne!" jeered witnesses to such transactions.

The rugged Soviets did not mind. But before they handed over the bread, they insisted on tasting the merchandise. Clutching a dainty bottle of cologne in their grubby hands covered with dirty rags in place of mitts, they would lean back to pour a little of the pale yellow liquid into their mouth.

"(Horoshii/Good!)" would be the verdict, and the bread would pass to our side.

Some lucky women saved all kinds of things when leaving the city that had been marked for annihilation. "Grab what you can" is a useful motto when opportunities for barter, an unavoidable companion of war and general collapse of civilized activities, loom on the horizon.

During the journey to Hanover we suffered tension and gloom, in turns, and discomfort constantly. We sat on the floor of a boxcar, enduring nerve-racking periods of long stops during air raids. We were just a part of the train, motionless and defenceless. We heard voices of the crew and their harried footsteps, as they ran to safety away from the train, leaving us in the railway car. Such stops between the gloomy periods were frequent and slowed down progress, severely testing our endurance.

"I don't believe the Allies could possibly wish us any harm." This belief in being exempt from the dangers of Allied bombing was at this point somewhat shaken--it offered no moral support and, more often than not, we had to break into one of the many marching songs of the Resistance to drown out any dangerous noises from outside.

The gloom did not leave us in Hanover when we were shown into an ugly barrack, divided into two rooms with a kind of washroom between them. This was to be our home God knows for how long. Dead tired, we fell fast asleep on the rough bunk beds, only to be awakened at five in the morning by a noisy railwayman who was supposed to be the boss. As he shouted half in German, half in Czech, urging the women to hurry and get "breakfast," his spacious, red countenance contrasted sharply with his dark navy railway uniform with its shiny metal buttons.

The "breakfast" consisted of a piece of mouldy bread and the already familiar hot liquid, rather inappropriately referred to as "coffee." We were to start work in a few minutes!

Though her eyes shone with steely determination, one of our two commanding officers looked like a little girl dressed in grownup clothes pretending to be a woman; the other, only slightly more imposing in stature, was equally determined to stay on top of the unpromising situation, and they soon had the totally dejected group form a respectably lined up platoon, gloomy faces twisted in desperately conjured smiles. The railwayman opened his mouth in disbelief at seeing his "slaves" marching in soldierly fashion, carrying shovels like rifles on their arms, and singing a lively marching song. Our work had to involve railways; therefore, the "boss" was a railwayman. Soon enough, we arrived at the railway tracks, which were frequently just hanging over the edge of large bomb craters. We had to fill the craters with soil, using our shovels to produce an even surface.

We stood silent in disbelief, thinking that only a raving maniac could assign such a task to women like us, who had never had anything to do with shovels, but there was no chance to argue with the collective wisdom of the functionaries of the Third Reich. Even more astonishing orders were coming.

First, we had to move huge freight cars along the tracks to clear the working area! Our bodies were cold and weak, exhausted by steady malnutrition, but the "boss" was already ordering us to take up positions around one end of the car and . . . p-u-u-sh! in unison. Incredibly, to our amazement, the huge box on wheels jerked and started to roll. Another triumph of German efficiency!

The days dragged on in continuous misery beginning with the "railwayman" yelling outside on the foggy late November mornings, and ending after hours of standing around the bomb craters pretending to work--the idea being to minimize contribution to the German cause despite the screams and threats of the *"Aufsehers."* [7]

The authorities conceived the idea that maybe they would get more useful work out of this lazy bunch of women pretending to be prisoners of war if they forced them to renounce their claim to military status. Almost every day we were presented with different forms of the same ultimatum--invariably sweetened with a promise of better conditions once any pretence to military status was abandoned. Such overtures were accentuated with the threats of withdrawal of food rations, and of other mortifications to punish us for our refusal to co-operate.

Evenings were spent around the small stove, which, as luck should have it, kept going. There were small successes and small celebrations.

The weather on the Great European Plain running across most of central Germany and Poland is at its worst in late November and early December. Days are short, and darkness begins to fall shortly after three o'clock in the afternoon. Fog or heavy mist reeking of the unhealthy breath of a large industrial city obscures any rays of sunshine even close to noon, so that the frost arriving later on in December is actually an improvement.

On one such depressing afternoon, we were marching back to the barrack after work--tired, but singing as usual, whenever given a chance of showing ourselves in the street. Hanover was no longer a city in the civilized sense of the word. Most of it lay in ruins. The road surfaces displayed holes and craters of various shapes and sizes, depending on whether they were the marks left by bombs or just shrapnel. There was no gas to drive civilian vehicles, so the roads were used only by pedestrians; that is, people not fit to be in the war--and such as they were, they did not do much walking in the streets.

---

[7] Guards

The nightly "carpet" bombing by the American so-called "fortress" aircraft completely terrorized the population and paralyzed its activities. Individuals encountered in the street appeared colourless, like mere shadows of their real selves. Other than members of the German military forces walking briskly in groups of two or three, and frequently uttering curses at the singing women, there were some people slowing down to give them a second look. They were the foreign slave workers employed in the gigantic "Hanomag" factory, which manufactured tanks. Some of them smiled and gave signs of approval, as if grateful for the sound of the marching song in this tormented place.

"Hanomag" was regarded both as a curse and a blessing. For in all the bomb raids night after night, it did not suffer a single hit. Sofie, a well-liked "miss know-it-all" and a budding comedienne, had an explanation:

"Of course, this factory is partially owned by an American millionaire; it will never be hit. Boy, are we ever lucky to be so close to it!" For better or for worse, our barracks were just across the road from the monster.

As we marched and sang, carrying spades on our shoulders like rifles, the images of the ruins of Warsaw we left behind less than two months ago appeared as a filter in front of our eyes, robbing our hearts of compassion in view of the devastation we were witnessing. Furthermore, a feeling of security, totally unjustified under the circumstances, seemed to absolutely separate us from the misery around us.

"I think soldiers going to battle must feel this way," I thought as we were passing three more members of the *Luftwaffe*. This bunch just passed quietly, staring.

"Look, there!" An excited voice suddenly interrupted the flow of the song.

A big boxcar on the railway tracks only a few feet away from us, suddenly started spewing a shower of potatoes onto the ground underneath it.

"There must be a hole, look!" one of our girls shouted.

The group was not allowed to stop and gawk at the appetizing accident; nevertheless, its pace slowed down to a crawl.

"Hide me," I commanded, prompted by a sudden idea.

Lowering myself to the level of moving legs and running almost on all fours, I started grabbing potatoes lying on the ground, stuffing them inside my heavy "*Kriegsgefangene*"[8] coat. With only seconds at my disposal, I emerged unnoticed to take my place within the marching column, triumphantly holding on to the loot at my bosom and stomach. I walked on gingerly, not only to prevent losing any of the precious cargo, but most of all to avoid severe punishment, should the theft be discovered. I felt strangely inspired to continue my "mission" after we arrived safely at our barrack. Surveying a row of expectant and hungry friends, I decided to crown my extraordinary achievement by acting in a most uncharacteristic manner; namely, by preparing a meal of potato dumplings that I had no idea how to make!

"Let's find stuff to burn." I was in command. "We need to boil something here."

The tired faces around me lit up with interest.

"Here, you can have this newspaper." Barbara brought out her impromptu umbrella that had performed as cover for her exposed head on wet days. "The weather's improved, and anyway, we won't be here much longer."

"You can have my old stockings; they are full of holes anyway," said someone else, throwing a pair of awfully worn out woollen tights on the pile.

As if preparing for a big party, my colleagues conscientiously gathered whatever they could, parting even with what had become an indispensable accessory of their misery. The primitive stove soon grew red with the heat of the flames eagerly consuming the gathered offerings, and the pot half full of water was shaking merrily on top of the stove. Just as the potatoes were carefully placed in the boiling water, wonderful warmth suddenly embraced the people gathered around the hot stove. We forgot the cold, grim barrack, and our faces blossomed with smiles and shining eyes.

The dumplings were consumed with bits of bacon carefully preserved from a Red Cross parcel received some time ago. Even the tasteless coffee seemed delicious. What a fabulous meal that was!

---

[8] Prisoner-of-war.

As a little girl, I would hang around the kitchen watching the preparation of meals. It was probably due to a subconscious absorption of that information, now stuck in my memory for so long, that transformed a curious little girl into a heroine, at least for one day! Being a heroine is fine, but my smiling friends and an almost happy expression on Kora's face gave me the greatest pleasure.

* * *

Kora went back to Poland after the war. In 1981, I was in Warsaw trying to locate her.

Owing to the scarcity of telephone directories in Warsaw, a lot of skilful networking was required then to find someone's number. I was lucky to have met a Polish translator who happened to know Kora.

The telephone--the dumb object that does not usually deserve much attention--in the city of my birth, more than anywhere else in the world, was an instrument capable of producing suspense, excitement, and joy. I dialed Kora's number. After a few moments of bluntly impersonal beeps, she answered. Indeed, suddenly speaking to my old guide leader was an unforgettable experience.

"Kora," I shouted, "we have to meet."

I could only hear my name repeated a couple of times and some disjointed sounds. It sounded like crying.

No, it's impossible! Good old Kora would not cry so easily, I was persuading myself, while slightly losing control of my own voice.

The last time I saw Kora cry, was inside the cattle box, all sealed up for the journey to a POW camp. The train was just beginning to move forward. Kora was looking out of the miserable little opening covered with a cross-work of wiring which served as a window on the world outside, when she spotted her mother standing out there totally distraught...

And here we were speaking to each other on the phone!

"Where are you?" she asked.

I was embarrassed to tell her that I was staying in this expensive hotel, where only high communist party officials and members of the government could afford to stay.

"Victoria?" she asked with an almost imperceptible note of contempt in her voice.

"Come for lunch tomorrow," I insisted. "I am attending the translators' convention at this hotel."

"Sorry, but all the government people go there," she protested. "I wouldn't feel comfortable."

"Well, at least come and meet me here, and then we'll decide."

She agreed. The next morning we embraced in the lobby, our eyes shamelessly filling with tears: she a white-haired, but serene, lady, and I a woman well past her prime. We were both so eager to talk that deciding where to go next seemed like a waste of time. Kora entered the dining room no longer concerned about who might be there, but later discreetly pointed out some well-detested personalities of the day being served by several obsequious waiters.

"If anything, they look well fed," I whispered to Kora.

Strangely enough, it was not the memories of our activities almost fifty years ago that made us talk a little breathlessly, as if time were running out, and there were still so many questions and answers. No, we spoke about those who had been our friends and companions in danger and misery. Some had died already, or, weakened by injuries and poverty, were ill.

The members of the Home Army who returned home after being imprisoned in Germany, or those who fought as part of the Allied forces abroad, became victims of the communist regime and its lackeys. They faced humiliation and denial of privileges, such as access to university; they were victims of vicious insults, false accusations, even imprisonment and death.

Kora's older sister, an officer of the Resistance, who lost one eye in the midst of an assassination attempt during the occupation, died a few years ago. There was not much happiness to report. I wish we could laugh, but I was no longer a giggling teenager of the early post-war years! More than ever it was overwhelmingly clear that our country found itself left far behind Western Europe, excluded from the bonanza of prosperous peace, despite its generous sacrifice of blood and lives for the cause of freedom.

TEN

Working on the Railroad

During my life, I have spent a fair amount of time in a variety of hospitals in different countries. The first time was in Hanover, when our hapless group of women was forced to work, while stubbornly insisting on retaining our POW status. As if it were not enough to have to endure the atrocious conditions of forced labour and grievous malnutrition, we also took on our German bosses in an unequal fight to prevent them from depriving us of POW rights, even though the latter did not seem to amount to much as it was.

"*Nichts zu essen, nichts zu essen*! [No food, no food!]" screamed the overweight railwayman outside the barracks during one of his morning shouting matches with our CO, Nika. He threatened repeatedly to deprive us of the mouldy bread, and the so-called coffee, when she once again refused to accede to his wishes and accept civilian status on our behalf.

In a couple of weeks, the damp cold coupled with inadequate rest and poor nutrition caught up with the youngest girl in the group, Ala. She got sick. The poor girl was lying on her bunk burning with fever, her previously pale face flushed, her eyes glowing in the semi-darkness of the barrack. Kora was concerned.

"It must be the 'flu," she was saying, hoping to reassure everyone including herself. It could be something worse.

One evening somebody started a rumour that the lot of us were to be returned to the POW camp. Not even realizing where such a place could be, we exploded into shrieks of joy, since no place could possibly be as bad; on the contrary, any place would be better than where we were right now. I decided to include Ala in the general rejoicing with kissing and hugging. We clung to each other for a moment. I was the second youngest, so we felt like sisters.

"We have to ask for a doctor," decided the commanding officer. Being sick under such wretched conditions could be dangerous. Miraculously, the doctor came next evening. He turned out to be a French POW who was looking after a sizeable contingent of French POWs working in the area.

"It is scarlet fever," he said after examining Ala. "There is an epidemic of scarlet fever around here and the Germans are anxious to keep it from spreading. The girl will have to be hospitalized."

Ha! The German fear of disease spelled a vacation from work for the whole group, since all occupants of the barrack had to be quarantined. When Ala was gone, I started to feel poorly. A terrible weakness and then hallucinations brought on by a high fever followed. The latter happened especially during the air raids, when everyone went to the shelter, and I had to be left alone in the barrack. Only Rosa stayed with me. Rosa did not consider it as anything extraordinary. She offered to stay and just sat there quietly crocheting. Nobody knew where on earth she got her crocheting from. She kept working even when the ground heaved repeatedly as bombs fell close by. Me, I could not care less--the sensation of "flying" was enjoyable; the magic world of hallucinations kept away fear.

Nevertheless, just before Christmas 1944, when the ominous red patches appeared on my thighs and stomach, it became necessary for me to follow Ala to this place of mystery and foreboding--the German hospital. Nobody knew what to expect there. Only the fact that Ala was apparently all right was promising. I was very weak when I was finally brought to the hospital. A nurse came and spoke to me, most certainly in German, but it took me a while to figure out that she was merely inquiring about my having a nightgown.

If memory serves me correctly, the picture of a fairly large hospital ward with a number of kids in beds, looking quite comfortable, comes to mind. By this time, a higher-ranking nurse attached her big, strong body to our little group and marched ahead to a smaller room. There, a mattress covered with clean, white bedding was lying on the floor in the corner of the room. The larger nurse fixed me with a decidedly hostile look, and motioned towards the mattress. This was to be my place. Maybe she did not know this, but such a bed was a hundred times better than the rickety bunk in the dirty barrack opposite "Hanomag" factory.

My fever abated in a few days but I was very weak and still contagious. The quarantine for a scarlet fever patient was six weeks. The prospect of spending at least five more weeks with the formidable dragon of a nurse was daunting, to put it mildly. Once my health improved, she had me doing little jobs around the ward. Her favourite assignment task for me was emptying the bedpans. She probably would joyfully have relegated me to some dungeon to peel potatoes all day, but professional pride forbade her to betray her calling, were she to entirely relinquish the duty of caring for the sick. I once heard her upbraid a young nurse for neglecting to take my temperature and failing to mark it on my chart.

"It has to be done, *trotz allem* [in spite of it all]," she sighed, casting a malevolent glance in my direction.

Although I was kept at a distance from the kids, some of whom were close to my age, one boy about fourteen years old, who was well enough and inquisitive enough, found me in my little lair. They must have talked about me, since he knew who I was. His visits were a welcome break in the monotony and vexations suffered under the dragon-nurse. However, the way he was trying to entertain me included divulging his plans to become a *Luftwaffe* pilot, and then go and bomb Warsaw.

"ZZZZ, BOOM, BOOM," he would elaborate, pretending to be at the controls of a bomber.

Once he caught me writing in my tiny calendar I used as a diary, and insisted on signing his name in it. There was no way to refuse, and I still have his message in the little booklet:

"*Zur steten Erinnerung an die Scharlach Zeit*--Willie" ("In everlasting memory of the scarlet fever.")

He probably never realized his flying ambitions, since the war was to end a few months later. My good or bad fortune in contracting contagious, though not too severe, diseases at appropriate times continued, as, one morning, maybe two days later, a nurse looked at me and shouted: "*Irene hat Masern gekriegt!*" Meaning I had contracted, appropriately enough, German measles. The red rash all over my chest and face was all too obvious.

The news seemed at first pretty grim. But then, I was transferred to a different wing, into a nice private room with a proper bed. To be on my own for the rest of the quarantine, away from my tormentor-witch, and visited by a pleasant enough nurse seemed heavenly--at first.

After a while, being left alone all day was boring and sad. I began missing Willie and even the obnoxious nurse. There was one compensation: I could speak Polish to myself without upsetting or alarming anyone. Although my German improved immensely, and later people even admired my "*echt Deutsch*" accent, the fact that there was no one to speak to in my native tongue had me worried. For the first time in my life, day after day, I had to exclusively use a foreign language. What if I forgot how to speak Polish? I was living proof of how much people could miss their native tongue, and, of course, if deprived of using it long enough, they could forget it.

Once, during the nocturnal excursions to the shelter due to the persistent air raids, before I made a pact with the night nurse to avoid them, I found a fellow prisoner working there. The man looked rather illiterate, but being a Soviet prisoner of war, he could have been speaking a language similar to Polish. Full of hope, I started a conversation. He was Belorussian, so I asked him if he could speak Polish and he said yes. My joy soon vanished, however, as I desperately tried to make some sense of his rumbling rhetoric; alas, it was absolutely beyond my understanding.

Outside, life continued in its miserable fashion with the nightly air raids on the city. The nurses had the horrendous task of gathering all the patients and leading them, in various ways depending on the state of their health, down to the shelter. The German adults and children were just as afraid of air raids as anybody else would be. They were a sorry lot, sitting there like actors in a mournful play, bundled up in hospital blankets. Once the speaker on the radio announced the approaching enemy aircraft, faces grew pale and tense not from sickness, but from fear.

Even though I could have perished with them right then and there, I suppose I could have gloated a little, because I had been the target when the horror was being dispensed by the Germans. But gloating is not the proper description of my feelings then. Rather, I felt superior in my certainty that after surviving the catastrophe of the Warsaw Uprising, nothing could harm me anymore, and there was no need to be afraid. Consequently, I asked the night nurse, whose duties included looking after my safety, to leave me in my room during the air raids. If she had asked, I could have explained to her that I considered the safeguards the hospital was able to provide totally inadequate anyway, and unnecessary in my case. And why all this fuss about a few bombs? Imagine, for over two months, I'd had to endure day and night the kind of bombardment that resulted in the complete destruction of our city. But I did not have to explain all that much because she was glad to have one less delinquent to look after, and she easily agreed to let me be. We became a pair of conspirators, and she showed her sympathy for me by bringing all the sandwiches left over after the evening meal every night, for me to devour. After my fever left me, I was perpetually famished.

Desperate in my loneliness, I befriended a mouse. It startled me at first; one evening I heard a mysterious rippling noise, impossible to trace. I got out of bed and went around the room. The noise stopped. When I got back to bed, it started again after a few minutes.

"This something must be a living thing!" I was overjoyed at having a companion. The little mouse was running around inside the fold of the blackout paper screen on the window.

It is now hard to believe and appreciate the depth of the feeling of isolation and abandonment that made me look forward to the nightly visit of the mouse, who was too scared even to come out and show itself. I just spied on it, waiting quietly until it inadvertently showed its little snout. Later, tempted by crumbs of bread, it would come out in full glory, and let me feast my eyes on it.

Christmas came and was celebrated by everyone in the hospital. It meant a little more food, and of slightly better quality. The big hero of the celebration was the "*Weihnachtsman*," a sort of Santa Claus adored by German children. The penetrating festive noises awakened painful thoughts about the gruesome ruins of Warsaw, which now served as a graveyard for thousands, including possibly my mother.

The friendly nurse said one day: "You will soon go to Neustadt." Hardly the location of my dreams, but to be polite, I inquired why.

"Here, too many air raids--over there--nice and quiet; all kids go there when they get better," she explained in the telegraphic style people tend to use with foreigners. If she expected me to jump for joy, she was disappointed.

"Neustadt! What difference does it make?"

But it did make a difference! Ala was already there convalescing, and we were put in a room with beds side by side. No more morosely keeping company with a rodent! We talked and cried and laughed. The large ward was full of kids in different stages of convalescence. The almost healthy ones clamoured for food and drink, keeping the nurses constantly on the go.

Since scarlet fever can lead to dangerous complications, not all were so lucky. There was a young boy who went deaf as a result of the fever and looked rather poorly. The other kids made fun of him. I found it rather barbaric that no one tried to teach them better. Well, that was not the only barbaric trait of this supposedly civilized nation.

Among the frequent visitors to the children's ward was somebody's mother, or maybe just a volunteer--in our case, a charming woman. She brought little goodies and the children loved her. She was known as *Tante Speck*, which means "Auntie Bacon." It was rather disarming and admirable, the way she tried to cheer up the kids with small gifts of candy or whatever else she had to give them. She was a happy housewife, modestly but respectably dressed. I gave her my full sympathy until one day she mentioned that her husband was away fighting the war.

"Where is he?" I asked almost sympathetically.

"In Poland. He is in the SS[9] . . ." I did not bother to tell Auntie Bacon how disappointing this information was to me.

Ala and I were now close to hale and hearty; well, actually it would take some time to regain the strength that the fever had drained from our systems--in my case, two fevers. Nevertheless, we started wondering how we would manage to get back to our camp.

First, how to determine where and which camp would be our destination. Then, how do we get there? The hospital was completely at a loss as to what to do with us. Worse, for the first time, since my

---

[9] The dreaded Nazi special service known for its cruelty and brutality.

arrival there, we actually came face to face with a doctor. He was a pleasant, youngish man. He had lost an arm on the Eastern front. He and the other staff had suddenly taken a consuming interest in my ability to speak German. A higher-ranking nurse even decided to investigate the rumour about how well I knew *"die Deutsche Sprache* [the German language]."

"Read this," she ordered, holding a small book under my nose.

After a while, she interrupted my reading and took the book away.

"Now tell me what you have read."

The story was simple enough for me to repeat its gist. The old nurse shook her head in disbelief: *"Junge, Junge* [Boy, oh boy]," she muttered. "She actually understands German."

The news travelled to the nice doctor, who began to draw me into political conversations, asking me questions like, "Who do you hate more, the Germans or the Russians?"

I was happy and grateful to the New Testament for supplying me with an answer to such a question: "I don't hate anybody," I said. This seemed more diplomatic than: "I love my enemies." I thought under the circumstances, the latter would sound sarcastic.

The good doctor also got it into his head that Ala and I should stay and work in the hospital.

"Why do you want to go back to some filthy camp?" he questioned me. "Would it not be better to stay here? It's nice and clean here; you could work for us . . ." I was horrified that he might insist and keep us away from our friends and our "army."

Two weeks after Christmas in 1944, some higher authority, giving orders significantly more powerful than my polite and necessarily feeble declining of the doctor's kind (he thought so) offer, was instrumental in conjuring up the appearance of a middle-aged soldier of the *Wehrmacht* [army], who arrived at the hospital precisely after the six weeks of quarantine, fully armed with a rifle, to escort us back to our "filthy camp."

I hope the nice doctor survived the rest of the war no worse off than he already was. He would perhaps have been happy to know that not everyone was so anxious to be back in a camp. At least one in our group decided to make a dash for freedom.

* * *

"What was she like? Was she pretty?" One of the ladies, a retired librarian, was particularly interested. Eleanore knew many languages and was more interested in the outside world than an average house-proud middle-class lady playing bridge, dropping names, and discussing far-and-wide-travel. In one way, however, she was very much like any other woman, and a majority of her compatriots close to her age--she was very careful to have her charming head always immaculately coiffed. She and many other ladies have perfected the technique of directing their first steps, no matter where they happen to arrive, to a powder room to inspect that precious hairdo. I somehow never mastered the trick of improving my appearance, though I frequently feel badly in need of it, before exposing myself to the gaze of welcoming hosts and other guests, who always seem to hang around close to the entrance. Hair and lipstick. Women of a certain generation apparently use both as a compound certificate of respectability. Nobody could suspect anything improper if the hair is neatly arranged and the lipstick properly applied.

Ours is a small circle of friends sharing an interest in the arts. We meet regularly, taking turns in hosting a meal. This time the meeting takes place in the elegant living room of one of the members, whose husband is a physician. As not nearly everywhere else in the world, all the physicians in this country are well off. The colour scheme of the room is admirable; soothing shades masterfully brought together to produce a surprisingly radiant combination. The furniture is in contrasting shades of walnut and fruitwood. The deep couch and easy chairs offer the superb comfort of exquisite upholstery. A coffee table and occasional tables are cluttered with delicate china bearing the remains of dessert.

Eleanore listens to what I am saying as I mention the name of the wife of a famous Canadian politician.

"A particularly gifted polyglot, her French was very good indeed; she was the only one who decided to leave our group in Hanover and try to escape to France. But she was eventually captured and sent back to the POW camp," I continue the story.

"What did she look like?" insists Eleanore.

There is no need to tell anybody now that my memory is failing me, that there were two girls who could be the woman in question. Both were named Alice, both spoke French, and they looked vaguely similar. One of them I met after the war in high school. I got to know the other one better during our stay in Hanover. She was known as "Ursel," but it was a nickname she adopted while in the Resistance. There was a great deal of uproar when she escaped. Still in the hospital with my scarlet fever, I heard the story much later. It was then that I looked at Ursel with renewed interest.

"She was a fairly tall brunette," I begin. Such a general description would be suitable for a composite picture of the two Alices. Perhaps, it would be a good idea to go to the public library and inspect more carefully the photograph of the author of a memoir, published by this lady in Canada, after she became Mrs. P., the wife of a well-known Quebec politician.

"She kept more or less to herself in the camp," I added. I remembered, but did not mention, that some girls looked with suspicion at her thick, almost black hair. Maintaining perfect personal hygiene in the camp was a challenge to be met with determination.

Laughing quietly to myself, I refrain from making the story overly scintillating, and decline to mention that one of them had a dazzling smile and the slow movements of an odalisque.

"Yes, she was very attractive in an exotic sort of way; attractive enough to catch a good man." There was no point in carrying on with the description.

The second Alice was not bad looking either, but not even close in the sex appeal department. She was a much more serious girl, and since she met and fell in love with her future husband at the Sorbonne in Paris, it was a given that she would have more than just a good knowledge of the French language, as demonstrated by the first Alice.

No wonder the mention of Ursel awakened so much curiosity; people frequently like to stay on the safe side and look for romance and adventure in the life of others rather than in their own. Romance can be very troublesome ultimately, so why not enjoy it from the sidelines?

Almost every time I travel by train, maybe because I do not do it often, my mind wanders back to the bizarre train trips I had to take under duress. Circumstances forced upon us by the war necessitated those undesirable, dreadful, and dangerous trips, where being transported as prisoners, we could not expect Pullman service. We had to be satisfied with boxcars, which came to symbolize the slavery and humiliation of the vanquished.

One exception was my last trip by train, courtesy of the German Reich.

Ala and I, first stuck in the German hospital in Hanover, and subsequently in the convalescent clinic in Neustadt, were both really looking forward to the trip back to our "filthy camp," as described by the German doctor. When confronted with our *Wachman* (guard) in the middle of January 1945, we were a little weary, but anxious to rejoin our friends.

The *Wachman* was in his forties, one of those scraped out from the bottom of the barrel. The barrel was close to empty after five years of a war that had exacted high losses in the ranks of first-class specimens of German manhood. Unlike my scarlet fever companion, Willi, the *Wachman* was too old to have grown up under the guidance of Hitler *Jugend* (Hitler Youth). Probably for this reason, he still appeared to possess human sensitivities. His name, we found out later, was Fritz.

As we started on our journey, he did not divulge any information as to where the camp was located, but since we headed for the train station, we deduced we were going to travel to our camp by train. The station was crowded with people trying to escape somewhere from the bombardment and hunger in the city. They were laden with bundles and were waiting for a train that no one knew when, if ever, it would arrive.

Irena on the train, Münster, Germany, 1945.

Ala and I were not supposed to see much nor be seen. Fritz, the rifle on his arm and stern look on his face, persisted in pushing us into out-of-sight corners, and then stood in front of us facing the crowds, making himself as big as possible. Perhaps he was worried about our military caps and our white and red armbands, which we were still wearing. However, people in the stations were too preoccupied with their own troubles to try and guess what those two young girls in dark ski outfits were up to. We were very skinny and our hair was cut short, so we both looked more like young boys.

Finally, the sound of a train, first in the distance and then approaching the station, penetrated the darkness of the late evening.

"Come!" ordered our guard, and he beckoned us to follow him. We stayed very closely behind him, as the throng started to press around us like a beast roused from slumber. Names were called out into the night; people were gathering in groups of families and friends.

"How are we going to get on that train?" we both asked ourselves and watched ruefully as a "regular" train--not a cattle train--rolled into the station.

But we underestimated the resolve with which Fritz was going to carry out his orders. Steering with the butt of his rifle left and right, and pulling and pushing the two of us in turn, he succeeded in barring the way to the nearest wagon entry until all three of us climbed on board. It was hard to imagine that many people got on that train, as it was filled to the rafters--not only with people, but especially with their baggage.

Exhausted by the waiting and now hungry, we stood at the entrance to the long corridor, happy to be moving at last toward our destination. Gradually, our bodies got into the rhythm of the wheels rolling over the track in a pleasantly steady movement. Wedged tightly in between somebody's gargantuan bundles, I must have fallen asleep. Suddenly deprived of the lulling motion, I felt a jolt; the train stopped.

"We get out!" said Fritz, pushing us down to the platform.

The train could not go on because the track farther on was bombed and out of service. It was dark. For a while the crowd leaving the train stood in disarray, not knowing what to do. Not our Fritz. We thought we were to cross the tracks and begin another agonizing wait, and again fight to get on board another train, bulging with a hapless populace.

But not this time. Our guard directed us to an underground canteen for travelling soldiers. We could go to the toilet--such as it was--and were given a cup of hot, very thin soup. There was no other food available.

Fritz navigated us into the darkest corner to sit at one of the long tables in the spacious but rather grim-looking hall, darkened by vapours emanating from bodies in worn-out uniforms. The place was full of German soldiers in various stages of relaxation. Most of them sat at the tables, visibly dead tired and oblivious to the world around them.

"*Cracow kaput* [Cracow is finished]," I overheard one saying. "We had to leave in a hurry. I'm telling you, the Russkis are chasing us!"

Then it became clear to us that this crowd of men, barely able to carry their arms, was what was left of Hitler's proud army. Defeated and running away, the men, falling off their feet with exhaustion and probably despair, were no different than conquered fighters anywhere. Maybe even no different from those conquered in the Warsaw Uprising. Warmed up by the hot fluid, I flattened my elbows on the table, and, imitating those around me, I soon fell asleep resting my head against my arms.

Almost the same routine was followed for three days. Though at a snail's pace, we kept going west, while the Eastern Front was beginning to cut into the body of the Third Reich. The German army on that side was obviously reduced to a band of exhausted, hungry and disillusioned men, who like the general population, were running out of places to hide.

Nobody paid any attention to us, and standing, as usual, close to the exit from the train car during the long and slow progress into the night, I thought how easy it would be to escape, but I had a strange feeling of being free already.

It was the Germans now, who, ensnared by the destiny of their insane leader, were hurling towards a dreadful disaster they were unable either to avert or to escape. If one could reasonably expect to experience a "closure," seeing our enemies, stricken by the Arm of Justice, collapse into the misery and despair they had brought to others, could be regarded as one. There was no doubt the war would soon be over.

In the meantime, we were better off with Fritz. He was our ticket to the army canteens, hot soup, and a place to doze off at the table. He also guarded us in more ways than one. Once, he even had to use his rifle to threaten three young "junkiers," who must have spent time in Poland and understood what our white and red armbands were all about. We had a few tense moments as they moved on our little group cursing: "*verfluchte Partisanten* [damned Partisans]," but Fritz stood his ground, bravely shielding us with his body, and holding his rifle at the ready.

When at last we arrived in Lathen, close to the Dutch border, it was evening. There were still a few kilometres to be covered, this time on foot. We left the town behind us and walked through a forest, which, covered by snow, seemed to shine in the darkness. It was strangely beautiful to be walking past the large fir trees carrying the white burden of snow, with their branches weighed down to the frozen ground looking like the paws of a huge animal. It made me think of the movie *Snow White and the Seven Dwarfs*.

But it was not at all comical. The ground was too slippery for our boots and we kept falling. Fritz was helping us by letting us hang on to the butt of his rifle. He also took turns carrying our bundles. I can imagine how happy he must have been to finally deliver us to the Niederlangen camp. We were welcomed with tears and laughter by friends.

Then, we slept for three days and nights, waking up briefly to drink hot soup.

ELEVEN

Freedom—Artificial or Real

The arts provide a magic and convenient entry into a world possibly more enchanting--or simply different--from that envisaged in everyday human life.

Many people around here travel regularly to Toronto to see a ballet or an opera or to attend a concert. These are intelligent people, entitled to being recognized as such, since a further development of the intellect by paying homage to the arts appears to be essential to be called "intelligent."

The proportion of snobbery to a real appreciation of the arts in their attitude depends on many factors. For example, different individuals generally enjoy different degrees of emotional or psychological comfort. It is quite conceivable that perfectly confident and self-satisfied persons may have no need at all to widen their horizons by embracing an art form; in other words, by delving into the expression of someone else's ideas, which everyone knows, can be regarded at times as totally crazy, if not distasteful. Even certain music falls into that category, but I have actually met people who astonished me by professing a dislike of any kind of music at all.

Most people do not have the time, perseverance or the opportunity to be well acquainted with classical, or any other music, for that matter. To be blessed with any degree of musicality is a gift, which many so endowed frivolously squander on noisy, easy music. Some become enamoured with one piece of classical music they happened to have heard at an opportune moment.

Just like Anna. I remember Anna's exhortations on the subject of "beautiful music."

"When I am dying, I would like someone to play Schubert's *Serenade*," she would say with a dreamy look in her eyes.

Far from perceiving it as a deficiency in my psychological makeup or as a display of snobbery, I accepted as a lucky break an invitation to visit our son in New York City and enjoy with him what one of the greatest cultural centres and the home of a superb opera organization had to offer.

It was not all a "cultural" event--it took two hours to drive to the airport at Syracuse, N.Y, followed by the hour-long flight to New York City. This time, because the plane was early, the passengers were treated to a flyover of Manhattan, with the pilot explaining various points of interest in "The Big Apple"--an unexpected pleasure. Paris, New York, Rome, and Beijing have all been fantastic to visit at different periods of my life. Although it was difficult to like the London weather, I also considered it good fortune to have been able to live there for several years.

It seems that the most enjoyable and free activity in a big city is walking in it. When my son, Roman, was working during the day, I walked. Block after block, I measured the expanse of the streets and avenues of Manhattan with my two worn-out feet. The bigger department stores I found too confining and too crowded. But even out in the street, it was hard to get away from the multitude.

One always got stuck with a group of people. Marching quickly ahead did not help. Red lights were setting an ambush at each corner, and with heavy traffic making it impossible to cross the road, trying to move away at a faster pace from the same group just didn't work. No wonder Greta Garbo wanted to be alone when she lived in New York City!

Some people passing by were pushing baby carriages. They were well dressed, sophisticated, and well preserved, like so many retirees in this wealthy place, but too old to have a baby! Discreetly glancing inside the carriage, I often discovered if not a pile of shopping bags, a little dog! Maybe later that night, the cultured couples would leave their pets with pet sitters and take off on a cultural expedition to one of the great palaces of entertainment in the city. Maybe they would be at the Lincoln Centre as well?

As planned, we set off by taxi to the Opera at the Lincoln Centre--the very hub of the opera world--even the most blasé world traveller would be thrilled to be there.

I was looking forward to the experience very much. Music figured prominently, but it was impossible not to enjoy the ambiance.

"Great seats," I whispered while we listened with anticipation to the sound of tuning instruments, and looked around at the audience in seats around us. Being called a snob would not have been offensive at this particular moment. The great chandeliers and the plush chairs lent a luxurious brilliance to dazzle anyone with even a modest capacity for enjoyment.

"Must have cost a fortune!"

"I'm a generous son," laughed Roman. "It's only money."

I was not troubled by the money that was spent for very long. We laughed looking at other people in the audience, who maybe found us ridiculous and laughed at us, too. I think a couple seated a few rows in front of us were the best--an elderly gentleman, white-haired and well dressed, was accompanied by a much younger woman which would not be anything unusual, except that her back, totally exposed due to the style of her expensive gown, was completely covered with tattoos!

We saw three operas on three consecutive nights in New York.

The opera in Toronto, though not yet as impressive as the great opera houses of the world, comes up with some great performances as well. Yet it is not very often that we even get to Toronto's Hummingbird Centre. John Vickers singing his signature part in *Fidelio* was certainly worthy of extra effort to participate in this celebration of glorious music. Accompanied by a woman friend, I joined the crowd filling the seats with eager anticipation. For some obscure reason, I fervently wished that everyone should be thrilled by the performance.

The second act was about to begin. The rising curtain revealed a grim prison scene and a half-starved prisoner . . . well, you could argue about the merits or demerits of the *mise en scène*. The music was the thing. "I think I'm going to cry." This announcement of mine surprised my companion.

"Why?" she asked. "You don't appear to be a crying person."

"I know what it feels like to be set free . . ."

* * *

After a few days of rest, Ala and I joined in the daily routine of the camp. When the euphoria of being back with friends wore off, our eyes opened to the misery of this "new" camp. It was located in the lowlands area near the Dutch border. The dampness and foggy atmosphere created unhealthy conditions for people and scarcely any better conditions for growing crops. There were no trees, either. The only product harvested in large quantities in this depressing corner of Europe was peat from the peat bogs, spread around as far as the eye could see.

The camp in Niederlangen was not new. Its history had many versions, though a predominant feature was its function as a penal camp: first, for all the enemies of Nazism in Germany, and then, for the POWs. The most morbid version described it as a "death camp," notorious for liquidating large numbers of troublesome prisoners.

"Ala, do you think it would have been better if we had stayed in the hospital to work there?" I asked my "hospital" companion, when she seemed particularly depressed one morning.

"No way!" she shouted, and almost immediately her mood improved.

"The doctor would have been really insulted if he knew that even stuck in this muddy hole, we would not consider his offer an option," I thought, very pleased with Ala's reaction. Desperate to be back with our crowd, I never gave Ala a chance to express her opinion until we were on our way back to the camp. Suppose she would have wanted to accept the doctor's offer?

Looking forward to a place like the camp in Niederlangen as a peaceful haven could be regarded as proof of insanity, but all the groups coming back from their mercifully short working spells were happy to be back with the rest of their friends. Some had a worse time of it than we did in Hanover. All were harassed constantly to renounce their military status. None of them did.

Soon almost sixty years will have passed since the yoke of "*Kriegsgefangene* [prisoner of war]" was finally lifted off our necks.

The end did not come abruptly; it took a long waiting period--our mood alternating between a blissful hope and a dreadful panic. Rumours abounded about what was happening in other camps: concentration camps, POW camps, and labour camps spread around neighbouring territories and all over Germany. Are we going to survive until freedom arrives? Are our liberators going to find a stack of corpses or are we going to be dragged out of here and finished off somewhere along the way to nowhere?

The Germans were unpredictable; even the kindly, middle aged *Posten* [guard] with whom we once conducted a conversation in German across the barbed wire, would, most likely, dutifully machine-gun us all down if given the order to do so. Especially when we laughed in response to his saying, with an embarrassed smile: "*Deutschland kaput* [Germany is finished]."

And worse, what about the yelling *Feldfebel* [staff sergeant], with a nasty habit of bellowing out his orders while marching, oh, maybe half a step behind the women and urging them to make haste.

"*Bistro, Bistro!*"[10] he would yell, using the full power of his considerable lungs. It felt like marching in front of a vicious dog capable of attacking at any moment. Keeping in mind that no self-respecting POW would ever rush to execute the command of a screaming guard, we dragged our feet. But it took a lot of courage to sustain a sluggish progress and not break into a swift trot in front of that psychopath.

Yelling seemed to be the order of the day in a POW camp. Nevertheless, after four and a half months of the dreary existence, a spectre of spring began to sneak up around us. Life as well as death continued--two women died, and nine babies were born.

April 12, 1945. The strange quiet around the camp announced a complete collapse of normal order and daily routine. The guards were silent and invisible; the women guards had disappeared a while ago. Nobody was fussing about the little "stoves" built with the large food cans that came from Red Cross parcels. Normally, the Germans were absolutely infuriated to see that the fuel used for this cooking method came from "German property," i.e. wooden boards from bunk beds cut into thin, tiny pieces to fit the ingenious "stoves." Removing a few boards from the bottom of the bed meant giving up the relative comfort enjoyed with a full set, but we constantly craved more food. Meagre but precious quantities of extra food came from Red Cross parcels, which

---

[10] Czech for "faster!"

were received with absolute joy. Each, albeit infrequent, arrival of such parcels, often damaged or retained by the guards, was followed by carefully planned culinary projects in which the firewood played an essential role.

A few missing boards did not make much difference until after repeated raids on the wretched bunks. We ended up having to sleep with our bodies suspended rather than resting on a strategically placed, diminished number of boards.

Around noon it became clear that all the guards had either escaped or were hiding somewhere out of sight. The atmosphere was pregnant with dramatic possibilities, but nothing dramatic was happening: There were no explosions, no distant artillery rumble, no visible or audible signs of any battle going on anywhere near. The prisoners were on their own, congregating in the barracks on orders of their leaders.

All of a sudden, the air was crackling with some not easily identifiable sounds.

April 1945, liberation of Niederlangen.

"What's that?" they asked each other. They moved towards the doors. The sounds were coming closer.

"Take cover! Get inside!" shouted the barrack leaders. But there was no holding back; the surge of reckless excitement quickly overpowered the instinct of self-preservation, releasing an insane desire to see what was coming.

"Motorcycles!" shouted somebody over the swelling noise of anxious voices.

"Men on motorcycles--two of them!" several women, who ran to stand as close as possible to the barbed wire enclosure, bordering on open fields, joined in the chorus. The motorcycles were approaching at breakneck speed, bouncing wildly on the rough terrain.

"They are black!"

The two solders on motorbikes were only a few metres away now.

"Black Americans?"

"Damn it! What Americans? We are Polish!" one of them shouted in Polish.

They were right there, their faces camouflaged with dirt and maybe soot. Something was written on the little red bands attached to their shoulders. Somebody screamed: "It says 'Poland!' It says 'Poland' on their sleeves!"

A deafening cacophony of emotional outburst filled the air. There was no longer any doubt as to who the liberators were--the men of General Maczek's First Polish Armoured Division, part of the Allied army on the Western front. Everyone's mouth was open but articulate sounds, if any, were wiped out by millions of decibels of triumphant roar.

Time stood still. Everyone was kissing and hugging everyone else. Coming out of nowhere, an enormous Cromwell tank waddled across the several layers of barbed wire surrounding the camp.

We were free . . .

* * *

Within a few days after the end of hostilities, the news of the "Women Soldiers" from Warsaw, recently liberated from the misery of the POW camp in Niederlangen on the Dutch border, had already travelled around occupied Germany. Our participation in the ill-fated Warsaw Uprising incited interest, and probably a desire to help. We were showered with accolades, especially by the Polish forces abroad, and very important as well, supplied with wholesome and plentiful food. We were transferred to a "better" camp a few kilometres away, the Oberlangen. The barracks were much more spacious and brighter; the bunks were replaced by normal beds.

Instantly, Oberlangen became a kind of shrine, a place to visit for every Pole, a place to look for relatives or girlfriends. They said it was like visiting a mini-Poland after five years of war. Many a daughter and a father, separated by the war in 1939, were reunited in the camp, and the lucky girl was immediately whisked away to England to enjoy, what we could only conceive of as a wonderful life. The rest of us were, one could say, wined, dined, and romanced, but still within the confines of the camp.

However, the world knew about us, and as a result, a pleasant surprise awaited a group of Polish schoolgirls who remained in Oberlangen camp--an opportunity to enjoy a glorious vacation at Mardorf camp in the summer of 1945. A part of the 30 Corps, Mardorf was the convalescent camp for the war wounded.

The commander at Mardorf was a great English gentleman, Major P. Among the men enjoying a holiday at the camp were the Welsh, the English, and members of the renowned Scottish Highland Division, whose uniforms were marked with an "HD."

The camp, set up at a medium-sized lake, was a pre-war resort, situated a few kilometres from Hanover. It was equipped with facilities for every conceivable summer sport. Several sailboats were moored at the sprawling docks; a variety of diving boards graced the shore and the inviting beach. The playgrounds offered an opportunity to play volleyball, soccer, and what have you.

The resort stables housed beautiful riding horses. The horses actually understood Polish commands, because they had been "borrowed" by the Nazis from Poland.

The group of us had been selected in response to an invitation sent by the British Command. Somehow or other, we all happened to be pupils from respected high schools in Warsaw. The Polish maidens in the midst of British soldiery--they could not be just anybody!

For what it was worth, I would always remember those two months as one of the most enjoyable and somewhat bizarre experiences in my life. Gosh, I can imagine my mother and my aunts looking disapprovingly at me dancing every evening in the canteen. Either a superb German civilian band or a lively British military band played all the latest hits. The dance floor was always crowded with young soldiers dancing with the Polish girls or with each other.

Apart from an occasional visit of the ATS (British Women's Auxiliary Service) girls, the Polish schoolgirls were the only females allowed on the premises. Major P. had a huge placard affixed at the main entry to the campgrounds, proclaiming our status as honoured guests of the 30 Corps, deserving of the utmost courtesy. There were German women working in the kitchen and at other housekeeping chores under the command of a Polish ex-slave worker in Germany, who was also liberated by the Allied armies. She was a very nice-looking lady in her middle twenties, and appeared to be on good terms with her underlings.

The resort occupied a large area on the lake and the adjoining beautifully treed acreage of picturesque countryside. The vacationing convalescents were billeted in small cottages scattered around the main buildings. We were occupying a large villa about half a kilometre from the main camp.

A great big "OUT OF BOUNDS" sign graced the entry to the garden. Its meaning was not immediately obvious to us; we were only just beginning to learn English, courtesy of the major.

"Do you know what it means?" we frantically asked each other; but no one knew.

The best part of the villa was a large sunroom overlooking the lake, shimmering at the bottom of a gentle slope. The furnishings inside, though clean and bright, were sparse and basic, but after our confinement in the crude barracks with grubby bunk beds, they seemed nothing short of palatial splendour.

Life had never been so good. Mornings, we would be swimming in the lake before breakfast. We would be returning to the villa joyfully swinging our bath towels, while three or four fighter planes would suddenly pass, roaring overhead.

"Here they are, the Dutch!" Basia would shout happily. The low-flying planes were not a deadly menace anymore.

The planes would turn around and zoom even lower, almost catching the roofs.

"One, two, three, Irka!" could be heard clearly over the roar of the engines.

"Play bridge tonight?"

"Knuckleheads!" would be the response from the ground, but the planes were already gone.

The exhilaration of youth, joy, and friendship blossomed during this international summer party, especially since the pilots belonging to the Dutch contingent were handsome and entertaining members of the air force. I suspect my mother and even my aunts would have been quite happy with our daily routine here. After breakfast, which was eaten in the officer's tent, we usually rested awhile, and then had a horse-riding lesson. That would occupy most of the morning. The riding master, a sergeant walking with the swagger of a real cowboy, looked like a smaller version of John Wayne. He called me "Smiler," and let me ride his own mount, a beautiful horse the colour of chestnut with a white blaze down its nose. I loved the gentle beast, but I could never be a fan of John Wayne or cowboy movies.

The majority of our group followed the same approach in dealing with all the men we encountered in the camp. Only one of our girls became romantically involved: with the assistant of the "quasi John Wayne," a handsome hunk of a man. It did not work out but Lala was so intent on landing herself an Englishman that she later married another member of the staff there.

I also had my suspicions with regard to Elisabeth. "Why are you giggling so?" I asked her one evening at dinner, again in the officer's tent, an almost elegant affair, were it not for our clothes, altered from men's uniforms.

"Don't tell anybody," she went on squealing into her paper napkin. "Jock kissed me."

"What? First Lala and now you!" Despite wanting to follow the directives imposed on us by our superiors, I was beginning to feel a little left out. But I knew Elisabeth was just "flexing her muscles." She was far too sensible to get seriously involved.

It was the evenings in the canteen that my aunts, not to mention my mother, would probably have found not quite *"comme il faut."* It was a time to relax, and different people had different ideas. Some men would sit themselves at one of the tables, and after having brought enough mugs filled with beer to occupy exactly every inch of the tabletop, stay there for the duration of the evening, happy not to have to totter back and forth to the bar to replenish the supply of drink. These types were not too eager to socialize but when they felt an urge to exercise, they would get up and dance some crazy jitterbug with each other, and be hailed by the crowd of spectators with howls of appreciative laughter.

Some men were sitting around and would come up to the tables occupied by the Polish girls and ask us to dance. Maybe our aunts would not approve, but we found them very polite.

We were curious about life in Great Britain, but conversation had to be reduced to a few words, for that was the extent of our knowledge of English. Nevertheless, the men tried to entertain us by carrying on conversations while dancing with us. The conversation was limited in scope, but occasionally hilarious because of those limitations. Everyone understood the need to maintain a pleasant atmosphere of friendly camaraderie.

I always loved to dance. When I started going to school at the age of six, one of the girls in our class was a straw-colour-haired little sylph named Lili. She was attending a ballet school. The very next day, there was a discussion with Mother.

"Mama, could I take ballet lessons?" I always chose a direct approach with my parents.

"Where did you get such an idea from, my child?" Mother's voice would betray just a shade of alarm.

"Well, this girl in our room--Lili is her name--she goes to ballet school," I explained, trying to be as convincing as possible.

To choose to be a ballerina as a profession for her only daughter did not appear very high on Mother's list of possibilities. Rather, such a profession, as perceived by Mother, who had me relatively late in her life, was completely out of the question due to its lack of respectability. I could not be aware at the time of all the traditional and cultural baggage that Mother's generation was carrying, but I sensed that attending ballet school could not be further contemplated.

My passion for dancing was transferred to sports and games, even to the point of interfering with other people's desire to dance! So many times at school, even as a seven- or eight-year-old, accompanied by a bunch of adventurous classmates, I would sneak up to the large gym in the part of the building belonging to the secondary school students. This was the best place to play tag: among the throng of pairs of teenage girls losing themselves passionately in dance to the strains of tangos or waltzes, or the latest American import, the foxtrot, being energetically played on the piano by an eager volunteer. So many times, chased by the shrieking dancers and delivered into the hands of a home teacher, we were sent to the principal's office for what remained of the long midday break, where a false promise of "never again" was extracted from us.

The war robbed my generation of the fun that teenagers all over the world expect as their due. Dancing and sports were out.

Now, riding the tide of opportunity, I was eager to learn new dances and new steps of what used to be in those days primarily ballroom dancing. It was an activity combining two of my favourite elements: energetic movement and generally agreeable music. My frequent partner was a "Tommy," as the Englishmen were popularly (and politely) known, so as to distinguish them from the Scottish "Jocks." His name was Paul and he was married.

One evening, as the music stopped, Major P. approached us just as Paul was about to lead me back to the table.

"I don't think you should dance with Ihra," the major said bluntly. The constant trouble Anglophones have with pronouncing my name was already raising its ugly head.

Paul did not show any embarrassment; but of course . . . the English know how to keep a stiff upper lip.

"I'm teaching Ihra to dance, Sir," he said quietly.

"I think she has already been taught enough," replied the major, leaving us in the middle of the floor to ponder his words.

We looked at each other, puzzled. For my part, I tried to figure out the word "taught." I had no idea what my partner was thinking. Major P's action could be considered surprising. Never for a moment did Paul appear to me as a romantic prospect; he reminded me of a middle-aged uncle. He was just a good dance partner, and there was no reason at all to suspect him of ulterior motives. So at first the major's intervention offended me.

He's read too many stories about Polish "sirens," I thought with annoyance. *Perhaps he enjoys reading biographies and has come across a number of famous people in history who had Polish mistresses. He might not have heard about Balzac, but as a military man, he must have read about Napoleon and "Pani Walewska."*

After brooding over the matter for a while, I decided that the major did what a good commanding officer would do: namely, whatever was necessary to ensure good conduct, and bring the straying soldier, whose wife hopefully awaited his return, just like Penelope awaited Odysseus, back from the edge of the precipice.

It also occurred to me later that no man in his right mind could regard me as a "siren," and that Major P. was most likely simply interested in protecting me!

TWELVE
The Lure of Independence

Without a leader or advisor to speak of, we twenty girls chose Tamara Leniak to negotiate on our behalf through all the pitfalls of the entirely new scenario at Mardorf camp. At first sight, a somewhat heavy figure of a girl with an inexpertly improvised hairdo, wearing, like all of us there, unflattering clothes totally devoid of anything remotely resembling elegance, Tamara would never be regarded as a "siren." Despite the latter, her lively and intelligent eyes, her engaging smile, and most of all, her throaty, alto voice had a power to beguile.

After our stay in Mardorf, Tamara and I attended the last year of high school, where social life, now flourishing after the long, barren years of war, was in serious competition with book learning. A few years later, we would find ourselves in London, Tamara and her husband living not very far from Ted and me, but in a better house, in a better area . . . with a baby girl born a few months before our baby boy.

Most of the time, Tamara was accompanied by her mother, and no matter what any young person might have thought, it had its advantages. Her mother was a doctor, and this profession put her on a pedestal. The daughter, as is usually the case, shared a little bit of the glory. Before getting married, she lived with her mother instead of in student quarters, which protected her against the unwelcome advances of men looking for a quick romance.

Tamara could play the piano. She would just sit down and bang off a Beethoven sonata, leaving all present marvelling at her memory and strength, if not virtuosity. I did not think about the lack of expression and subtlety in Tamara's playing; I was just simply envious. The war years were really hard on our family after Father's death. Love of music and moving my fingers over the keys whenever I found myself in the vicinity of a piano were all I had.

Her piano-playing prowess apart, Tamara could be regarded as a perfectly ordinary girl with perhaps a little more maturity than is usual for her age. Perhaps because of all the above, as a married woman and mother she seemed to know everything about babies and what to do with them, while I was completely ignorant of such things. When our first baby, Roman, was born, I relied heavily on books and the advice of the pediatrician, both of which, at that particular time, put forward some outlandish, quasi-modernistic ideas.

One evening, when Roman was about four months old, Ted and I eagerly accepted Tamara's invitation to bridge. We walked for several blocks, pushing the baby in its carriage. When Tamara proudly introduced us to her apartment, we felt surrounded by luxury. There actually was a separate bedroom for the baby.

Gradually, as time went by, Tamara began to appear less and less like a suitable friend, and more and more like a silent reproach. Her charming smile and excellent manners, her being "just so" began to chafe. I was almost glad to hear they decided to immigrate to the United States. But the perfect family was not entirely perfect. Not perfect enough. We heard later that Tamara fell in love with another man while travelling on the ocean liner to New York, and left her husband. Maybe her mother's protection only smothered her natural disposition to welcome romantic experiences; or maybe her husband, a good many years her senior, was more the choice of her mother than her own.

* * *

It seems that only Major P., the cultured, handsome man who seemed to know all about well brought up young ladies, might have sensed Tamara's capacity for passion as much as her mother tried to quell it.

One evening in the canteen at Mardorf camp, Tamara was asked to play the piano. She seated herself at the upright piano there and went through the Beethoven *Apassionata* with her usual not overly subtle vigour. When she was done, everyone present applauded; it was truly impressive to be able to perform such a difficult work from memory. Interestingly enough, the major noted with a slight lisp that he seemed to cultivate:

"When you fall in love, you will be able to play this sonata more passionately."

The poor Polish girls in ill-fitting army clothes were once more reminded of their possibly dangerous sexual potential. The major in all likelihood merely thought of something clever to say and ended by being prophetic. The next moment, completely unaware of the weight his opinion would carry with us, he got up from the wicker armchair in which he was relaxing, clapped his hands, flashed a charming smile, and promptly changed the subject.

"Time for our English lesson, let's go!" He urged our perplexed group to follow him into one of the quiet, side rooms where he would conduct a daily lesson. He was just like everyone's uncle.

Too bad he soon grew tired of giving lessons, leaving us hanging on to a few words and phrases we managed to master. Too bad, as well, that his debonair charm and sophisticated brand of quasi-cordiality spelled trouble for raw simpletons like us . . .

The vacation spent at Mardorf camp managed to elevate our expectations to, frankly, unreasonable heights. When we came back to Oberlangen, it could no longer pretend to be anything else to us but a dolled-up POW camp with our middle-aged female commandants attempting to maintain army discipline among a hormone-driven juvenile and young adult community of women, eager to taste what living in freedom had to offer.

The ladies were exerting Sisyphean efforts trying to raise the banner of virtue and purity, while facing numerous legitimate concerns dealing with the moral behaviour of such an incongruous crowd. Occasionally, getting frustrated by the scarcity or apparent lack of success in reaching the conscience of the unruly individuals, they wandered onto the wrong side of the boundaries of absurdity.

"Why do you have your breast pockets undone?" one of the female captains would chastise a startled girl, wearing the smallest size of a man's battledress, our usual attire at this stage. "Do you want someone to put his hand in there?" she sneered.

In a matter of minutes, everyone in the camp was talking about the open breast pockets and somebody putting his hand in them. The willingness to maintain army discipline was already seriously weakened; it was deemed no longer necessary by a considerable number of ex-POWs, and was now in danger of succumbing to an often uncouth derision.

The four of us: Elisabeth, her sister, Lala, and I were quietly plotting an "escape"--back to Mardorf.

"Remember when we were leaving Mardorf, Major P. said, 'See you later.' What else could it mean? He wanted us to come back!" argued Elisabeth, trying to convince us.

"I don't think he meant that at all. It was just something to say," I tried to play for time.

"I am sure Major could help us to go to England. Imagine, we could study there," persisted Elisabeth.

The temptation was so great that we were ready to ignore the snares of the insufficiently mastered language, and embark on an adventure with possibly regrettable consequences.

The behaviour of a foreign person with its subtle, unknown to us, nuances had contributed to our reading the signals incorrectly. But staying put was too difficult. Quite a few people with various connections had already left for England, Belgium, or Italy. Why should we stay?

We figured we were not a "real army" and our army role was played out. We felt somehow betrayed and tricked out of the right to make decisions about our own future. However, breaking away from the camp so soon after the German capitulation, when the country was still in the throes of post-war convulsions, possibly still dangerous in places--such decisions could not be taken lightly. We were pining for the freedom of the wide world out there, but a little afraid, too. The news the next day forced us to decide quickly. Our group was to be assigned to sentry duty. To add insult to the injury, we were to be armed with wooden rifles!

"Now, do you want to stay here?" Elisabeth asked triumphantly.

"Enough of playing army!" was the reply.

The same evening, helped by our loyal friends in the Armoured Division, we got in a small army van and hid ourselves under a pile of blankets. We left Oberlangen forever.

Hitching a ride to get to Hanover, and finally to Mardorf, was not difficult. Hitchhiking was the only means of transportation available to DPs, as we were known by the Allied command--we were displaced persons. A large number of members of the Home Army, both male and female, were incorporated into the Polish army units under the British command. But we were too young to stay in the army; we were destined to go to school. And we decided to go to school in England. As for the dangers of our journey, the most perilous situation happened when an American navy officer stopped to give us a ride at a side road, not an Autobahn, and he was driving his--or rather his CO's--limousine at ninety miles an hour!

Major P. received us very kindly and invited us to stay as long as we wished. We were assigned one of the small cottages on the grounds. The camp seemed empty, since it was already September and many convalescents had gone back to their units.

It seemed like the subject of our transfer to England would have to be broached carefully at the nearest opportunity. In the meantime, Lala was flirting with her future husband, and Elisabeth's sister was dreaming about surprising her sweetheart from the Polish Armoured Division in London, where she imagined they would meet unexpectedly. Elisabeth and I were having arguments about all kinds of silly things; we both realized that our dream was not worth much in the face of reality with its laws and regulations, all seemingly too difficult to overcome.

After a couple of weeks of somewhat forced fun, Elisabeth and I took it upon ourselves to confront the major. He answered with his awfully attractive smile: "Why, Elisabeth and Ihra, I would love to help you to come to England, but it cannot--"

Whatever he said after we did not understand, although he tried to speak slowly and clearly. At this point we didn't care what else was said. We only heard a big, fat, NO.

Severely disappointed, we suffered a momentary shortage of ideas as to what to do with ourselves. But shortly after, a liaison officer from the Home Army headquarters in Emsland came to notify us about the opening of a high school in Maczkow.

"I am going back to school, and I hope you will come too." I was glad it was turning out this way.

"Tommy and I are engaged to be married," announced Lala. "I am going to England with him."

Although Lala never concealed her plan to marry an Englishman, we were speechless.

"Are you sure you will be happy as his wife?" Elisabeth asked finally.

"Oh, yes, I know what I am doing," Lala sounded so grown-up and determined. "The three of you do not understand at all," she said. So we let her be and left on the journey to Maczkow, by way of our Canossa.[11]

Actually, our Canossa was a little place in northwestern Germany called Hange, where we had to mend fences with our lady commandant. At the entrance to an imposing villa, a corporal receptionist acknowledged our arrival rather absentmindedly. This seemed to be a good sign. The commandant of Women Services of the Home Army, Major Yaga, was a handsome woman with big blue eyes, too piercing to be alluring. She was wearing an elegant khaki ATS uniform; somehow her shiny black hair was piled up inside a military service cap.

"What do you have to say for yourselves?" she asked. Her tone did not match her severe military demeanour; obviously she would have preferred to administer a stern reprimand but had probably been advised to be lenient. There was no point in explaining, so we just meekly apologized for our sudden exit from Oberlangen, and the obvious neglect of assigned sentry duties. The lady commandant called our behaviour insubordinate and caused us a few anxious moments by asking: "Where are your military virtues?"

Out of respect for her, we did not say anything. Luckily for us it was a rhetorical question, and she did not wait for an answer. We would not know what to say, and anyway, her question now seemed funny. Strange how a few months ago we were ready to risk our lives to maintain our military status!

---

[11] To "go to Canossa" has the meaning of "to eat humble pie."

"*Tempora mutantur* [times change]," came to my mind. At school, I was good at Latin.

In the end, sanity prevailed, and back to school we went.

The school was actually for German kids. The small German city of Harren was quietly dreaming on the banks of Ems, and perhaps it did not deserve its fate. On the other hand, being situated in the midst of Nazi concentration camps within endless miles of swampy peat bogs, where slave labour was used to harvest the peat and do the farm work, it probably grew rich on the backs of the enemies of Nazism. And so, the time came for the city to pay its dues to the unfortunate.

In May 1945, thousands of freed concentration camp inmates, wartime slave workers, and ex-POWs had to be given food and shelter, before their existence, brutally suspended at the edge of an abyss by the occupant and the vagaries of war, could be helped along towards safe, and possibly happy, goals. Among those throngs of maltreated human beings were children growing up and becoming teenagers. Accorded a nearly subhuman status, they had endured severe emotional deprivation due to the absence of nurturing care and moral guidance.

Following the liberation of these people, their basic needs were provided for in quickly organized camps. Luckily, the military government set up by the Allied forces also acknowledged the necessity of helping the inmates of the camps to escape boredom and despair. People had to be given a chance not only to improve their living conditions, but also to regain their human dignity; their moral and cultural needs were to be addressed by appropriate organizations. Living conditions made as normal as possible were seen as necessary for the healing process to begin. And so a project unprecedented in its scope was undertaken in which a quiet little town on the river Ems was emptied of its German population. In its stead, a crowd of foreigners, Poles in this case, homeless, though not through any fault of their own, occupied the place over a period of three years.

The town was under the special care of the 30th Corps of the British Army on the Rhine, and particularly the 1st Polish Armoured Division, which shared the duties of the occupation of Rhineland. Its CO was General Stanislaw Maczek, and therefore the German city was given a temporary Polish name--Maczkow. The administration of the town was taken over by Polish functionaries best suited to perform particular duties in the circumstances. The task of finding such personnel was not difficult, since the people liberated from various institutions of oppression came from all the strata of Polish society-- from simple workers to artists, lawyers, physicians, and university professors.

One of the landmarks of the town was a fairly large school building. It was promptly filled by about three hundred secondary school pupils, hoping to eventually obtain their high school diploma. The teachers were primarily recruited from among the ex-POWs and other liberated groups. Even some soldiers serving in the Division were given leave to attend the school.

When we first presented ourselves in the principal's office as candidates for the final grade of secondary school, the year was 1945. It was not in England but in this small German town, Harren, on the Ems River, which had been temporarily taken over by Polish authorities.

Elisabeth and I emerged triumphant from the preliminary session designed to assess our qualifications. The principal, like the majority of the teachers in this school, had been an officer, and had been taken prisoner during the *Blitzkrieg* in Poland in 1939. After spending five years in an *Offlag* (prisoner-of-war camp for officers), he was happy to teach anybody.

Furthermore, one of the commissioners in the school was the Latin teacher from our high school in Warsaw, so there was no problem.

Elisabeth and I were installed in a little hotel, the only one in the city, until another building suitable for a young ladies' dormitory would be ready. By virtue of the circumstances, Elisabeth gradually became what appeared to be a "special" friend.

It turned out later that in order to get the matriculation diploma as quickly as practically possible, some people lied to get into higher grades than those for which they were qualified; furthermore, some of our classmates had not been to any kind of school since the beginning of the war. Consequently, though the teachers were conscientious and highly proficient, the tempo of acquiring knowledge could not be very rapid. For the two of us, not quite a year out of the classroom from an excellent teaching institution, the schoolwork in this situation presented no extraordinary challenge, leaving us with ample free time.

Since we had spent most of our lives in Poland's capital city, we soon found living in the small town too monotonous. The life in the hotel where we were lodged, especially compared with our recent life history, was quiet to the point of boredom. The hotel was actually more of a boarding house. Nevertheless, the social standing of the other residents, including a retired army officer and middle-aged, respectable ladies busy with charitable activities, added considerably to the prestige of that modest place. All aspects of life in the town were commented upon at meals.

"Disgraceful how some of the young girls dress to go to church!"

"If I were the mayor I would close that café on X Street!"

It was really trying to have to listen to such conversation.

Eventually, Elisabeth and I became friends with another, younger student, occupying an adjacent room. Her name was Krystine, and she was exceptionally beautiful. She was not very tall, rather dainty and delicate, and had brown curly hair and green eyes. Her smile was as sweet as her nature, her movements graceful. She projected an aura of innocence bordering on helplessness, and since she appeared unaware of her captivating appearance, Krystine's beauty inspired affection and the desire to protect rather than envy her.

Mr. Gradecki, the teacher of German language in the school, was the one person that Elisabeth and I disliked. A charming bachelor with a knowing smile and dreamy eyes, he notoriously bewitched the female population. His very presence raised the temperature in the classrooms, for he would indulge in flirtations with older schoolgirls.

As far as we were concerned, we would rather die than admit he was attractive. To us he was the personification of a piteous, self-styled Casanova, who we imagined could flourish only in this unsophisticated town. He was the type that would graciously accept the admiration of important matrons, but would be equally interested in hard-working maidservants.

It was probably different for Elisabeth, who had already been engaged at an early age, but for me, sexual attraction and interest in boys and men were still overshadowed by my mother's veiled warnings about adventures with the opposite sex. My acquaintance with that section of humanity was somewhat expanded during the Uprising, though not always inspiring admiration. At that stage, nothing had happened yet to eradicate the childhood memories of the boisterous youth of my brother, and to effectively shake my conviction that boys and young men, with a few exceptions, were to be regarded as unrepentant troublemakers. However, there was an even more powerful reason to dislike Gradecki--Krystine had fallen in love with him. The shy glances and sudden colour on her innocent face whenever she saw the wretch were all too obvious.

One late afternoon, Elisabeth and I had nothing to do, and the Gradecki affair suddenly came to weigh heavily on our minds.

"I wonder what Krystine's mother thinks about it all?" I began.

"She may be under his spell too." Elisabeth emphasized her disgust with an expressive scowl. "Well, if the person closest to her won't rescue her--"

"We will!" I completed the sentence. "Imagine the gall he has to even consider marrying this angel!"

I started to dig into my books and papers immediately. I found two large sheets of drawing paper. We worked till the wee hours of the morning, delighted in the hope of not only chastising Gradecki, but also putting some spark into the otherwise monotonous town existence.

"They'll have something to talk about in this sleepy hotel!"

The next morning, a large written obituary, the fruit of nearly an entire night's labour, graced a wall in the market square. It proclaimed the following:

"M.W. Gradecki, age forty, passed away as a result of excessive romantic emotion. With his passing, our town has lost the heart and soul of social activities. He has left a great number of bereaved ex-fiancées, prospective wives, and others who loved him deeply."

The man was only thirty-five, but we thought it would really cook his goose if we made him forty! In the lower left corner of this solemn proclamation was a P.S. "An auction will take place where some valuable effects of the deceased will be available. Items for auctioning include: a dozen scented handkerchiefs, a photo album full of pictures of beautiful ladies, and a copy of the deceased's memoirs."

Nothing happened at breakfast, but on the landing, I overheard a young woman saying to another:

"And only yesterday he was telling me he loved me . . ."

The perpetrators left quietly for school. On our return in the afternoon we found the inhabitants of the hotel beside themselves with excitement and righteous indignation.

"What kind of scoundrel conceived such an awful joke?" fumed one of the ladies.

"It's not a joke, it's a crime," corrected a retired colonel from the corner of the room.

We were a little dismayed at being called scoundrels, but felt gratified that, according to plan, the affair was receiving wide and vigorous attention. Too soon, however, a messenger arrived and asked us to go and see the principal, at once! Elisabeth went into the principal's office first, and after the interview, I was not allowed to see her. I could not fathom what went wrong.

Maybe a caretaker spotted us when we sneaked out at three o'clock in the morning to put up the obituary, I thought.

The principal was a large man in his middle fifties. He was breathing heavily as I entered; it got me worried for myself, but then, I thought, maybe he had asthma.

"I know everything," he paused for breath and, by now I felt sorry for him, "Your friend confessed and I know you two are responsible."

Then he put some papers in front of me. They also were fake obituaries announcing the untimely demise of Mr. Gradecki! Of course, in appearance, they did not come close to ours, but still! Apparently, Gradecki had many enemies in the town on the river Ems; we merely started the ball rolling. One look at the obituaries convinced me that whoever wrote them did not mince words; they were stressing the point less than delicately.

"You didn't write these, I hope," thundered the principal.

"No, Sir!"

"You realize you created a public scandal? I will have to consult my colleagues on how to deal with you two, but I tell you we cannot be too optimistic. Everyone is shocked by this--" He paused in search for words and more air. That was all.

The next few days, people in the town talked of nothing else; Elisabeth and I were in the limelight. Even a reporter from the local paper came to interview us but we refused to talk to him. As a punishment, we were officially suspended from the school for one month but were able to attend classes so as not to waste time in preparation for the approaching matriculation exams.

Some of the teachers treated the whole thing far less seriously--a college prank, they said. We were reassured by this benevolent group about our future in the school. It became known that even some of the senior municipal officials laughed their heads off at poor Gradecki and the way he was sent packing so swiftly and efficiently. Elisabeth and I did not mind that a considerable portion of the community (most of all the older people) disapproved of us. But Krystine, in her own gentle manner, also turned against us. The poor girl suffered with her beloved.

As for Gradecki, he extracted some kind of apology from us two culprits. He had no choice but to magnanimously accept it. His career as a teacher in the local school was over. He left town, and maybe found better hunting grounds somewhere else. But the story of the phony Gradecki demise does not want to go away. People still remember it and give me their opinion on the subject.

* * *

One summer in the early nineties, we had the Maczkow High School reunion in Poland. We were on a bus on the way to visit a renowned baroque cloister and a cathedral some thirty kilometres from Warsaw. It was a nice day and the passing scenery interesting.

I was enjoying looking out of the window, when a woman, one of the students from the school in Maczkow, requested permission to sit down next to me. Lowering herself into the seat, she said: "You know, General X thought that the joke we played on old Gradecki in Maczkow was really refreshing considering our situation then . . ."

I was not at all prepared when she suddenly opened the conversation this way because, being a bit of a "stuffed shirt," she'd had nothing to do with the obituary affair.

"He said it testified to a magnificent resilience of the spirit of our young people," she continued, ignoring the look of surprise in my eyes. Her impudence temporarily robbed me of the ability to control my facial muscles. I was even not quite sure whether my mouth was wide open or not.

"Wait a minute!" I was finally able to articulate, "Weren't you one of those goody two-shoes who would have nothing to do with us after the scandal exploded?"

The woman, now in her sixties, was Krystine's friend, and fifty years ago commiserated with that naive young girl suffering from the effects of broken childish dreams. Of course, she regarded us then with utter contempt--maybe rightly so! Now, determined to earn points in her social climbing exercise, she wanted to win popularity at high places by assuming partnership in the activity she once unequivocally condemned!

"Well, you know I had to be careful; the school--" she started to offer a lame explanation. I was laughing now and that seemed to restore her confidence.

"Could you describe exactly how you did it?" she continued her quest demurely, but I was annoyed by now.

"Listen, I am not terribly proud of what we did; I guess it was okay at our age. You will have to rely on your own memory, sorry."

We continued together in awkward silence, smiling at each other with insincere smiles. I was really disappointed at not being able to anticipate the vagaries of human behaviour. . .

Has she regressed to her teens in her old age, or have I lost my sense of humour?

The incident revealed how I've lost touch with my own background. Savouring the pleasure of visiting the country of my birth, I got out of step with my own kind. I abandoned common sense and expected everyone to be perfect. The "old cobwebs" can really clutter up the minds of people obliged to move away from their roots. Being "displaced" requires much adjusting, and the wanderers run a risk of losing touch with the steadying support of their background. Sadly, they also lose the opportunity to unravel old issues; they are denied the options available to the natives within their community and family. It is easier to be in your own country among relatives and school friends. By the same token, people moving away learn to expand their outlook to wider horizons--maybe experiencing fear at first, but hopefully growing stronger and also more tolerant.

Krystine and I have no quarrel about the Gradecki affair; when we meet, be it in Warsaw when we both come to visit, or in other places, we act like good friends from the past. On the other hand, Elisabeth, who has remained closest to her roots, writes querulous letters.

* * *

Trying to reform people or make life more interesting exacts a price. The world proved to be determined to stay dull, and sided with the small-time Casanova. As a punishment, Elisabeth and I were relegated to a lower class accommodation on the outskirts of town. Though our good friends stuck with us for better or for worse, we earned one more minus in the eyes of the establishment, and consequently could not afford to make any more "mistakes."

In this town "borrowed" from the Germans, the army was our benefactor. The military authorities were looking after our immediate material needs and helped to run the city, as well as the high school. Among our schoolmates, who were members of the Polish 1st Armoured Division granted leave to attend to their education, was my future husband, although at the time neither of us had any idea what was going to happen about four years later. In comparison with the DPs, such as we were at the moment, the members of the Armoured Division were very well off. Their life was perfectly organized by dutiful sergeants--all they had to do was to attend to their homework.

They also had leave. They could go away to those far-away, fabulous places and then tell us, probably with shameless exaggeration, just to tease, what a great time they had there. These were glimpses of a better life just around the corner. There were cities not ruined by murderous aggression; there were people living in comfort who had never seen mouldy bread--never eaten it and never craved it. There must be stores with elegant clothing and dainty ladies' shoes. With the spectre of annihilation removed, people's minds would gradually turn to more carefree interests.

Except for those gnawing concerns about what had happened to our loved ones . . .

We found out from our military classmates about the activities of the Red Cross agency, which was located in Brussels, and which conducted family searches in response to inquiries.

If all this talk succeeded in planting adventurous thoughts in our fertile minds, this particular information about Brussels helped them to blossom into a powerful obsession. We were determined to visit this Mecca of the army, presently occupying Germany, to try to find out about our families and maybe savour some of the city's attractions. Yet the obstacles blocking the way to carrying out this desire seemed insurmountable.

Only military personnel could get permission to travel throughout Europe, using the available means of transportation. The magic word was the "pay book." It opened doors; it yielded favours. No one paid us anything; we did not have a pay book.

I asked the principal of the school if we could go to Brussels to inquire about our families.

"You don't have to go there," he told me. "Just wait and the inquiries will progress far enough to have the information reach you here, so don't worry."

"It's easy to say, 'don't worry,'" I said to Elisabeth back in our room.

We were silent for a while, and then Elisabeth said, "What we need is a document with our names on it, giving us permission to travel and stamped with some official seal, right?" She had an inspired look in her eye.

"That's about it."

"Well, we have a document like that!" she announced triumphantly. I was just trying to think hard, and then I remembered. Yes! The document in question was the pass we obtained from the military authorities to travel from Mardorf to the school in the German town, Harren. We only had to find two things to proceed with our plans: the said document, and a place called Harren in the general vicinity of Brussels! After some feverish searching, we found the piece of paper we imagined to be so powerful! And indeed, there was a place called Harren close to the Belgian-Dutch border. We set out on what was to be our last mission, our last act of conspiracy. I guess some habits are hard to break.

THIRTEEN
Life Begins After the War

At the railway junction station in the German city of Münster, the night train to Brussels dazzled us with its impressive exterior--it was not a cattle train. Servicemen and women of all ranks were boarding leisurely. Though not quite sure whether our fake documentation entitled us to be there in the first place, we were anxious to board regardless. We were rushing to hide on the train, away from the sharp eyes of the patrolling military police, who, we thought, might regard us with suspicion. We climbed on board, deliberately choosing a third-class car, and stood in the corridor, happy to be there and not knowing what to do next. Apart from the occasional "Excuse me" from people trying to pass us on the way to various compartments, nobody spoke to us. We were greatly relieved when the train started to move and we were still on it.

Major P.'s English lessons did not take us very far, so when an elegant British officer approached us, we had no idea what he was saying at first. He was a skinny fellow with a yellowish moustache and not at all like the handsome Major P.

"I beg your pardon?" I managed to resurrect in my memory the phrase we repeated several times with the major, it being more polite than, "Come again?"

"I am Major . . ." (Another major!) "I am in command of this train; I would like to escort you to your proper seats, since you cannot possibly spend the night out here." He spoke slowly to make it easier for us to understand.

Our poor knowledge of English perhaps stood us in good stead. At least we did not say anything stupid. He invited us to follow him to first-class, which was the designated train section for travelling women in auxiliary services, as dictated by military protocol. Unable to find any room, as all compartments were already occupied by some women but mostly by male officers, he invited us to his own compartment.

"Oh, oh . . ." Elisabeth and I exchanged glances.

But we did not have to worry. The major was charming but absolutely correct in his behaviour, and soon bade us "good night," saying he would share a compartment with his friend. We looked at each other relieved.

"Fine conspiracy," Elisabeth and I had the same comment. "How inconspicuous are we going to be, right in the CO's compartment?"

We started giggling nervously. Soon we grew tired and decided to relax. It was not difficult to enjoy the luxuriously comfortable velvet upholstery. The light of the early morning alerted us to the hazards of our situation.

We hoped to be discreetly out of the compartment as soon as the train stopped in Brussels that morning at 7:30, but no such chance. The major appeared with the last jerking movement of the train coming to a halt. As polite as before, he steered us personally towards the sergeant, seated at a table set up at the exit from the platform, who was checking the documents of those newly arrived. No possibility existed to mix with the groups of other passengers and sneak out of the station. Instinctively obeying the military procedures, everyone present was in the process of leaving the train in a rather disciplined way, and then formed orderly lines in front of the sergeant. Only Elisabeth and I were totally out of this game, and felt like a couple of scared chickens.

"The major must have suspected us, and now we will get it," said Elisabeth in despair.

"Wait, we aren't in mortal danger and nobody is going to beat us up," I tried a little "pep" talk. The important piece of paper in my hand, our surrogate document, seemed to generate vaguely optimistic vibes. No one had needed to see it so far. This would be the acid test.

When our turn came, the sergeant was temporarily distracted by a person in front of us who asked him a question. A brief conversation disrupted the rhythm of the proceedings. The sergeant, trying to re-establish the tempo, barely glanced at our "pass" and, smiling politely, handed us a slip for a hotel stay in Brussels. He even pointed out which hotel--just across the square opposite the Gare du Nord. Heaving a sigh of relief, Elisabeth and I congratulated ourselves on such a piece of good luck. Imagine staying in a luxury hotel instead of some crummy hostel for DPs!

The hotel proved to be of the highest standard. Let us say the women in auxiliary services were treated with the utmost delicacy, a practice that seems to have been abandoned in recent warfare. An official-looking lady in a smart ATS uniform politely asked us for our pay books. We had been lucky enough so far, but now we could not proceed without the magical document, the pay book. We must have looked pitifully lost, because the nice lady suddenly said, "Why don't you have a good rest now and come to see me when I come back on duty tomorrow at noon"--at least this is the gist of what she said after many attempts to help us understand her.

Needless to say, we took full advantage of the hotel amenities, including prolonged sessions in the bathtub, and an excellent dinner, not to mention sleeping in superbly comfortable beds. However, we left immediately after breakfast the next day, feeling a little guilty only because we would have no chance to thank the polite ATS lady for her kindness. Otherwise, we felt we had a right to all these comforts-- maybe even more right than others, considering how long we had been deprived.

Human beings create rituals, establishing barriers of distinction from other groups so as to preserve a place in historical continuity. We were marked for failure on two counts: one, because we broke one of the rules set up to uphold the military rituals; and two, an even more blatant transgression, we were different from the accepted models!

Heavens, were we ever different! We stuck out like sore thumbs in our ill-fitting uniforms and men's army boots, clumsily exceeding our feet by at least two sizes. Yet the trip was an unqualified success--after six years of experiencing denial, fear, and destruction around us, we delighted in the beauty of normal life in a charming city.

Our triumphant and somewhat illegal attempt to return to civilization brought also, at least for me, a relief from the constant anxiety concerning the fate of my family. There was a letter waiting for me at the Red Cross office.

"It's good you were able to come to Brussels," said the woman volunteer handing me the letter. "It could have maybe reached you in a few months, but maybe even never."

I looked at the white envelope trying to figure out its contents. I made a clumsy attempt at opening it. The woman in the office handed me a paper cutter. My eyes picked out words at random. My mother was safe! She did not perish in the ruins of the building where I last saw her. I embraced Elisabeth; we were both crying.

For the first time in a long time I felt really happy. Happy and grateful--grateful for human kindness overriding the rituals and privileges of exclusive groups. Grateful to the major, the commandant of the train, the sergeant checking the documents at the station, and the ATS officer at the hotel, who could find it in their hearts to overlook our ridiculous uniforms and our crude army boots, to respond to a cry for compassion which they might have read in our eyes.

School life continued uneventfully, until shortly before the final examinations were due to begin in the spring of 1946, when Mother Nature interfered with a colossal flood. Holland, Belgium, and a large portion of Germany were under water. The occupying armies assumed responsibility for the safety and essential supplies for the population. While Elisabeth and I were diligently studying for the final exams, higher powers decided that we should be transferred to the villa occupied by our military schoolmates, which was situated on high ground and closer to the school. Their commanding officer, Lt. Mark, who was also our classmate, was probably instrumental in bringing about this change.

The floodwaters were rising visibly. When Elisabeth and I, with barely enough time to get a few of our things, climbed beside Mark in the driver's seat, the water was already reaching our ankles. He had come in a huge truck to personally carry out the order.

People in low-lying areas had to move to higher ground in a hurry. Families with small children required assistance and special attention. Fortunately, there were not too many of them in Maczkow, and their needs were satisfied without any major problems.

Naturally, most people regarded the unexpected emergency as a darn nuisance, and it must have been a financial disaster for the countries affected. In a somewhat twisted way, the girls invited to the

Polish armoured division with pontoon, flood of 1946.

military quarters enjoyed generous hospitality and were treated like princesses. The flood was hardly a concern, although the river Ems claimed all the lower parts of the town. We were trying to study and avoid the interference of unusual attractions, such as sorties in large army pontoons to get supplies. The pontoons were far more interesting than the studying and won out. Were we thoughtless or just used to disasters?

The matriculation exams came and went without too much trouble. Unfortunately, Elisabeth did not make it. Surprised and terribly disappointed, she decided to stay in Maczkow and retry her exams in six months. For the successful candidates, the immediate future was less clear. Maczkow would not survive forever, and although it was delightful during our school year, plans had to be made for the future. Anyway, Maczkow was starting to wear me down. The familiar one-kilometre walk from our quarters on the shore of the Ems to the school building on the main street, and further past the small marketplace along the street, where the villa occupied by our military schoolmates was located, grew steadily more irksome, enclosed as it was within the framework of the architecturally typical German homes. Its limited perspective as a small town stifled my spirit. Like thousands of DPs all over Europe, regardless of location, I was becoming a disgruntled victim of the depressing inactivity and absence of focus in my life.

Getting away from Maczkow became urgent for one more reason. About halfway through the school year, romance started to pull at my heartstrings more seriously than any previous fleeting emotions, its progress this time more dignified than the hasty scamper of a scared rabbit--as it used to be like.

Take, for instance, the embarrassing experience with Mol. Mol wasn't his name, only a nickname he used in preference to his Christian name because Mol was proudly describing himself as a communist. Of course, his friends knew Mol was not a "typical dumb" communist, but an idealist and an intellectual.

We had long discussions on the steps in front of the school building . . . I was just about the right age for the final high school grade but Mol, like a majority of students there, was older. Like me, Mol was a member of the Home Army and had participated in the Warsaw Uprising, and was subsequently serving in the Armoured Division. I was impressed by his intelligence and idealism, and felt flattered when he showed interest in me. His enthusiastic plans for improving the human lot were so admirable.

"We would be crazy to go back to the same pre-war government," he was saying. "Communism is the right idea. People will be equal; there will be no unemployment."

Although we did it frequently, we did not discuss politics all the time. On the contrary, our military classmates, being in a relatively prosperous situation, frequently hosted parties at the villa they were occupying. Usually, a buffet dinner was followed by dancing to the best live bands Germany had to offer. Such were our spoils of war!

During one party, I felt hot after an energetic polka and tried to cool off in an adjoining room. I sat on a sofa furiously fanning myself with a small handkerchief, anxious to rest quickly and not to miss too many dances. Mol entered the room. He had a serious air about him--hardly suitable, in my opinion, for what was to follow. I did not see him dance; maybe dancing was just a frivolous pastime for him or maybe he did not know how . . . It did occur to me, though, that this was not an occasion for a serious discussion, but I remained seated as he lowered himself onto the sofa next to me. We were alone.

He started to mumble something not very clearly. I thought he said something like: "You are driving me crazy," and his face was suddenly coming very close to mine. Before I knew what was happening, he kissed me hard. It reminded me of the kiss I received during the Uprising--an innocent kiss from a frightened boy--but this was an act of aggression. I left the room quickly.

Good and wise friends are rare, and I felt badly disappointed, as though I had just lost one. The incident drove us apart, since from then on I avoided being alone with him. Another student in our class, Wanda, an intelligent, charming girl impressively steady and strong in dealing with the world in general, accepted not only Mol's attentions but also his views, and the two became a couple. Wanda was nice. She had a round head with a lot of blond hair. Her face was very sweet, but her figure was a little too full in the opinion of her girlfriends, to which she was perfectly indifferent, since Mol liked it. I suspect Wanda regarded me and my girlfriends as immature nitwits.

Somehow or other, I had gained a reputation of being one of the bright kids at school, and was often asked by my classmates to help with homework. It was fun to play "teacher," explaining things to people older than I and of higher rank. In emergencies, due to extreme lack of imagination or sloth or the pressure of time, I even "lent" them my own work. Such was the case when Vince, who was also in the Armoured Division, asked me to help him with his Polish essay assignment.

"Put in some mistakes, otherwise the teacher will be suspicious," he asked humbly.

When he came to collect my contribution to his passing mark, I came down to receive him in the quasi-recreation room of our modest quarters. It looked pathetically small and even more shabby with two handsome men in smart battledress standing there in the middle of the room.

"I came with a friend," Vince announced unnecessarily, since I could see for myself.

I had noticed Ted around the school a few times before, but both he and Vince were in a different room. Now I started to imagine that he had noticed me as well, and wanted to meet me. I was just dreaming! Balancing on a very shaky gangway at this point of my life journey, I could not contemplate any commitments. But that is how it began.

In the meantime, I was contemplating my future on one of those early summer days, when sunny weather urges you to go out and start something great--plant flowers, go for a long hike, or build a sandcastle. When Elisabeth called that the manager of our quarters, Sergeant B., wanted to see me one day, I felt gloomy and discouraged about my lot. Liberated from some camp or other, the manager was a well-meaning person appointed to take care of the building in which we were lodged. She looked so like a corpulent housewife that her uniform made her appear comical.

"I have received notice that Dr. X is organizing staff for the military hospital in Schleswig. He has some personnel already, but would welcome girls to train as nurses. Have you ever considered working as a nurse?"

"I have to think about it," I said after a pause. It was rather scary to have to discuss such an important decision in my life with a female sergeant whose qualifications for such a role I hardly trusted.

"It would be something to do for a while and wait for other opportunities. I could also enjoy staying on the famous Island of Sylt." Elisabeth and I were in our room scratching our heads. Well, Elisabeth had already decided to stay and repeat her grade, but she had a plan in mind, too.

"Why don't you go?" she asked excitedly. "You could take Greta with you. I don't want her to get so close to Frank." Greta said many times that she loved Frank, but both Elisabeth and I considered him too old for her. At twenty-eight, he was over the hill in our opinion.

Elisabeth was concerned and exasperated by her younger sister Greta. Elisabeth considered herself in charge, but Greta would not accept any authority, least of all her sister's. Beautifully built, with a charming gamin face framed by masses of brown hair, she towered over other girls. She looked very mature, and sexually she was; only her eyes betrayed the little girl inside her heart and brain. The power to seduce men was perhaps just a novelty, which she enjoyed like a new toy.

Was Elisabeth's apprehension due partly to jealousy? Frank, the man Greta professed to love, was initially Elisabeth's boyfriend, until he found out, very early, that Elisabeth, though flirtatious, was essentially a "good" girl. More at ease with the already sexually active younger sister, Frank let Greta lure him away from Elisabeth.

With memories of the summer of 1945 in Mardorf still fresh, the decision was finally taken in the summer of 1946 to venture to Sylt Island, situated on the North Sea along Germany's border with Denmark. The North Sea was not as hospitable as the inland lake the year before. The fresh wind chilled us to the bone, and coats had to be worn on the beach. A pre-war vacation spot for the German upper crust, the island had a luxury hotel with large windows overlooking the sea. Part of the hotel actually housed the hospital with exclusively Polish patients and personnel.

The three of us, Greta, Eva, and I, arrived to an overwhelming welcome from the matron, Rena, a lady in her late twenties, maybe less. To us then, everyone over twenty-two and projecting a little bit of authority looked ancient. She was a brunette with a shy smile and pale eyes of nondescript colour. The doctor in charge, on the other hand, seemed to me too young to be in charge of the hospital with only a medical student to help him. Indeed, the whole institution was in a state of flux pending more cooperation and assistance from the military government--MilGov for short.

The whole region of Schleswig-Holstein seemed to be low on the list of priorities of the new authorities, and was left to drift along with groups of Polish ex-POWs, created semi-spontaneously according to traditions governed by age, rank, and experience. The staff of the hospital on Sylt, as well as its patients, was recruited from such groups.

Having dismissed my previous failure to embrace nursing as immaturity, I cherished a vaguely construed vision of taking care of wounded war heroes. It eventually collapsed for lack of much factual support. Most of the patients were army officers recovering from minor complaints or surgeries such as varicose veins and haemorrhoids. Since no one was particularly interested in teaching us anything apart from very rudimentary rules having more to do with hygiene than medical care, our training proceeded at a snail's pace, and finally, not at all. Anyway, Rena suspected us of having designs on the medic, who was perhaps her lover.

This scenario was typical of the problem-ridden situation in Germany after the war--crowds of displaced people not knowing what to do, waiting for something to happen.

The political situation in Poland prevented large-scale repatriation of Polish POWs. We were all suspended in limbo. Nevertheless, in about two weeks we were transferred to a proper hospital in Schleswig with a great red cross on a white background painted on the roof. The more conventional location did not in any way alter our activities. Even so, the time in Schleswig was not a total loss. We met many different people; we had fun; we even did some work at the hospital, which included playing bridge on evening duty with the recovering patients.

I remember only one wounded and seriously ill patient. Once a week, one of us had to watch him during the night. Some dreadful hallucinations he was having made him tear off his bandages and terrify us with his screams. Maybe he was a hero, or maybe just a victim.

Two important things happened to me in Schleswig: I realized once and for all that I am not cut out to be a nurse, and I met Margaret.

The first time I saw her, she impressed me with her assurance and elegant bearing, not at all diminished by the horrible uniform adjusted from men's battledress that we were all obliged to wear. She introduced her fiancé and that was that. I assumed I would never see her again.

FOURTEEN
Widening Horizons

In the fall of the same year, a call came out to the ex-POWs from the Warsaw Uprising or, as the MilGov put it, DPs, to consider a trip to Italy courtesy of the Polish 2nd Corps. Apart from the opportunity it offered to see that spectacular country, and visit the cemeteries of Polish troops fallen during the Italian campaign, especially on Monte Casino, the purpose of this trip was not made immediately clear. The authorities described it as an educational excursion for students. Judging later by the vintage of our fellow travellers, one had to allow that people of any age could be studying something.

I could not leave Germany without seeing Ted, who was still in Maczkow awaiting his matriculation exams.

When I last saw him before leaving for Schleswig, he had said very quietly, "I may be going back to Poland."

"I am going to Italy!" I could not refrain from shouting and jumping down from the truck that stopped in front of the students' house. It was my exhilaration at seeing him again. There was not much time--we said our sad goodbyes. Would this be the end of our friendship, perhaps love? His usually playful eyes betrayed an unusual seriousness. I was happy to see this, and again, it made me sadder.

"Tough!" was the laconic comment of the slow-speaking Richard, Ted's best friend in the army who was to figure prominently in our life later. His best girl left for the repatriation camp to return to Warsaw and he had to stay. Richard's mother and sister were about to arrive in England by way of the Middle East and Africa. After the Soviets occupied the eastern part of Poland in 1939, Richard with his family and thousands of Polish people living there were expelled from their homes and forcibly taken to Siberia and other far-flung areas of the Soviet Union. They were set free in 1943 so their men could join the Polish forces under British command. Now their families were to join them in England, if they so wished. Richard avoided showing emotion by turning his back on us. There were many other couples who had to part as well . . .

Without knowing what awaited them in that presently unknown Poland--hard work in the best-case scenario, political persecution or even prison in the worst--many of our friends went back, mostly to fulfill family obligations, to look after ill or aged parents or maybe to look after a family farm.

Once again I was in Hange, my previous Canossa, and there, to my great joy, was Margaret. She had arrived from Schleswig and joined us with her mother.

This time there was no lecture on military virtues; we just had to undergo verification and be assigned to an appropriate group. The women's commandant of the Home Army gave us her blessing on the journey to Italy, and waved to us as we were leaving in a long, dark green column of trucks. The transport trucks belonged to the British Army on the Rhine--the famous BAOR with its emblem of a black boar jumping merrily in a white field. The Army of the Rhine was probably tired of taking care of all the DPs and ex-POWs, whom they could not absorb in their ranks. Let the Polish 2nd Corps worry about them for a while.

Needless to say, I, Eva, and Elisabeth, who decided to chuck her matriculation efforts at least for a while and come with us to Italy, cared little about all such technicalities, including the fact that we were pushed from one place to another without any apparent reason or plan. We were travelling through the most attractive part of Europe, and the late September weather was great and getting even better as we drove farther south. Food and shelter were provided. I had a photo of Ted in my pocket to look at from time to time, and wonder about the inscription: "To my dear wife."

It only seemed strange to have an "older" person with us. It was tacitly assumed that Margaret's mother might pose a little bit of a problem.

"I cannot sit right at the open end of the truck," she complained soon after we started on our way. She was uncomfortable with the heights even in navigating gentle hills. Wait till we get going through the Alps!

One of the girls sitting farther back happily changed seats with her, and all was well until Margaret's mother found something else to complain about. The poor lady personified the cares and worries besieging the minds of mature people.

While the youngsters were eagerly looking forward to whatever surprises the next stop in an unknown place had to offer, the older people, having lost at this point the fruits of half of life's labour, did not particularly enjoy being moved around like pawns in somebody else's chess game. They felt victimized by fate and unscrupulous politicians. While we were willing to enjoy the adventure, their primary interest was to know where it would all lead. I can understand now that these were not the conditions middle-aged women, as they were in those days, could relish. As for me, it was one of the most exciting trips in my life.

Still in Germany for the first couple of days, we spent one night in school buildings somewhere in Bonn--the second in renovated military barracks vacated by the now nonexistent German army. Entering France, the column of trucks moved like a giant khaki-coloured snake along the highways, less spectacularly efficient than Hitler's autobahns. One of the trucks collided slightly with a walnut tree, one of many that bordered the highway in the vicinity of Grenoble. The column stopped under a shower of walnuts still clothed in their outer green shells.

"Wow, let's get some!" We jumped down in a hurry and grabbed as many of the green balls as we could carry. The rest of the journey that afternoon was spent trying to extricate the darned nuts from their protective cover. When someone eventually noticed how black our fingers became, it was too late; the powerful stain could not be washed off for several days.

Still with black hands, we stopped for "tea" somewhere in Switzerland. The night was spent in a barn on mountains of hay. The delight of the hay fragrance added to the exciting view of the Swiss Alps--a feast for the eyes--and to the crowing of roosters accompanied by the gentle sound of cowbells. Waking up on an exquisite, sunny morning in this paradise was nothing short of living a fairly tale.

We were treated by the farmer, no doubt grateful to find his barn still standing, to freshly baked bread, eggs obligingly provided by squawking chickens, and delicious cheese and fruit. Who could ask for anything more?

Visiting Switzerland many years later, I wondered what happened to those hospitable Swiss farmers? At that time, with the memory of war retreating further in the past, most people there seemed to dislike foreigners, regarding them as a somewhat lower form of life. In Geneva, the Swiss try hard to completely ignore foreigners by looking "through" them; in the countryside, they torment them with extravagant prices.

"I am getting awfully sun-baked," I complained a day later, looking in the mirror of an old powder compact that Margaret and I shared between us. Constant exposure to the sun at the face of the mountain we continued to climb created "ideal tanning" conditions, but we had no lotion to protect ourselves.

"Here, put some Vaseline on your face." It was Margaret's mother, reaching to me from the back of the truck. "I got a few jars from first aid," she explained triumphantly, for it was the advantage of maturity with its foresight winning over the recklessness of youth that she was demonstrating, and not for the last time, either.

"Thank you so much," I said. It is impossible to estimate how many more "sun spots" would be presently fighting their way to the surface of my face, were it not for the foresight and kindness of this mature woman, whom we tended to regard as a bit of a nuisance.

We arrived in the historic city of Parma--actually, there are no places in Italy other than historic ones. Our clothes, showing almost a week's worth of crumpling, and our faces covered with a thick layer of Vaseline threatened to be an embarrassment in the city streets, even though we were better off than the majority of people wearing shabby civilian clothes. But the European population in those days was accustomed to people in all types and shapes of uniforms. Gradually, even the most self-conscious of us forgot the petty concerns about their appearance as they let themselves be overpowered by the excitement of seeing the places previously known only as names in textbooks. It was a continuous feast for the eyes under the permanently cloudless, blue Italian sky.

Our trucks, everywhere they stopped, were immediately surrounded by the local people searching for something to buy. Very often it was salmon conserves. Having very little money, our bunch of girls was only too pleased to part with something we considered very dull, and far less tasty than fresh fruit and "*gelato*."

"Salmon, salmon?" hopefully insisted the men brave enough to approach our encampment in the city square at lunchtime. Imagine dozens of individuals, whose faces could have been lifted from the paintings of the Masters, noisily milling around the trucks and repeating their mantra: "Salmon? Salmon?" And around us, this corner of the universe resplendent in Renaissance finery was a scenario undeniably worthy of the brush of a great painter, but it proved to be too troubling for our military "guardian angels," who kept chasing the people away.

In Turin, some of our escorts invited us to one of those divine nightclubs, with a dance floor under the stars, where we danced to the strains of the sweet music of a real Italian band. Such music is fit for Italy only; anywhere else it sounds terribly schmaltzy. We were even dancing with the Italians. I remember one young man invited me to dance, and looking unswervingly into my eyes, he kept asking: "*Contenta, contenta?*" All I could do was laugh a silly laugh. What else could I do? My severely underdeveloped diplomatic skills were not suitable for international circles.

The music stopped after midnight. It was time to go home, even though home was only a truck in the marketplace. It was considered safer to stay with the convoy for the night. We had to sleep inside the trucks with sentries guarding not just us, but also an even more precious cargo--the tires. The war had been over more than a year, but the economic situation in Italy was close to desperate, and the military personnel, especially since our convoy was manned by the forces stationed in Germany, did not feel all that comfortably secure. Rather poignant was the incident in the nightclub when one of our escorts, maybe too full of the Italian wine, was not ready to leave when the dancing was over. He asked brusquely, what happened to the music?

"*Finito*," explained the manager.

"*Finito, Italiano!*" shouted the inebriated sergeant, and we all gasped when he removed his six-shooter from its holster with an unsteady hand; the crowd of club guests took a precautionary step back. Luckily, his less belligerent colleagues overpowered him quickly, and our whole party left in a flotilla of horse-drawn carriages with snow-white seat covers.

When I visited Torino years later, it was just a wealthy, industrial city--with no excitement whatsoever!

The bloodthirsty behaviour of our sergeant made us very uncomfortable. We were trying to excuse it by assuming that he still blamed the Italians for being on "the other side" in the war. Apparently not everyone was convinced the war was over; the sergeant still needed to experience "closure," such as is needed after any traumatic ordeal. In view of the later political developments, a closure after the trauma of war, as far as we were concerned, had been a colossal disappointment. The political climate in Europe did not bode well for our country. Travel to interesting places, nice food, and good company could not protect us against the feeling of deep anguish in response to bad news arriving in twos and threes at a time.

The worst was yet to come. A few months later, the legitimate leader of the Polish Socialist Party, who hoped to come to terms with the post-war assembly of pretenders to power in the "new" order, had to escape from Poland to avoid prison, maybe even murder.

Much earlier we lost General Sikorski, the lynchpin of the Polish wartime diplomatic and military efforts abroad; he was killed in an apparent airplane accident over the Rock of Gibraltar.

The pre-war map of Poland was recklessly torn to pieces by Marshal Stalin, by cutting off generous portions of the territory to suit his fanciful plans for the Soviet domination of Europe. Where did it leave all the Polish inhabitants of these regions? Where would they be going back to? Everyone felt a persistent anxiety over the future, but they tried to keep it quiet. The time in Italy was our vacation, an opportunity to gather strength in preparation for hard times ahead. It was generally rumoured that tough decisions would have to be made sooner or later. There was no point in tainting our educational trips with life and death worries. These were left for later.

Our educational excursion led us to Rome, which has to be close to the top on the list of my favourite cities. No matter how impressive I have found it before, every time I visit, I find something new to admire.

Even so, I will never be as impressed by Rome as the very first time when we arrived in army trucks, following the trip schedule arranged for us by the Polish 2nd Corps in 1946.

"Look how they have bombarded here!" shouted little Eva as we were passing the Coliseum.

"Ha, ha, ha!" the rest of us could not stop laughing.

"What? Why are you laughing?" asked a perplexed Eva.

I know it is mean of me, but every time at the sight of this unforgettable ruin, I recall my first look at "real" ancient history so memorably accentuated by unabashed ignorance--and it always makes me laugh.

Camping in tents in Porto San Gorgio beat the hotel on Sylt. The Adriatic Sea, just at the bottom of the hill, was far warmer than the North Sea. Dressed in swimsuits consisting of men's trunks and elaborate scarf arrangements to cover our bosoms, we practically lived on the beach. The sea bathing season was over as far as the natives were concerned, so we had a lot of privacy. Still, some local youths came out to challenge us, and did swim in the vicinity.

We slept in large tents (six girls in each), set up in the park surrounding an impressive mansion, requisitioned as the school for Polish girls wanting to finish high school, the same way it had been done in Maczkow. The owner of the mansion, said to be a prince, came to visit occasionally. He was either really demented or pretended to be so. He addressed us all as "*Signorina Polacca, multo bella, multo carina*" and asked for cigarettes. We were advised to ignore him. Anyway, we were too busy swimming and playing ball on the beach.

"Some people really have it difficult," said Martina, one of the schoolteachers, as we were sitting on the beach one day. "Look at Mirka."

I turned my head, following the direction of her eyes. A sweet-looking young girl was relaxing on a blanket. She was crocheting. She was just like one of us, except that she was obviously very pregnant. My experience with human relationships was very limited at that time, and having grown up on a diet of myths about virgins who chose death over dishonour, I was ready to blame the girl before feeling any anger at her partner.

"How could she do a thing like that?" I said from the top of my ignorance tower.

"They are very much in love, you know," Martina tried to explain a little about life.

Apparently everything was going to be under control; only there was not enough time for them to get married.

"I am sure she will join him in England and everything will be fine," Martina continued, in an effort to wipe that expression of doubt and disdain off my face. I was actually thinking about Lala, who got herself married to a total stranger, a person from a different country and of an unknown social background, just to go to England.

"Don't worry, the fellow was from the Armoured Division; he will be honourable." Martina was visibly concerned about my reaction.

Maybe she was sorry she told me about Mirka. I did not say anything. I just thought to myself, *what some people are willing to do to be allowed to go to England!*

"I hope she will be very happy." I sincerely hope she was.

In the midst of all the pleasures, excursions to Rome, Capri, Predapio, Assisi, to mention just a few, we seldom had time to ponder our future. More enterprising and older people probably were more concerned, and tried to make plans while looking for opportunities and worrying. The more frivolous enjoyed the present.

But even the future promised to take care of itself when it was announced one day that we were actually to leave for England at the beginning of November. The Promised Land, the place we wanted to visit so badly, became easily attainable all of a sudden. It seemed that from that moment on, life's problems began to fall off by the wayside, a quasi-paradise had thrown open its gates, and our Italian adventures suddenly paled in comparison.

Not that the Italian sunshine was less delightful, or that walnuts and *gelato*, the best in the world, were any less enjoyable; our stomachs were still being progressively stretched by generous portions of both, while we feasted our eyes on art sublimely presented in all forms.

"You look deliciously round!" Colonel P. greeted me on top of St. Peter's Dome, which both of us happened to visit in Rome at the same time.

"I think it's time to cut down on walnuts and *gelato*," I suggested to Elisabeth, who complained about losing her willowy silhouette the same evening.

Long forgotten was the pernicious past--the danger, the spitting soup, the bombing, the POW camp, the politics--or was it? It is hard to imagine that nobody was concerned about what would happen once we arrived in England. Who was going to support us? The war was won and the victorious armies would be going home. But what if, as a result of political deals negotiated behind his or her back, somebody's home was now in a foreign country or under a hostile government? Would anyone want to go back then? Higher powers must have been spending time shaking out the bag of incredible problems. Talk about a Pandora's box!

By the middle of November, we set out from Verona on the way to Calais; it was raining. Sunny Italy was saying a weepy goodbye. Almost everyone had something to say about Verona, the city of Romeo and Juliet. It became vaguely irritating when one was looking through the rain-sprinkled windows of the train. Later, the heating in our compartment stopped working. We kept visiting other compartments in search of warmth, but at night we had to snuggle under the German army sheepskin-lined greatcoats that each of us had received as part of our soldier's pay. Nobody had taken those coats very seriously; now we were happy to have them.

While the Swiss and then the French scenery was there for us to admire through the Pullman windows, rumours, the bloom of prolonged immobility, sprung copiously from fertile brains.

Summer 1946: on top of St. Peter's in Rome; Irena is on the right.

The life of dark-haired Masia had been messed up by the war. She lost both parents during the occupation, and was practically on her own from a very early age. She was reasonably good-looking--tall and statuesque, with wavy dark hair and large brown eyes. Her beauty seemed to be all external, spoiled by something not quite wholesome about her personality, a certain lack of freshness, not to mention innocence. Although she was known to indulge in escapades with men to the point where her respectability could be questioned, we felt sorry for her and never showed our disapproval--there was enough of it from others. She hung out with us from the time we left Germany.

When she walked into our compartment so deliberately, we guessed from the serious expression on her face that she was in a hurry to share an exciting secret with us.

"Guess what?" she gushed out after closing the door of compartment behind her, and signalling with her "top secret" body language. "I am being offered a part in a movie about the Home Army--an apartment in London, all expenses paid, salary, the works!"

We knew there was more, so we waited for her to continue.

"There is only one catch." She heaved a sigh and looked at each of us in turn. Masia had told us her secrets before, and we knew what to expect. This story had a new twist to it, and Masia was going to get to the point anyway. There was no need to interrupt her with questions. Her silence was designed for theatrical effect.

"The catch is, I have to sleep with him!" she seemed to unburden herself--half relieved, half still weary of this compromising scenario she had to contemplate and decide what to do about. Masia knew how to dramatize a proposition.

"What are you going to do?" Margaret asked politely.

Clearly, Masia was not asking for advice. The poor girl was maybe trying to make us envious. No one was making such offers to any of us.

"I wonder who it was?" whispered Elisabeth when we were alone in the compartment.

"Do you think it's all true?" asked Eva.

We did not know about any romances or any intrigues happening on the train. It was quite long, and as it rumbled on through the Brenner Pass and on towards Calais, some relationships could have developed.

Only women occupied our car; furthermore, we were still too full of memories of the people we had left behind in Germany to be interested, even if some men happened to visit.

The other story, which turned out to be true, was that General Anders, the commander of the 2nd Polish Corps in Italy, was going to cross the English Channel at the same time as we were, and that he was actually travelling on the same train! Apparently, we were the last military transport to leave Italy for England.

* * *

A somewhat prolonged waiting period in Calais, before we boarded a boat to carry us towards the white cliffs of Dover, gave people with money ample time to make arrangements, designed to ensure that the influx of their cash into Britain did not contravene any British rules. The rest of us were watching the parade of fellow travellers and getting impatient.

The first impressions of the Promised Land were quite disappointing. After such a glorious time in Italy, the weather, above all, seemed designed to give sinners a taste of purgatory. As for the food--well, we had to keep reminding ourselves how much worse the wartime POW fare had been.

Each morning, at a camp inherited from the long-departed American troops, began with porridge unappetizingly similar to wet cement, and sausages climbing out of their skins to take a swim in deep grease, the identity of which was kept secret. It would be bad enough to have to get up and bear witness to such unpleasantness. To make it worse, on the way to the canteen, we had to wade through puddles permanently fed by rain or drizzle from a grey morning to a grey evening. After a few days, the question was: why could we not stay in Italy? Well, the camps in Britain, abandoned by troops going home, were filling up with the Polish military units arriving from the Continent. After having been demobilized, the British hoped they would go home to Poland. It was to be a matter of a few months, maybe a year.

We were being invited to other camps for dances and other entertainment. I befriended a very pleasant ex-Home Army corporal, although Elisabeth kept reminding me about Ted. He was still in Germany about to do his matriculation exam. Later, some wicked tongues spread a rumour that Ted failed the exams. According to some, he was not good enough for me without his high school diploma. I was getting irritated at people poking their noses into every little detail of my private affairs. Elisabeth and I started to have arguments much more frequently than ever before. It became very important to me to end this eternal life "en masse," so characteristic of camps. An opportunity presented itself quite unexpectedly in a best possible scenario.

The Department of Education of the Polish government-in-exile was advertising scholarships financed by the Polish Treasury. The demobilized members of the Polish units and ex-POWs were invited to sit for competitive exams in London. The successful candidates were to be awarded scholarships and accepted as students at London University.

"Of course we will try," Margaret and I told each other, excited and ready to start packing for the trip to London. The exams were scheduled just after Christmas, to be completed right after New Year's.

We boarded a train in the railway hub of Crewe. This time we were armed with all the necessary documents and high hopes. Too bad Elisabeth could not be with us. As the train proceeded towards London, the two men sharing our compartment offered to share lunch with us. They were two Highland Division soldiers. I cannot remember what rank they were. As always at this stage, our conversation in English was very limited, which they both made up for with animated talk and laughter for our benefit--two bewildered damsels. They did not mind too much when we refused sandwiches but they became downright upset when we declined their offer of tea!

Making absolutely sure they heard us correctly when we refused the tea caused an unexpected reaction. One of the soldiers suddenly jumped up in his seat. Was our refusal to take tea so barbaric to them?

"Tea!" he shouted to make sure we could understand. "Tea saved my life! I was in water up to here." He made a line with his hand just under his chin. "It was cold, very cold; hot tea saved my life," he repeated several times.

We did not understand how he managed to drink hot tea while standing somewhere in water up to his chin, but we did not ask; he probably told us during his lively tirade--we just didn't get it.

Our first glimpse of London happened to be the busy area around Victoria Station. It was an early evening illuminated by traffic lights and neon signs in various colours and intensities. We stopped at the edge of the sidewalk, taking in the scene. An immense satisfaction overwhelmed us--we had arrived! So lasting was the wonderful impression I received on that fateful evening, that during the almost nine years we subsequently lived in London, the area around Victoria Station leading up to Hyde Park Corner was my favourite spot.

"Are you looking for something?" a nice middle-aged man asked politely.

"Chester Street?" It was fun to be actually carrying on a conversation in English.

The man was pointing up the road and explaining where Chester Street was. Good thing we already knew it was a couple of blocks up and to the left because we only managed to catch a few words of his explanation. But we enjoyed pretending we understood.

The majority of candidates would not know any English, so the exams were conducted in Polish. They were not really very hard, but we had to wait two weeks to find out whether we both passed, which understandably kept us in suspense. We had four subjects to cover. Two exams were scheduled before New Year's and two after. To whip up even more excitement and make that first trip to London truly memorable, Margaret's cousin and his friend unexpectedly invited us to the New Year's Eve party in the famous Polish "White Eagle" Club, located in one of the mansions just off Hyde Park. We foolishly agreed to go.

Among the elegant people in evening clothes, were two girls, ex-POWs, dressed in their best shabby uniforms. I was proudly wearing a woollen khaki pullover, the best piece of clothing I owned at the time. It was boiling hot. My poor mother, she ought to have seen me there! When I was small and listened to the Cinderella story, totally enraptured, mother would tell me about the first ball I would be attending when old enough.

I would be wearing a beautiful, long, white, or maybe pink, gown, with flowers in my hair and dainty little dancing shoes. Well, Cinderellas we were, only the fairy godmother left us in the lurch. Even so, in all the years I have known Margaret, neither one of us has ever expressed regret at attending that elegant New Year's ball!

FIFTEEN
Perplexing Options

Who can ever forget walking happily along Oxford Street in London, one of the most fabulous streets in the world, especially on a rare sunny day? And particularly, after successfully passing the entrance exams and obtaining a scholarship to study at one of London University's colleges? I still could not believe how fortunate I was. Only twenty candidates with the highest marks were accepted for the Department of Economics and Commerce. I was lucky number thirteen. It made the difference between going to work as an *au pair* and being a legitimate student.

Running along, dodging people rushing in the opposite direction, colliding with those wishing to take a more leisurely pace, I suddenly saw Mol and Wanda. His not so terribly handsome face wore a broad smile. Surely, it was his masculine charisma that interested girls to a degree that normally would be due to a taller stature and more harmonious facial features than those fate had bestowed on Mol. In fact, in his battledress and the black beret of the Armoured Division sitting on his head at an aggressive angle, he looked more menacing than handsome.

"Finally it's all arranged! Here, look!" he shouted over the traffic noise while waving some papers.

Wanda seemed a little confused. On this sunny day in London, Wanda had no appetite for making decisions; the desire to at last enjoy life and love was strong . . . Mol, faithful to his ideals, wanted to go back to Poland.

It was so easy to go back to Poland . . .

"Everybody wants us to go back." I smiled my sitting-on-the-fence smile.

Especially the Polish post-war government, which we did not support, and our British friends . . . This I kept to myself.

* * *

A significant experience regarding our British friends comes to mind. I was visiting Margaret in Queen's Gate, one of the most prestigious avenues in central London. The imposing mansions along this wide boulevard had fallen on hard times, and most of the stately residences were chopped up into one-level flats or even single rooms to house the hordes of the newly arrived in London or those made homeless by the blitz. Margaret rented one of the servants' rooms on the top floor.

As Margaret was one of the least important tenants there, her name was not displayed on the panel at the entrance, and so there was no bell to inform her about the arrival of a visitor. I stood on the sidewalk on the opposite side of the road, well in view of her window, hoping Margaret would notice me and throw me her key. I had come at the appointed time . . . yet, nothing happened. There was only one thing left to do.

"Margaret!" I shouted. I felt stupid and embarrassed for making myself the object of attention for what seemed to be half of the borough of Kensington.

The reaction was instant. An irritated middle-aged woman, obviously endowed with a powerful pair of lungs, leaned out of a second-floor window. "Go back to your country!" she screamed.

* * *

But even more disappointing was our friend from Mardorf, the major.

In civilian life, Major P., the former commander of Mardorf Camp, was a solicitor. Shortly after settling down as a London University student with a furnished room in the vicinity of Notting Hill Gate, I invited Elisabeth, who was still at the camp, to visit for a few days. We hit on the idea of renewing our friendship--well, our acquaintance--with the major. After all, he gave us his name and address in London when we were still in Germany.

"He probably never supposed we would actually be in England one day," suggested suspicious me. Frankly, I was more concerned about embarrassing the poor man by descending on him like creatures from another world--which we were.

"Oh, don't be daft! He was so nice to us back in Germany, maybe he will give us some advice."

There was no way Elisabeth could be dissuaded, so off we went to see him in his office in the city. Charming as before, Major P., in his expensive civilian attire, was even better looking than in a major's uniform, though his fabulous long legs, which he enjoyed displaying when wearing Bermuda shorts as part of his summer uniform, could not be seen. His breeding did not allow any slips in immaculately polite behaviour, and although we two looked precisely like the stateless wanderers we were, he took us to an elegant café decorated with expensive, highly polished woodwork and populated by stuffy middle-aged men in starched collars. He proceeded to instruct us about the British ritual of serving tea, the same as can be admired in the high society plays of G.B. Shaw or Noel Coward. He asked me to pour; I was mortified and barely managed not to destroy the teapot or any of the cups.

The conversation was limping along somehow--our English must have been "painful to the major's ears." And what did he say after listening to our story?

"Go back to Poland!"

This cry of the British, growing impatient with the multitude of foreigners arriving on their doorstep, echoed the exhortations of the Polish communist government. It was so easy to go back. Unfortunately, the eventuality of any subsequent desire to leave Poland seemed too remote to contemplate. Nobody foresaw how awfully difficult it would be.

My mother wrote in one of her letters: "If you can study abroad, stay there. It would be a shame for you not to get a good education." I recognized this advice as a warning against going back to Poland, and I was actually beginning to be frightened of returning.

At first most of the Polish students, including me, considered our stay in England as a prolonged educational excursion prior to going back to work for the benefit of our country. The grim news from behind the "Iron Curtain," as the occupied area was being called by Winston Churchill, was gradually distorting those plans. A string of escapees from the unfortunate countries under Soviet domination related stories about the brutal hardships forced upon them. Severe food shortages and the lack of all kinds of basic supplies added to the misery. Future prospects were not very encouraging either, since Stalin refused to let those countries benefit from the Marshall Plan.

Travel abroad required passports, but passports were not readily available. In Poland, people had no right to apply for and hold on to their passports, unless permission to travel abroad had been granted by the authorities. Obtaining such permission, however, depended on gaining favour with one or more boorish party officials through bribery or other distasteful methods. Little by little, Poland, along with the other Central and East European countries, came to be regarded as a prison; once arrived there, a huge iron gate would close behind you.

Yet Mol and Wanda decided to go back and did.

There was not much news about them. Probably because keeping in touch with the "rotten West" was frowned upon by the communist regime.

Besides, quite apart from the political situation in Poland with its grim news and nasty rumours, we were pursuing and developing life quite interestingly in London, and gradually, most of the former friends spent less and less time pondering the lot of old Mol and Wanda. After all, they themselves were responsible for their actions.

An item in the Polish émigré press caught our attention one day. Mol's father, a highly decorated resistance fighter, had been arrested in Poland and executed in prison for alleged treason. After that, everyone was anxious to hear about Mol.

A few months later we were sitting, as we often did, in Margaret's cosy little room on top of the "mansion." Our friend Staszek arrived and announced that Mol was dead.

"But he was a communist!" Margaret made an effort to argue Mol's case, as though someone could grant him pardon and return him to the world of the living.

"Well, Mol was an intelligent person and an idealist--" Staszek, assuming an air of authority, was explaining the obvious, so we wouldn't let him continue.

I barged in: "Stalin 'adjusted' communism to suit his plans."

"So what happened?" asked Margaret.

"After the death of his father, Mol apparently began to break down when he finally realized that his ideals did not fit reality. His career was going nowhere. He was gradually forced into a poorly paid, lowly pencil pusher's job in some little hole of a place . . ."

Moved by compassion, I thought about our not very serious and brief "romance." One more valued human being had fallen victim to a brutal and corrupt power.

* * *

Though life in London offered hope for the future, not everyone knew how to handle the offer. The best choices were made by those who decided to face whatever happened next armed with a university diploma. Others, unable to shake off the gloom of bad news from behind the Iron Curtain, were like a flock of lost sheep. Not knowing where to go and feeling unwelcome where they were, they had trouble deciding on the next course of action. Some threw themselves into politics, hoping to influence the events; some, giving up on higher education, went to work determined to build a new life in England; but the majority vacillated between trying out different plans and having some fun.

Admittedly, for most of the time, I belonged to the last group. The distraction of "history in the making" stamped out my ability to focus on anything. I found studying extremely hard. My decision to study Economics and Political Science was a wise choice considering the international situation, but my English then was barely at a germinating stage, so that my ability to absorb knowledge easily was severely reduced. Even if I managed to learn a little, I could hardly communicate my knowledge to the professors, be it in spoken or written form. It did not help, either, that some of the professors were actually Polish, and had only just mastered the English language themselves. Though perfectly correct grammatically (I suppose), they turned into perfect crushing bores during their lectures. Faced with a stack of textbooks for English-speaking students written by highly sophisticated people, I dreaded the task of reading them at my slow, nearly analphabetic pace. My brain grew tired just looking at the recommended reading.

No wonder I took every opportunity to escape from my little room in a house belonging to an Irish family. The problem was that I was not immediately aware of the importance of studying in order to get a degree. Before, learning had been always easy for me, but here in London, serious, non-stop cramming was necessary to acquire the proficiency in English that I needed to tackle the course textbooks and the recommended journals, such as *The Economist* or *The London Times*.

The other, worse, obstacle to my studies was my attitude of being "the kid in a candy store." Deprived of the pleasures associated with growing up in a prosperous and peaceful environment as a teenager, I was positively dazed by my new and independent life. It did not interest me very much when Elisabeth finally decided to return to Poland. As a matter of self-defence against depressing perspectives and sad situations affecting many people, I found myself drawn to a hedonistic approach to life with *carpe diem* [seize the day] as a suitable motto. Naturally, my fellow students provided a lot of distractions. There were only two of us girls in a class of twenty-odd men ranging in age from about nineteen to thirty years. Only two of them were married. Lacking self-discipline, I frequently preferred an interesting date to settling down to study alone in my minuscule room. Worrying about the future was not going to prey on my mind and spoil the fun.

Margaret, my best friend then--and hopefully now--was different. Margaret was definitely focused, and pursued her studies with determination, to the extent that Margaret's mother--yes, having a mother was definitely an advantage--was despairing of the lack of "mirth" in Margaret's demeanour.

Young girls not interested in studying had other options. Many mature, lonesome ex-officers demobilized in England, abandoned the idea of returning to the "old country," as well as in some cases returning to their wives. Consequently, a young girl could find a good, if slightly "aged," husband. Indeed, many girls my age married considerably older men--assuming that no wife anywhere was awaiting their return. Such marriages were regarded as a means of securing the future.

Future . . . The future was *so* important, since it remained, for many of the ex-service men and women, and particularly for the DPs, pretty shaky.

One of my fellow students, a small guy looking a little like Scotty Hamilton the skater, was my particularly devoted friend. To look at his insignificant frame, it was difficult to imagine him as a sailor on a Man o' War, but that is what he said he was. There was no reason to suspect him of lying, especially since he had photographs of himself on a battleship to prove it. He lived with his married older brother, whose Scottish wife, Betty, spontaneously assumed the role of my guardian angel. Using her considerable connections in London, she had found my little room right off Sloan Square. The rent was so low, that even though the toilet was outside, the place became an object of envy among my fellow students.

The home of this Polish-Scottish couple, Mr. and Mrs. R., was far from luxurious, but for me it was a haven of comfort and what the Germans call "*Gemutlichkeit* [cosiness]." It was such a joy to sit down at the properly laid dinner table, with friendly and cheerful people around it, and eat a modest but lovingly prepared meal. I did not mind that Betty pictured me as an innocent lamb at the mercy of the beasts of prey; she kept inviting me to her home, probably to keep an eye on me-- and forbade any even mildly racy talk in my presence. In military life, especially in wartime, pretentious behaviour is usually abandoned, and we were still very much in a military kind of atmosphere. The jokes the men would want to tell did not always pass Betty's approval. For instance, there is a particular Irish joke that I recall.

"Well, there is this poor village, you see," Betty's husband began. "The parish priest walks along the road and suddenly sees a little girl of about eight years old coming towards him. The little girl is holding a rope at the end of which there is a cow."

At that point, the speaker would stop talking to allow for a chorus of "oohs" and "aahs," expressing polite and eager anticipation of what was to follow.

"Well, you see, the cow is not behaving very well; it pulls and yanks at the rope with all its might so that the poor girl is almost falling over trying to walk forward. The priest watching the scene feels sorry for the child. He asks, 'Where are you going with that cow, little girl?' 'I am taking it to the Brown's bull, Father,' she answers in a very businesslike tone. The priest is shocked. 'What kind of people entrust a small, innocent child with such a crudely primeval mission? Poor little child,' he thinks. Then he turns to the child and almost shouts indignantly, 'Couldn't your father do it?' 'No, Sir,' answers the girl, 'it must be the bull!'"

The outburst of laughter was suddenly silenced--the lady of the house was not laughing. "I am really cross with you," she said to the guilty male. "Irene is not even nineteen!"

It was not very hard to tolerate or even to welcome the lady's protective passion--until . . .

One day during lectures, I was notified by young R. (the petit sailor) that tomorrow a special occasion would be celebrated at R's residence and I was invited to dinner. "Make yourself even more pretty," he joked.

Having almost forgotten the "special occasion" until it was time to go, there was not much I could or desired to do in preparation. My closet contained only one other dress--both my dresses had been donated by UNRRA, an international organization taking care of refugees. People said the clothes came from movie stars in America, but such a claim could not be readily supported by their quality of fabric or design. Anyway, the dress was sort of fuchsia in colour and the fabric was crepe-like. It was perfectly simple and had short sleeves. Its only decoration was a piece of ribbon in a contrasting colour, about five inches wide, stretched across the chest just above the bust line. I had taken advantage of an opportunity to exercise modest creativity, by buying, some time ago, a piece of pretty, colourful silk to replace the rather worn ribbon, and also to make an attractive, matching sash.

Forget about a hairdresser. First of all, it was expensive; second of all, the British hairdressers were not accustomed to fine hair and their efforts, genuine or not, ended in disaster. Was it before a dance or a special date? I remembered once returning home from a hairdresser, looking in despair in the mirror at my reflection, which suggested a half-drowned chicken. I barely had time to wash out the wretched hair, and set it in the usual fashion--with bands of fabric cut out of old underwear!

When I arrived at the R. household that fateful day, the hostess came to meet me beaming, her pleasant honest face flushed with excitement.

"Come, Irene dear, I would like you to meet somebody!" she intoned.

He could have been about forty, not old by any means, but to me he seemed ancient and unpleasantly eager. He looked at me with a wide smile, revealing a well-installed set of teeth. I was sure he smacked his lips. He was seated beside me at the table.

"Mr. Komer is on his way to Argentina to take over a position as chief engineer in this South American concern . . . what was the name of it again?" announced Betty after dinner, when we all were sitting around enjoying a cup of tea.

"Fantastic, Joe, old man," Betty's husband commented with great gusto. "Congratulations. When do you leave?"

"As soon as I arrange all my affairs here," replied Joe. I thought his eyes, moving slowly from face to face, came to rest deliberately on me.

I smiled back at him, not suspecting any ulterior motives. Betty R. beamed some more.

Maybe two days later, she suddenly appeared at the Lyons Restaurant opposite the South Kensington Station, where I came frequently to lunch with friends from the chemistry department. Betty, carrying some parcels, since her inborn industriousness would not allow her to cruise around the city without attending to at least two or three errands, planted herself at the table, and then rushed off to get herself a cup of tea along with one of the nondescript pastries usually available at the establishment. She radiated a joyful confidence in life and the world in general.

"Mr Komer--you know, Joe--was very happy to have met you the other day." Betty's eyes were boring into me like two screwdrivers, but she did not detect any of the signals she so dearly wanted to appear. I simply drew a blank. Total ignorance of the "apropos" was so obvious from the expression in my face that Betty started to get impatient.

"Mr. Komer, the engineer--he was at our place for dinner, don't you remember?" she asked incredulously.

My life was so full--lectures, dates, political meetings, dates, studies, outings with fellow students, dates, dates . . . I was young, full of energy and *joie de vivre*. How was I expected to remember an "elderly" person who was at the R.'s? Somebody new was always there.

Ignoring my lack of response, Betty continued: "He would like to meet you again. He is a very serious gentleman; very well off, too." She hesitated, not knowing how to broach the subject of Mr. Komer's intentions. "I would advise you to think about your future, dear . . ." she continued after a brief pause.

There was that "Future" again, with a capital F. It was not to be ignored, by any means, but couldn't it wait until later? I was at a loss for words; my diplomatic skills at this moment were not equal to the task. I simply had no comment. Betty, seeing me apparently deep in thought, decided her mission was crowned with some success and left, repeating an invitation to tea on Saturday. "Don't forget, dear!" she added, as she rushed off.

So when Saturday came, it was time to face the challenge of Betty R.'s and Joe Komer's conspiracy. Out of the closet emerged the fuchsia dress from UNRRA. I dressed with grim determination. The Future presented one of its uncomfortable aspects. Why? Of course, they could not know that I was not looking for marriage. Probably because my mother always annihilated any speculation about a possible career for me with a wistful sigh and a recommendation that a good husband is the supreme fulfillment of a young woman's future aspirations.

I appeared at the R. household suspecting, or rather knowing, that this might be my last visit in this friendly home. It was a sad prospect. After all, I had no family or more mature close friends to offer advice or simply sympathy, other than this half-Scottish, half-Polish family. I did not mind that they occasionally asked me to babysit their toddler; not a very exciting pastime, but I gladly did it to repay their kindness.

Joe Komer was already there, smiling and apparently very satisfied with himself. Later, probably by design, when we were left alone in the room, he asked me to have dinner with him one day. I looked up at his face, already covered with a network of middle-age wrinkles, his smiling eyes immersed in the sockets a little too deeply--it was hard to decide whether to laugh or be indignant.

"Mr. Komer," I began.

"Please, it's Joe," he corrected.

I stood up, so did he.

"Joe," I started again shakily, "I . . . I don't know what Betty told you . . . I . . ." It felt as though I were going to tell off my uncle or a professor--terribly impolite; the man had been unlucky enough to stumble on someone so little inclined to think about the Future. At least three names of young women of my acquaintance who would be happy to pursue this adventure came to my mind. Should I tell him?

"I am very busy right now," I heard myself saying, and immediately realized half-truths would not work.

"That's fine, I will wait until you find time," he chuckled awkwardly, "but don't keep me waiting too long; you know I am leaving for Argentina."

Of course Joe Komer, a mature man, well educated, well situated in this world, is going to Argentina to a great job. It would be stupid of me to think that he will not console himself rather quickly. Me, I will throw my lot in with the young people who still have to establish themselves. No need to feel sorry or embarrassed.

"I mean, I wish you all the best, a very happy life in Argentina," I held out my hand and he took it. He was no longer smiling. He raised his eyebrows and whispered:

"Okay."

* * *

So the Future with a capital "F" had temporarily taken a back seat to the present with its grinding and whining, but for the most part hopeful, if lots of work and good sense were fed into its greedy entrails.

The first hurdle was the entrance examination. Many failed it on account of an inadequate command of the English language. Some people had to try it several times.

The Special Entrance, as it was called, was scheduled three times a year. The worst part of the English exam paper was the précis. Everyone could learn a few decent sentences by heart and work them into an essay, but with the précis, understanding of the language was on trial. It was generally known that a précis should be shorter than the original article, and based on that principle, different methods, where ingenuity substituted for knowledge, were employed.

For some candidates the method was to leave out every other sentence. Others considered it too radical, so they left out only a few sentences and the words they could not understand. Others resorted to drastically cutting out the whole middle part and copying the beginning and the end of the article in its entirety. No wonder so many failed. Margaret and I were directed, after our first (failed) attempt, to take a very intensive English course for foreigners.

"This is going to be very interesting," announced Margaret after the first session. "We are six in our group--an Egyptian, a Belgian, a Swiss, and three Polish people. And you know, that tall handsome man is a nephew of W. [a well-known Polish writer]!"

"Don't indulge in any dreams, Margaret," I warned her. "Judging by her sweet smiles, Miss Davis, our teacher, wants him for herself."

Perhaps because Miss Davis wanted to see more of our attractive compatriot, we got a couple of invitations to tea and had an extra opportunity to practise a "debonair" English.

Both Margaret and I passed the entrance examination on the second attempt.

Our scholarship covered tuition and a modest life style, so apart from studying, it was necessary to work at odd jobs during vacations to provide means for "extras." Job-hunting was a popular pastime, but jobs of different kinds were fairly easy to come by. I had compiled quite a list of more or less unpromising kinds of work, most frequently waitress jobs.

Unfortunately, there was no perfect job. Waiting on tables in a fairly upscale restaurant (usually Greek in those days), brought better tips, which made up most of a waitress's income. The basic pay was microscopic and hardly worth mentioning. No wonder that a hierarchical system favouring the senior members of the staff prevailed in the British enterprises, where the amount of take-home pay was a function of experience in serving the public. Thus in the retail sector, there was the commission, and in the restaurant business, tips. In a smaller restaurant, run with less traditional tyranny, the boss could decide to give a younger, less experienced server a chance to get good tips. He would let her wait on the more popular tables. Unfortunately, the price for serving on tables close to windows, or those in discreet corners, was often rather exorbitant--it necessitated "being nice" to the boss or to the headwaiter. No, thank you!

The longest tenure in my career as a waitress was a job in the Selfridges' ground floor cafeteria. It was my favourite department store, as well as that of many London ladies. Its mock splendour of fake columns adorning the façade overlooking Oxford Street would unfailingly try to dazzle a pedestrian taking a short walk from the corner at Marble Arch. I regarded it as one of the friendliest landmarks in the centre of the city. I still do. Though not very far from the super-elegant Park Lane with its out-of-this-world hotels, when visited again after several years of shopping in air-conditioned North American department stores, Selfridges' appeared stuffy and outdated. Conceivably, modernization and "people marketing" robbed the store of its traditional British charm. *Are You Being Served*, the British TV sitcom, was undoubtedly based on the "life and times" of the old Selfridges' department store.

Every morning, dressed in a kind of mauve uniform with a small, light blue apron and a light blue band on my head, I marched past the sinfully fragrant and brilliantly polished cosmetic and perfume counters on my way to the cafeteria at the back of the ground floor area. The other waitresses, of whom there were four, were usually already there, endlessly arranging the settings on their tables. Helen was a bit dumpy and had a face like that of a fat man pretending to be a woman; Nina, about my age, was very cute, with a tiny waist and a charming smile--a real example of English beauty. But the best tables in the place, close to the wall, near the entrance, and generally offering the most pleasant ambiance, were permanently served by two classic specimens of the experienced waitress--Betty and Jean. They were neither young nor very handsome, but they "had been there for years," and that was what counted.

The atmosphere was comfortable because there was no "man" problem. The head waitress, dignified in her navy suit, which was designed to distinguish her from the underlings, had conservatively arranged yellowish hair and a bittersweet, polite smile. The smile was there on her face when she first began to try and persuade me to come to work on time. It gradually deteriorated into a grimace, expressing disappointment at my lack of devotion to my cafeteria server duties.

Needless to say, I was waiting on the least advantageously placed tables, but I accepted my fate without murmur. The others tolerated me to a greater or lesser extent. Betty, the dark-haired Scottish lass, seldom spoke to me. Jean, the tallest woman there, with a face carefully and thoroughly plastered and powdered with make-up, pretended to have a devil-may-care attitude, but her professionalism was impeccable. Having spent close to a lifetime on the job, she could spot high-tipping guests right at the entrance, where she would hover over them and direct them to one of her tables.

However, even if one of her tables was free, and unpromising guests happened to be approaching, she would act generously and direct them to a less busy colleague. Nevertheless, despite those manipulations, the staff as well as the customers liked her; maybe because of, among other things, the dirty jokes she enjoyed telling them.

Though her nose was rather prominent, she did not look too bad; the light blue headband worn jauntily on her tightly permed hair gave her a sort of gamin style, and when she passed by, she would send me a friendly wink

In addition to the privileges enjoyed by employees at Selfridges', the girls could eat their fill of the less popular sandwiches and drink all the coffee they wanted, at appropriate times, of course. There was also a ten percent discount on all purchases at the store--too bad; most of the time I could not afford the other ninety percent.

Like most people employed in "survival-sustaining," hopefully temporary jobs, I occasionally wondered whether the effort my parents and I had put into preparation for the Future was all wasted in our current situation, considering that the Future meant landing a decent job and having an enjoyable life as a participant in a sophisticated society. Not so much the primary education, but the secondary and university education seemed at times to be necessary just to offer opportunities for making "suitable" friends--especially since friendships begun in early youth often last "forever." Unless, of course, one is forced to move to another part of the world.

London 1947:
Irena is second from
the left in the first row
with a group
of students at the
Economics and
Commerce Department,
London University.

SIXTEEN
Parting of Ways

The garden outside is overgrown with lush vegetation due to all the rain. Hopefully, the time Ted and I spent digging and planting will pay off this year. Maybe the usual calamities perpetrated by various varmints ruining the painstakingly designed flower and shrub displays will not amount to total devastation. Anyway, it is too wet to go outside. Staying indoors gives me an opportunity to do some paperwork.

My weekly appointment book bears witness to my fairly animated social life, sports, and charitable activities. I know many people. There are so many charming, witty, attractive, clever, companionable women, but not one is really an intimate friend.

Actually, I have to admit, *it's my own fault; I'm too much of an introvert. Being with people frequently becomes a chore--I probably depend too much on Ted. It seems I feel relaxed and comfortable only with my immediate family. Unless there is something specific to be done, even just playing a game with other people, I stay in my little shell built of my emotions, ideas, and memories--some of them inaccurate. I suppose others have their own shells moulded to particular specifications, as well. Anyway, true friendship is like a good marriage; some people will never experience it.*

A letter, marking a gradually deteriorating link with Europe, arrived today from Elisabeth. Her letters have never been very positive, and are getting worse as she grows older. In response to the murkiness of irritation submerging more generous thoughts, I am undecided as to whether to continue the correspondence. Generally, it is nice to hear from people, but this is a querulous letter--a litany of complaints addressed to the whole world, including me. Despite her complaints, it is I who should have envied her. All this time she has stayed in Europe, her mother still alive and close by. Elisabeth is taking very good care of her mother.

While her sister and her own daughter chose to move to the far corners of the world, Elisabeth remains loyal to her family no matter how difficult the situation.

We both have had basically the same upbringing; both ready to follow the guidelines our mothers provided to keep us on the path leading towards our future life as honourable women. We had the same preparation to guide us down the road, but the road in my case took an unexpected turn. I journeyed under different conditions. Elisabeth married into an influential family in Poland and even had a nanny for her kids, while Ted and I were counting every penny in London.

Anna, my enigmatic ex-sister-in-law, was also doing well . . .

They did not have to work hard--as hard as we had to, at times. Admittedly, they belonged to a fortunate select few, and comparisons are no longer accurate anyway. The incidents involving these two phantom figures from the past could now be easily dismissed as irrelevant, but like a foreign country's stamp in my passport, they left an indelible mark on my consciousness. Even when judged as insignificant in the general scheme of things, those echoes from the past may have altered my approach to friendship, family--maybe to everything.

We generally seemed to get along better when we were all in difficulties, than now when times are relatively good. Before, everything was straightforward and clear. We understood each other easily. Recently, however, I was puzzled, even a trifle upset, and did not know how to react when Elisabeth suddenly sent back a neatly wrapped parcel to me. It contained the letters I had written to her from London and later from Canada, after she returned to Poland. Some time later, she let me know she was offended that I did not thank her for that gesture.

I decided to write and offer thanks and apologies, but not before I finally had the courage to read some of the letters. It was an emotional and humbling experience. Nobody said it was easy to get into one's old skin; gigantic self-confidence and high hopes bordering on arrogance did not fit me anymore. Life's challenges should not be addressed with such a condescending frivolity, and yet I found this overblown bravura appealing. I had to admire the boundless energy and the all-conquering verve I displayed in my attitude during what I remember as not a very easy time.

Gradually, looking through the airmail pages densely covered with my high school handwriting, I began to befriend my former self. I decided to call upon this other "me" to take over, anytime I felt intimidated or fearful and weary . . .

Here is a letter I wrote to Elisabeth after leaving the hospital in London:

London, 24.6.1947

Dear Elisabeth, I just managed to narrowly escape the gravedigger's spade. This violent and hair rising experience I owe to this horrible doctor in Doddington, who, not being able to recognize an attack of appendicitis, practically abandoned me--just like that. You see, exactly a week ago I got sick in the same way. Luckily my landlady, on seeing my face take on a beautiful rotten green colour, while I literarily turned myself inside out with pain, had enough presence of mind to load me into a taxi, and she and Margaret's mother took me to the celebrated St. George's Hospital on Hyde Park Corner.

Eight physicians proceeded to torture me one after another; finally it was decided that I have to undergo surgery--immediately!!! So here I am now with a big hole in my belly perpetrated by a very handsome surgeon, Dr. Nicholls. (Wasn't that the last name of your Scottish boyfriend?)

However, here I had an opportunity to be convinced of the undying affection of S. who spent the entire day in the hospital awaiting the end of the operation and my recovery. I think he must have been crying, because the nurse described him as a "tall, young man of about nineteen" (he is twenty-three).

He blamed himself for being a thoughtless egoist, ignoring my feeling poorly once when we were in the cinema. And Margaret moved me to tears, bringing me her own, freshly laundered and ironed nightgown, since my landlady, for some reason known only to herself, instructed her of my absolutely needing one--I had my pyjamas. It seems that in England and Germany as well, hospital people are paranoid about nightgowns.

Anyway, every evening between six and seven o'clock, I have to hold on to the eight-stitch cut on my belly, so it won't burst open, when my visitors try to entertain me. It really hurts when I laugh.

I am full of admiration for the hospital. It is cheerful and nice; all nurses are pretty, sympathetic, and polite. Medical care is carried on to excess. I think Polish doctors perform the operation, but then leave the poor delinquent to manage by himself. (I am kidding.) Here, every part of your body has a caregiver in the person of a nurse or a doctor. Fortunately, all the vexations of this kind are already behind me and I shall be now left in peace.

Margaret has postponed her birthday party until I will be released from the hospital. I will have to spend some time in a convalescent home for people without home support. An official-looking person came to visit me in my hospital room and asked if I have any money to pay for my surgery. I said, "No." She asked me, if I have anybody who could take care of me when I come home. I said, "No, I live alone." I answered all her questions with a "No." I had no family in England, no money, and a very uncertain future. I was a student on a modest scholarship--that's all.

She didn't ask any more questions and just put my name down for the convalescent home in Wimbledon . . .

* * *

My friendship with Elisabeth had a chance to renew itself in 1968, when my daughter Marta and I took a trip to Europe.

It was full of surprises from the very beginning. We were to stay in London at Margaret's house. At the same time, her husband was due to lecture in the United States, so given that, we were supposed to get keys to the house from a mutual friend (whom I did not remember). He was to wait for us at his house.

Confusing dates can happen to anybody. Though it is not a regular feature in my arrangements, I happened to forget this time that one does not arrive on the other side of the Atlantic Ocean the same day one leaves the American continent in the late afternoon.

Expecting no problems, we arrived at Heathrow Airport the next morning eagerly awaiting marvellous events. It was our first visit to London since our departure from there for Canada some thirteen years ago.

"Here we are!" I announced triumphantly. The taxi actually deposited us in front of a house on the right street, and bearing the number as indicated in Margaret's letter--no mean feat in London, where the same name may be shared by a multitude of terms including street, place, court, gardens, mews etc. I was pleased with myself for having negotiated the fare beforehand, the way I was instructed by knowledgeable people back home.

The taxi driver set our suitcases in front of the house and left with the money I gave him. We looked over the rather unremarkable, though pleasant, building, and used the door-knocker to alert our unknown friend to the fact that we had arrived. Nothing happened.

"Maybe he is asleep?" said Marta.

"I will knock harder."

But my repeated, persistently harder knocking had no effect other than attracting the attention of more and more neighbours. Curious stares from people emerging on both sides of the road started to embarrass us, and reminded me of the time I was calling on Margaret in Queens Gate during our university days.

"I hope they won't tell me to go back to my country," I mumbled in frustration.

"What?" asked Marta.

"Nothing, just reminiscing."

Finally a fellow across the road, who was ostensibly working on his windows, and had already spent some time on a ladder while keeping an eye on us, decided to approach us.

"He's not in, is he?" he sympathized.

"No, he isn't." There was nothing else I could say. "Do you know him?" I ventured.

"Oh, rather slightly; well, he must be at work." He divulged this information after surmising we were not likely to be dangerous, but he decidedly suspected we could cause trouble.

"He was supposed to meet us here today," I explained meekly.

The man from across the road smiled a crooked smile, probably thinking his naughty thoughts. It started to dawn on me that he had every right to suspect something fishy. Margaret's friend was probably close to her and my age. Marta was obviously my daughter, so I could be a long-lost or abandoned girlfriend finally deciding to claim paternity support for our child--no less. While I was trying to assess the situation, another neighbour, this time from next door, approached.

"What happened to the British people?" I wondered silently. "When we used to live here, people minded their own business; they would never come and poke their noses into some stranger's affairs!"

After I refused the offer of the ladder to climb up through the bedroom window, it was decided, with the neighbours participating in the lively discussion, that we should phone the absent owner of the house at his place of work. Here, British reticence took over, for no one was willing to invite me in to use a phone. On the other hand, it could be that, fearful of being accused of breaking with tradition, the British were reluctant to embrace modern conveniences such as I now needed.

"I am not on the phone," announced the next-door neighbour with a touch of pride in her voice.

Nobody knew for certain what the name of the missing fellow's employer was, or what he was doing, or making. I was directed to a nearby store to use the phone there. Using all my powers of both logic and intuition, I managed to find the number of a telephone, which was subsequently answered by a person who knew the fellow we were trying to contact. After lengthy explanations on both sides, we finally reached our destination--Margaret's house--with no further problems.

We enjoyed a few wonderful days rediscovering London--Marta was not quite three when we immigrated to Canada. During the nine years we lived in London, there was never time to visit the Tower. This time, we went there. It was a moving experience--I never expected the old place to play so much on our emotions. Particularly touching was the powerful spirituality and charm of the small, whitewashed chapel where Anne Boleyn prayed before her execution.

We then left for Yugoslavia--"Marshal Tito's kingdom"--to keep a rendezvous with Elisabeth. This was to be our first meeting face to face since she decided to go back to Poland, more than twenty years ago.

Needless to say, I was excited and nervous about the meeting. Excited is understandable, nervous--maybe about seeing the reflection of my much older self in her probing look!

Our British Air plane landed in Rome to the usual airport noise. From the crackling bedlam of many hoarse-voiced speakers, a depressing announcement about the Alitalia flight to Dubrovnik delay let itself be barely heard, and was to our disappointment, clearly confirmed at the departure gate. The Da Vinci Airport in Rome is not any worse than other airports, but we were not looking forward to a long wait with nothing more interesting to look at than the huge, rectangular windows, which had plenty of time to imprint themselves on my memory. At first, we were sitting quietly waiting to be called, if not for our flight, at least for lunch or for some explanation.

When nothing happened during the next four hours, I decided to speak to the nearest official, expecting to hear apologies and maybe be offered an invitation for a glass of good Italian wine. Ha! My demand for explanation and/or food was met with an offer of arrest by security.

The only scraps of news available to the waiting passengers was a rumour that our plane had been commandeered by high communist party officials on their way to Yugoslavia, and would not be available to us until the evening.

I have arrived after midnight in strange places before. This time it was in the exotic city of Dubrovnik. We witnessed one manifestation of efficiency: I was being paged loud and clear. Imagine my surprise on hearing my name being called on the loudspeaker to retrieve a message in a place where virtually no one was supposed to even have an inkling of my existence! Unfortunately, the message was from Elisabeth, who had waited to meet us at the airport. After the long delay, and unable to find out what had happened to us, she had to take the last ferry back to her island.

Not only were we alone in a strange city, without any hope of finding a place to sleep; what was worse, we were behind the Iron Curtain! Fortunately, before we left, we had prudently obtained a Canadian passport for Marta, who was British-born. At least we would stay together, wherever they put us. A miraculously found taxi deposited us in front of what was to be the best hotel in Dubrovnik. We were told there were no rooms available. Try another hotel? No,

Ma'am! The taxi driver mercilessly abandoned us and our luggage on the sidewalk, and promptly drove away.

"The plane was late." I tried to pin the guilt on the hotel clerk; after all, it was his officials who had deprived us of transportation.

"But you have no reservation, Miss," the clerk was speaking patiently.

"I am not leaving the hotel--"

"But there are no rooms," repeated the clerk.

And then I felt proud and happy to be a Canadian citizen. A woman with a young girl, also a mother and daughter, heard my unsuccessful pleading and offered us the hospitality of their room. They were Canadian. It did not matter that their room was so small only Marta could sleep on the floor between the two very narrow beds. We were very touched, and I felt gratified that at least we moved in the right circles. The hotel management showed its magnanimity by permitting me to sleep in the beautifully furnished, spacious lobby. I was given a pillow, which I used to cover our passports and money, and a blanket, and was politely bidden "good night."

Church bells and crowing roosters awakened us at four in the morning. Coffee and buns were being served on the veranda, overgrown by fragrant flower bushes, and overlooking the sea. The sun had already risen and was shining brightly. Sitting there with mugs of coffee, we were surprised at the absence of insects, which are such a nuisance in some of the most spectacular places in Canada. Feeling a new surge of energy, we gathered our possessions and walked down to the quay. It was already crowded with people waiting and getting into, or already sitting in, all kinds of boats. Apparently, most of the boats functioned as ferries.

"People get up and go to work so early here," commented Marta, who could have done with a little more sleep.

"We will sleep in tomorrow." My assurances were only partly sincere; first we had to find Elisabeth on the island! I had to look into her letter to find its name: Lopud.

The lively scene around us and the loveliness of the place were incredibly appealing.

"We'll have to come back one day for a family holiday."

In spite of the charming scenery, however, it was difficult not to feel rather helpless at times, and I needed to use a good deal of my mental and spiritual resources to make myself act decisively. Looking down on the quay, I picked out a man in the crowd who appeared to be reliable and smart. We stopped and put our suitcases down with determination. I made myself approach the man.

"I would like to hire a boat," I began in English. As there was no reaction, I switched to German:

"Do you speak German?"

"*Ja*," answered the man, showing a little more interest.

"I have to go to Lopud Island as soon as possible." I was suddenly aware of my limited funds. Imagine! Hiring a boat! Millionaires hire boats. But I had to try.

"I would like to hire a boat," I said now in German, afraid of what the man would say.

He remained silent, but I had to endure a careful examination of my countenance, as though my true value and actual intentions could be read in my face. I was making myself appear as friendly and honest as I possibly could. I was also hoping the man would be sufficiently impressed and prepared to do business with me--a prosperous tourist. Now the people waiting on the quay surrounded us and stared. Marta began to squirm next to the suitcases.

"Well," said the man finally, "this will cost you a lot of money."

I will never forget the way he emphasized "*viel Geld*"--a lot of money--and repeated it several times. This might have been the most important haggling of my life!

"How much?"

The man was obviously playing for time--not knowing how much to charge--unwilling to charge too much so as not to scare the customer away, or to cheat himself by asking too little.

"*Viel Geld, viel Geld . . .*" he kept repeating, the working of his brain mirrored in his facial expressions. As the boats began to leave the quay one by one, I thought my whole life suddenly depended on the decision of this obscure boatman and a little-known island, the existence of which I would have remained ignorant, had it not been for a series of coincidences.

"*Wieviel Geld*? [How much money?]" I asked impatiently, hardly able to stand the suspense.

"Nine dollars!" he blurted out.

The almighty dollar. I tried hard to conceal my great relief. *Let's not look too pleased.*

The man happily emptied his boat, telling the people already in it to go and find some other way to get to their destination. Once again, it was the working class getting the short end of the stick in "worker's paradise." Soon we were installed in the fairly large boat looking really empty now with only the three of us and a couple of suitcases and small bags.

There is nothing that separates those who depart from those remaining behind more decidedly, than a powerful motorboat leaving the shore. You can watch a departing train for some time, even a plane after it has taken off, but a motorboat is almost immediately lost in the distance and in a different medium. At the same time, the people in the boat, losing sight of the shore equally rapidly, are left with a sense of excitement, conveyed by the expanse of water speedily traversed, that they are surely going to meet head-on with a wonderful adventure.

Nevertheless, it did take time and not a little worry on my part before we would reach our destination. Marta did not mind. She enjoyed being on the water, and was completely won over by our "captain" when he instructed her how to drive the craft, and let her do it for a while. For me, on the other hand, not knowing how far we would have to travel, the journey became a source of disappointment and anxiety, which increased each time we passed another island. Each time, I would point with my finger, and ask, "Lopud Island?"

"No, no," he invariably answered with a little chuckle.

When almost an hour had passed, I stopped asking, so as not to emphasize what he must have perceived as lamentable ignorance on my part, and instead I started to suspect foul play. How easy would it be for this fellow to put us on some isolated island, take all our money, leave us there, and no one would be the wiser. The wisdom of my decision to hire a boat without inquiring at some reputable agency was certainly questionable. While I was struggling with my suspicions, the man just sat there silently surveying with true sea wolf's eyes the seemingly limitless waters of the Adriatic, which were from time to time punctuated by distant islands.

In the end, when I had almost given up hope, he turned to me with a broad smile and announced: "Lopud Island."

Looking in the direction his finger was pointing, I could not see anything.

"You have to look through these," he said, handing me a pair of well-worn binoculars.

Well, indeed a barely visible blob on the horizon was growing larger, until we came close enough to distinguish its rocky terrain with unexpectedly dense vegetation.

"This is Lopud Island?" I asked incredulously.

"Yes, Lopud Island," he repeated.

"But there are no people!" I objected.

With a pacifying gesture of his hand, he made the boat jump, accelerating rapidly. We took what seemed to be a wide turn away from and then toward the island. It was shaped like a huge croissant--its outer edges overgrown by bushes and trees surviving somehow in the rocky terrain. It seemed totally deserted. But as soon as the boat turned around the island's tip, a beautiful beach and a village with many houses built picturesquely on ascending terraces came into view. A fairly wide level strip ran along the inside edge of the croissant. There were no cars. The only means of transportation were the boats to connect the island with the outside world, and probably donkeys to carry people to the various heights of this enchanting corner of the world. There was a church and a convent. The boat swung around to a large quay, and I immediately spotted Elisabeth. She was looking great. Browned by the sun, her figure was lovely as before; only her face wore the unfamiliar signs of age--a network of fine lines.

SEVENTEEN

New Family and Emotions

In the Spring of 1947, after a year of study, the second test was set up for us by the university--the intermediate examination. The entire student body stiffened, some in sheer fright, some in grim determination. With extended scholarship funding at stake, the usual trivialities were chased away from student brains by the sudden awakening to the importance of being successful in this exam; a wave of feverish emotions wiped out most of our *joie de vivre* and sent unfamiliar panicky tremors through our hearts.

Just when I was spending days of what seemed like an eternity studying in my room, the last section of the Polish Armoured Division arrived from the occupation of Germany. One day, my landlady's knock on the door pulled me up from the depths of the British Constitution.

"Irene, your soldier is here."

And there he was. Still in uniform, transferred by friendly spirits from the shores of Ems to the borough of Chelsea, Ted was standing demurely in the narrow entry.

Now was the time for a different kind of joy, a different kind of concern; it was the time to really test maturity. We soon got engaged and were thinking seriously about the future. But how quickly could one lifestyle be dropped for the sake of another, even though personalities fashioned by no longer valid routines would now cease to exist? Unexpected opposition to our plans was mounted by people who suddenly revealed their claims on us--claims on me I never suspected they harboured.

Irena and Ted in London, 1948.

Although Ted and I had already become good friends at the high school in Maczkow, our situation was so precarious then, that neither was ready to make a serious commitment. We could find ourselves who knows where, whether it be responding to the needs of our families or to developing political situations.

When we both became students in London, there was no reason to resist any further the delight of mutual attraction--we were going to get married. I was surprised, though not at all concerned, that it did not seem right to some people. Margaret's mother, who liked to consider herself an authority on matrimony, disapproved, and, though nobody asked their advice, a group of my fellow students voiced objections.

"You ought to consider it very seriously," urged Margaret's mother. "This may not be the right choice."

I was probably an entertaining companion. I was asked out on plenty of dates, but managed not to get involved with anyone. The only person I really admired in first year was Stan K. He was very intelligent, a great gentleman, and he looked fantastic in his naval officer's uniform. It was fun to go out with him and make all my girlfriends envious. When Ted arrived, I stopped dating Stan; he left London shortly afterwards to study somewhere else. I was not the reason for his leaving, but it would be very flattering to think I was.

Ted and I were the first couple to get married in this large group of Polish students in London. Colonel P., the commandant of the Home Army Division in which I had served in the Warsaw Uprising, "gave me away." Everyone was just so wonderful. A deeply moving surprise was the generous wedding gifts we received at a reception in our honour.

However, life was not easy. I lost my scholarship when Roman, our first baby, was born. My interest in studying economics and political science shrunk to zero in the presence of my powerful maternal instincts. So what? After the arrival of twins two years later, any career plans of mine had to be put on a back burner. With three little ones to look after, living in a different world and on very little money, we could not carry on as before. Our friends did. I hardly ever saw Margaret. My situation in England was vastly different from Elisabeth's life in Poland, after she went to live with her family in Cracow. In 1951, I wrote this sour letter to Elisabeth from London:

Dear Elisabeth, your first letter must remain unanswered. I had to work during the summer to help us out financially. Usually, Ted gets a job during breaks in studies, but some old injury causes pains in his leg or pelvis or chest and back, so he could not do it this time.

I exercised my money-earning skills by running off my feet as a waitress in a restaurant in one of the largest department stores in London. The usual housework was waiting for me at home as well.

In addition to having virtually no time for anything as it was, we were visited by Lilka M. with her husband and little boy. I nearly went nuts when she insisted on regaling me with the most gruesome stories about women trying to abort unwanted pregnancies, after I told her in confidence that we were worrying about my missed period. If you ask me whether Lilka has changed, I would say she's grown a little fatter but her intellectual development is not impressive.

Ted and I couldn't help feeling panicky and discussed all kinds of possibilities--needless to say far beyond our means. Finally, we decided to stick to traditional morals; at least we could afford it in the short run, and a few days later the problem resolved itself. Phew . . .

Lilka, her husband, and their little boy are sailing in a couple of days on the Queen Elizabeth for the United States. She is very disappointed with friends who left and don't write--I wonder if she will.

She is hurt by the silent treatment from your sister Greta, her dearest friend, who promised to write from Argentina. By the way, Greta will have to wait for the giant book you sent for her--I cannot afford the postage now--maybe before Christmas.

We celebrated my becoming one year older in a very pleasant atmosphere. Stan Z. came with his future wife, his second. Roman celebrated by throwing up and staying sick for a few days. Afterwards, the poor thing got a terrible cold when we were visiting an old classmate of ours--do you remember Danka K.? So we had some more sleepless nights. Roman is beginning to utter some more civilized sounds that actually resemble words like: daddy, mama, yes, no, give, etc. Pity that he's carrying on a battle of wills with me when it comes to potty training. I sometimes doubt whether the melancholy hours we spend side by side with him on the potty, will ever be crowned with success, freeing us from the laundering of nappies.

Thank you for regarding me as a cheerful creature, but I am really a sourpuss; I don't really like anyone here; I get annoyed especially by women preoccupied with cooking, babies and money (!!!). Am I paranoid? Or maybe it's my sorry fate to be deprived of nice and interesting acquaintances, and to be exposed only to the company of bores. I, myself, am probably to blame for not being able to find these types interesting, and perceiving them only as structures consisting of stomachs, asbestos hearts, and prehistoric notions (if any).

One exception is Tamara Leniak, but they live very far from here; she's expecting another baby, and they are planning to immigrate to the US as well.

You have no idea how difficult it is to hang on to even some vestiges of intelligence, and to preserve a serene outlook on life, when surrounded on all sides by kitchen utensils, money problems, and daily doses of neighbourly gossip. My persona is breaking into two: one--a reasonably good wife and mother, the guardian of the family abode; the other--a phantom following close behind the first--ugly and constantly whining, maliciously upsetting our happiness . . .

The letter exploded with grievances, directing them where they could do no harm. Ted and I were never miserable. Because of our war-torn past, we appreciated our happiness all the more. Still, at the time, when I was bemoaning the lack of interesting companionship among my neighbours and acquaintances, Elisabeth was rubbing elbows with the international elite--including Graham Greene, no less. We had to leave such pleasures until some time in the future.

Elisabeth sent me a photographic story about the Warsaw Uprising. The impressive photographs appeared too contrived to honestly recall the drama of those two tragic months almost seven years ago. My closest companions from the Uprising returned to Poland. What was happening to them, nobody knew. Warsaw was completely destroyed, and people taken away by the Germans to different camps were returning after the war to find ruins in place of their previous homes. Most painful was the criticism poured on the heads of the commandants of the Resistance for starting the Uprising when they did. The Polish communist government, no doubt following instructions from Moscow, blamed them mercilessly for the tragedy.

No effort was spared to erase the Warsaw Uprising from memory and from its honourable place in the history textbooks. The people of Poland were given an early lesson in "thought control."

At the time, a neighbour invited us to watch Orwell's *1984* on television. It was a rare treat, since no one we knew owned a TV set in England in those days. That night, I woke up in a cold sweat, terrified by monstrous nightmares.

This could be happening anywhere, and it's already happening in Poland. My imagination was literarily choking me. My hope in the future was destroyed.

"What happened to you?" Poor Ted was asking for an explanation. Fearful my panic might be contagious, I did not mention the story. Part of the problem was that after the birth of our children, my overgrown sensitivity to the international situation was capable of inducing suffocating fear. Suppose there would be another war! Nuclear war! The disappearance of my youthful sang-froid left me defenceless against those horrors.

The spectre of war such as what happened in Warsaw in 1944, with its cruelty, betrayal, and destruction waited, thinly disguised, to emerge at the slightest provocation to scoff at our naive faith in a better world, the faith that upheld us struggling survivors.

We decided to immigrate to Canada as soon as Ted got his degree.

The Szpak family, London, 1955.

Dear Elisabeth . . . your letter, such a wonderful surprise, wandered across half the globe before it finally reached me in snow-covered Canada. Although yesterday was still warm, winter began in the early morning today with high winds and snow.

I haven't written to you for a while so I'd better start from the very beginning. So, Ted left for Canada the 20th of May, and I stayed on in London with the little ones. For two and a half months, I was wasting with longing and worry. Fortunately, friends helped to keep up my spirits; you must remember Tonia and Alf, and Zosia P.

Zosia P. was with us in Mardorf, and now lives with her husband not very far from where Ted and I lived in London.

Ted found work very quickly. He had to borrow money so that the kids and I could set sail across the Atlantic on the 29th of July. The

voyage, my first long trip by boat, was really great fun. The kids--
we have three now: Roman and the twins Marta and Olek--were
tearing around the boat in their usual energetic manner. Fearful that
they might find themselves overboard, I had to literally hang on to
them incessantly--and considering that there are three of those
rascals, that was not an easy job.

The boat was sort of luxurious, the weather beautiful--I really had a
ball. Most enjoyable was to sit as close as possible to the bow and
see the opposite end of the boat (I think it's called the stern) go up,
up . . . and then come down again. I heard that it makes people sick--
well, I must be lucky. On entering the St. Lawrence, we were
feasting our eyes on the panorama of hills overgrown with trees,
little houses here and there, and countless small isles. It reminded
me of the Rhine Valley. Remember, how we went through it on the
way to Italy?

The train travelled from Montreal to Toronto all night. At that point,
I would have preferred the European train with compartments. Here,
the cars are spacious and comfortable, but there is no privacy in such
a car, especially, when you want to relax and sleep. Nonetheless,
since there are no longer free trips for immigrants, the journey cost
us a lot of money, and debts will have to be paid off. But you know,
Ted makes three times as much money as in England, and it
shouldn't take us long.

Ted likes his job very much--it's a good practice and his efforts are
well received. My heart jumps for joy because after years of going
without, we'll start to reap the benefits of Ted's education.

Needless to say, Canada is different from England. The weather is a
little like in Poland, though in this particular region, a lot warmer.
No more fog and drizzle daily. We are forty kilometres from the US
border. The food is superb and the shops well stocked. Housing is
much better. With central heating and modern conveniences
everywhere, housekeeping almost feels like fun and takes less time.
I have time to read in the evenings--I buy books or borrow them
from the local library.

Don't think of Canada as a wild country with Indians ready to
pounce and scalp people. All the "accessories" for cultural life are
in place just like in other countries. We presently live in Burlington,
a rather small town situated picturesquely on Lake Ontario, which

seems as big as a sea. Lots of fun for kids. We can spend every day on the beach, enjoying a permanent vacation all summer!

We are hoping to buy a car next spring to explore the country and look up friends living in Toronto and elsewhere.

After arriving from London, everything here seems small and somehow provincial. But in this country, your ego expands as you inhale the aroma of wide-open spaces and optimism for the future, and you drink the nectar of freedom. There is more of it here than anywhere else . . .

My husband Ted is a survivor like myself. We have understood very well what happened to us and how we got where we are now. For the first few years of our marriage when I stayed home with Roman and the twins, there was no need to try and "fit in" the world outside our home. My brief excursions to the outside world always had something to do with our being short of money. We were in debt and also needed money to help our families in Poland. To my frustration, my artist brother, Stan, rather than stooping down to the earthy affairs that interested me, particularly with regard to Mother, wrote letters tuned to his romantic outlook on life. Mother was slowly going blind and could not write anymore. My hands were trembling every time I opened a letter from Poland, bringing news about the life of both our families, in what we knew were very difficult circumstances. It had to be our most nagging concern then.

"Stan fell in love again with some angelic woman," I would say dejectedly after glancing through the pages. "He never answers any of my questions; it looks like he never even reads my letters!"

Ted would then try to console me somewhat half-heartedly:

"Maybe he doesn't want to worry you?"

After Anna divorced him, citing irreconcilable differences, life in Poland for Stan and Mother became morbidly grim, with no prospects for improvement; I could help only from abroad. Much as I longed to see my mother and enjoy the feeling of returning home, my "past" was all wrong in the eyes of the communist authorities in Poland during the Stalinist era; they would most likely consider me an undesirable troublemaker. What happened to my university colleague, Peter, confirmed the reality of worrisome notions shrouding the thoughts of immigrants hailing from the Central European countries, and even of those already settled in Canada.

One day in August, nineteen sixty something, we were sitting on the beach at Lake Huron, as we did every day after supper that summer. Neighbours and friends arrived in small groups leading younger children by the hand, surrounded by older boys and girls frolicking around and jumping in the lake. Then one group arrived with an unexpected guest--Peter W., another ghost from the past.

Not one of my favourite colleagues from the university, actually. The ghost was big and somewhat ungainly, but he carried his reputation of heroic partisan well, which he obviously enjoyed and maybe even nurtured.

We were re-introduced by a common acquaintance.

How many years is it? I asked myself, wondering whether it was my patriotic duty to like him; or should I treat him as an integral part of pleasant memories? Now, a couple of decades later, he appeared somewhat less overbearing, less of a "Mister Fantastic."

Maybe, like all of us, he grew up a bit, I thought.

We sat around on lawn chairs or on the warm sand. It turned out that Peter was planning to visit Poland in the near future. Everyone regarded him with some envy and a large dose of apprehension. In the early sixties, people did not go to visit behind the Iron Curtain very often--especially people heavily implicated in anti-communist activities during the transition period after the war, when the Soviet-sponsored Polish communist government was taking over.

A lively discussion on the pros and cons of Peter's decision ensued. Instead of light-hearted banter, the people in swimsuits, sitting on the white, sandy beach of magnificent Lake Huron burdened themselves with grim forebodings, because fear and worries troubled them even in their new existence.

A few weeks later, as if to prove the whining pessimists right, the Canadian press proclaimed indignantly that: "A Canadian of Polish extraction was arrested and imprisoned while visiting his family in Poland."

It was too cool by then to sit on the beach, and the discussions continued during parties in people's houses, or in the places of employment, or anywhere else when two or three people were together.

"I don't envy Peter his encounters with the secret police," was the one remark that said it all, "they hit hard."

It took a few months of such "encounters" and an intervention by the prime minister of Canada to free Peter from the clutches of the communist "masters." Still, many of us would not abandon the hope of some day going to Poland, if only for a visit. Thinking about my friends from the Resistance, most of whom returned to Warsaw or never left the country, I felt like a player dropped from the team.

A rare opportunity to improve the flow of communications was provided by a friend's mother over in Canada on a visit from Poland. When she was returning home to Warsaw, I asked her to look up my family.

The information we received was not good. My mother lived with her two sisters in their house on the outskirts of Warsaw.

"There were three elderly ladies; they looked rather poorly," said our friend. We accepted the lack of details as a tactful reprimand.

In my mind I heard this sad voice saying, "Do something more to help, will you!"

Working as a waitress in London restaurants during university vacations was the only type of work I knew. My other ambitions set aside, I did what any immigrant would do: I worked at a low-paying job. Evenings and Saturdays, when Ted was at home to look after the children, I waited on tables at a nearby restaurant. It was rewarding to think about being able to help. But, maybe unfairly, I felt that being a waitress prolonged my sojourn in the sphere of peripheral members of society, which is the lot of any freshly arrived immigrant, a person tolerated rather than heartily accepted.

That was depressing. However, I almost lost my mother in the ruins of Warsaw; now I had to help her live.

The ideal time to visit might never have come, but it was necessary at least to wait until we became Canadian citizens. When we finally went, we were too late to see Mother. Unfortunately, she died in 1960, just a few months before we could get a visa. I was upset and felt considerably less inclined to visit Poland. When we did decide to go, because there were still many good reasons for it, our first trip turned out to be quite nightmarish.

Poland was more depressing than I ever expected. People were boorish, and who could blame them--poverty and ugliness had taken over the city of charming and familiar old places. But the desire to find and enjoy the company of people from the Resistance and schoolmates outweighed by far my loathing of boorish officials.

I braced myself for our meeting with my brother Stan. He, his third wife, and their young son led a really bohemian life in a godforsaken village not too far from Warsaw. We had to hire a taxi to find him. There were taxis, but since they were fewer in number than the people wanting to use them, the taxi driver had to be willing to actually take on some passengers. In other countries, taxis are queuing ready to be hired, but in Warsaw in those days, people heading home from "work" had to stand in line and wait for a taxi driver who happened to be driving home in the direction the passenger desired to travel.

"Excuse me," Ted addressed a driver reading a paper inside his cab. "Could you drive us to J.?"

No answer. Neither the man nor his paper changed the initial position. Ted was speaking correct Polish and repeated the same question at a higher volume. Nothing happened.

"Maybe he is deaf?" we wondered.

The man shifted his feet as if in protest and continued to read. Ted persisted: "I'll pay in dollars," he said, flashing a greenback not too far from the man's face.

That did it. Without a word, the driver folded his paper and opened the back door of the cab for us.

The trip to Stan's house took us along a few kilometres of highway, and then across a medium-sized village with one modest road. We drove along as far as it went and then continued cross-country, the car sinking in sand almost halfway. By this time, the driver was happily counting the dollars he was going to charge us, and even volunteered to come and drive us back to the city!

When we arrived, words cannot describe my feelings: an indefinable mixture of compassion, pity, shame, and anger. Stan was overjoyed to see me after almost twenty years; his wife was visibly moved and just held back her complaints, which we could read in her worried eyes.

"It's impossible to find a place to live closer to the city," was all she said, trying to explain.

Is this the Poland we were fighting for? I thought, while struggling to find something cheerful and uplifting to say.

Warsaw itself had changed into a grim, pseudo-Soviet city with grotesquely wide streets and ugly apartment blocks. The streets inspired feelings of depression and hopelessness, even more so than during the German occupation. Then, at least the hope for a victorious end to the war could sustain the people.

All aspects of life in the city such as are taken for granted in the West presented a problem. The famous communist full employment economy created a society based on a nonsensical premise. People were paid for doing practically nothing. The pay was not very good, but excellent, considering how little effort was required in exchange; no one was ever fired because there was nobody out there waiting to take the job and maybe do it better. The stores were poorly stocked, and salespeople, guaranteed always the same wage and lacking incentive to sell anything at all, largely ignored prospective customers. Customers in the stores, clients in the service centres, passengers in the trains and on the buses--everyone was always dependent on the unpredictable humour and far from consistent goodwill of the functionaries.

Warsaw under communist rule, as experienced on our first trip, became unbearable after a few days. Totally frustrated, we took the first flight out of Warsaw, which happened to be to Copenhagen. The contrast between this attractive, seemingly carefree city, with its Tivoli gardens, and that other city, the obscenely neglected Warsaw, could not be more crushing. It unveiled for us in vivid colours the infamous spectacle of our share of the victory over the Nazis.

EIGHTEEN
Two Different Worlds

Vancouver is really beautiful. If it were not for the rain, probably everyone would want to live there. It is blessed with an abundance of fabulous views, a cosmopolitan atmosphere, with its multi-coloured population, and elegant stores. The magnificent ocean vistas, however, are threatened by the intrusion of gigantic apartment blocks rising to high heaven and obscuring the most spectacular scenery. Only those able to pay will be enjoying it.

Walking down the street, women are accosted by well-dressed beggars claiming to be in desperate situations. One man particularly avoids male passersby.

The same evening, my daughter, Marta, and I sit in the elegant dining room of the Four Seasons hotel. The way dinner is being served it feeds not only the stomachs, but also the egos, of the guests. The snobbery of the so-called "high-class" atmosphere, particularly overpowering in better than average restaurants, tickles my funny bone. The perfectly ordinary people, who, seduced by the attentions of ubiquitous waiters angling for a good tip, regard themselves as suddenly grown in importance, should realize how ridiculous they are. On the other hand, people like good food, and it should not be held against them that they can afford to eat in such expensive restaurants.

Superiority and class, badly mixed up with each other, are often the two misunderstood concepts used recklessly to humour the undeserving. Children, in what are known as good families, are taught decency and good manners. Should they aspire to superiority when they grow up? Or by doing so, would they forfeit the claim to real class?

Better abandon such philosophical ruminations before they bring on indigestion.

Marta and I are in Vancouver to see the Worlds--to bear witness to the annual glamour of the Figure Skating Championships. Sitting around the rink, surrounded by the impressive interior of one of the colossal venues of Canada, a hockey arena, we watch the dazzling riot of colour and incredible grace. Some of the most handsome people from unheard-of countries are represented here. Names exotic to Anglophone ears advertise nations unknown to most people; nations that appeared on the world scene after the breakup of the Soviet Union.

"These competitors come from the Soviet machine for producing champions," explains Marta to some interested spectators around. She used to compete herself and went through a rigorous training in her early teens, although not half as rigorous as the training forced upon the candidates for the former Soviet figure skating world team.

"I have read the book by this Russian girl in pairs, what's her name . . . ?" one of the fans who annually returns to witness World's volunteers her bit of knowledge.

"Ekaterina Gordeeva," prompts Marta.

The woman describes how the coaches mistreated the girl skaters. "It was horrible."

It is mostly women who are milling around in the crowded aisles, laughing and waving now and then as they spot the familiar faces of other "regulars" in the distance. The men are present in smaller numbers; they are less flamboyant, rather withdrawn. In Canada, the men have hockey--figure skating belongs to women.

After a break, the American ladies' champion is on the ice; she is favoured to win again. The champion's performance is so good it is boring; she repeats flawlessly the tricks everyone has seen her do a thousand times before. In no matter what kind of competition, I get bored seeing the same person winning all the time.

Figure skating championships are so popular that local employers buy a number of tickets for their staff to enable them to enjoy at least some events. I am sitting next to a different person every session. Members of a broker's office staff take turns occupying the adjoining couple of seats. This time, a young secretary sitting beside me eats constantly. She has finished her bag of munchies, and her hand keeps on reaching into the bag of her friend. She will need another "crash diet" soon.

The women's magazines show the way: food recipes, make-up, clothes--oops! Dieting for the too fat, to the point of starving if necessary. Then the eating cycle starts over again as an inevitable ingredient of entertainment.

"Lose thirty pounds by Christmas!" announces an ad for slimming drugs. They are irresistible when coupled with a photograph of emaciated models in glamorous outfits.

Marketing success due to a dramatic juxtaposition of food and glamour is amazing. To strike a balance between these two frequently conflicting aspects of the so-called good life, and in so doing to make a fortune in sales of diet and exercise products, is nothing short of a stroke of American genius. The ladies have a right to everything--they are worth it!

Break for resurfacing the ice. People move up the steps in droves like so many streams rising onto the promenade surrounding the arena. Hundreds of fast-food brands are sold at food concessions, whetting appetites. Waiting consumers form long lines. Soon the whole crowd takes part in an orgy of food and drink. They eat and eat and eat . . .

What inspires such jaundiced comments?

My being separated from family and friends has led to a "double life" syndrome. Most people, free of consuming interest in the living conditions of some distant land, are fully aware of one kind of life only--usually that of their own and of their family. Constant participation in the life of loved ones through letters, and whatever else has seeped through the media, has made me, without my actually desiring it, an expert on life behind the Iron Curtain. Endless opportunities to compare the affluent life in the West with the life over there, not to mention the life of the majority of the population on our planet, have generated antagonistic thoughts.

Food and drink are closely associated with parties the affluent natives give to show off their homes, especially after they have suffered the expense and inconvenience of renovations. The hostess leads the guests into a just-enlarged or just-rearranged living room, or a patio, or what have you, and for her the real or pretended admiration on the faces of the guests makes it all worthwhile.

"We thought we would like," she will say in an almost apologetic way, "to have more light"; or, "more space"; or more whatever.

My appreciation of good taste is quite sincere, especially since occasionally the "viewing" is the best part of the evening. People come in--couples for the most part, but widows and divorcees, too. Very chic widows smile the noncommittal, Mona Lisa smile, so as not to appear too forward and yet at the same time, not to discourage attention such as may be forthcoming.

Mrs. Laker is in the process of divorcing her husband. She discovered he has been having an affair. She would be astonished to see how much the "other woman," whom I met at the club, resembles her; apparently Mr. Laker likes exotic brunettes, for both his "choices" are distinctly different-looking.

Mrs. Laker is wearing black to match her hair; her *maquillage* has been carefully applied, and her rather short skirt makes her look younger than I remember ever noticing.

"How lovely to see you, how are you?" she murmurs softly to me, making me suddenly feel how old and dowdy I must appear beside this energetic businesswoman. Mrs. Laker's eyes are darting around the room while she answers my inquiries about her family. Giving in to her excitable nature, she bemoans the state of her daughter's poor health and goes into much too much detail explaining the symptoms. Ted wanders off to get a drink.

The crowd gets denser, and suddenly other people are in front of me--it's time to start another little chat. Someone else joins us, and while an animated discussion occupies the others, it is safe to wander away.

Ted, who is in the other room, gesticulates with one hand, holding a glass of red wine in the other. He is probably telling one of his stories people love to hear so much. Anyone speaking freely and spontaneously about personal life experiences would fascinate them, since Canadians are not really a spontaneously acting lot; they surround their real thoughts and feelings with an impenetrable curtain of hazy formality coated in good manners. We, on the other hand, have a lot of stories to tell.

Perhaps because of his robust self-assurance, Ted has the endearing quality of telling stories that do not necessarily show him off to the best advantage. I know them all by heart . . .

"I cannot stay beside you at a party because you tell the same stories over and over," I complain.

"That's because they are true!"

Will the gap between two different worlds ever be bridged?

* * *

On that beautiful, sunny morning of September 11, 2001, I was at the tennis club breathing in the fresh, cool air--such a relief after excessive heat and drought. I marched to the court I had booked, past the centre court where two ladies were getting ready to play:

"I heard something awful on the car radio as I was driving over," one of them spoke very distinctly so that it was not necessary to stop and listen. The words were coming loud and clear, but the sense was so surprising and baffling that my mind, seconds before preoccupied with racquets and tennis balls in my bag, suffered a jolt. So much so, that I was unable to call on my usual cool approach to news from the United States to prevent myself from feeling apprehensive.

"A plane actually flew into a World Trade Centre tower, and then another plane flew into the second one, and something is going on in Philadelphia . . ." the woman's voice gradually faded as I mechanically continued on my way.

We played our game thinking the trouble would go away. But the trouble grew even more incredibly dreadful an hour later. People bewildered by the news turned to strangers in the stores and in the street to exchange expressions of shock and disbelief.

The cycle of hatred never ends. Cadavers and ruins mar the beauty of this earth when violence erupts like a plague at different times and places. This time, a saga of unprecedented terror, death, and devastation began unfolding on the territory of the greatest power on earth. Worse still, it was to set in motion a tidal wave of annihilation, destroying more and more human beings and unleashing economic disasters for months and years to come.

"You need to create a new language to say something about what happened that hasn't been said already." Ted and I sat glued to the TV exchanging irrelevant remarks.

"They are trying to mould public opinion."

"They are creating a show out of human tragedy."

"The president does not look very sure of himself." I repeat what I had heard somewhere before.

"It's not so easy to know immediately how to respond to a terrorist attack of such magnitude." Ted always defends and has hardly ever been critical of America--perhaps because he has regularly watched CNN, particularly since the Gulf War.

By sheer coincidence, Margaret and her companion, also a good old friend from university, flew over from London for the celebration of Marta's second marriage, and were staying with us for a few days during that time. One evening, we watched a video of the Warsaw Uprising together: also a tragic story featuring colossal destruction--a whole city disappearing in ruins, dust, and smoke. But the tragedy of the 1944 Warsaw Uprising could not be shown or documented while the communist regime, supported by the Soviets, continued to be in power in Poland.

Most of the film footage, recovered from a hiding place, was destroyed by the authorities to remove all references to the betrayal the Warsaw population and the insurgents suffered at the hands of the Soviets. The tape was all that remained of the films shot by the film crews of the Polish Resistance during the actual fighting. In true Orwellian "1984" style, these events had to be wiped out from the nation's memory.

Although survivors struggled valiantly to publish their stories during the more than half a century of communist rule, it is only now that books about the Uprising can be freely obtained in Poland. And not exactly freely: a persisting shortage of paper imposes limits on the number of published books. It is no wonder that the Warsaw Uprising has not been getting any publicity. Nobody paid any attention because nobody knew.

Even so, tragedies occurring in other parts of the world usually pass across the field of vision and hearing of CNN's viewers, to be forgotten or obscured sooner or later by other tidings deemed more important. The tragedy of September 11, 2001, will never be forgotten or forgiven in North America.

It was intriguing to observe that the CNN program, just like the Warsaw Uprising tape, showed people praying in the churches. The CNN announcers did say and show everything they possibly could, and kept on speaking, desperately trying to soothe and heal the nation's wounds. They summoned literally all the powers in Heaven and on earth to cope with the unbelievable happenings, hereto unprecedented in the USA, even to the point of displaying what would normally be controversial religious symbols.

On Becoming a Canadian

I felt that I truly embraced life in Canada only after I started my professional career. When our three kids started regular school, I returned to my academic studies in a variety of ways, depending on local circumstances and opportunities. Five years later, after trying out different disciplines from mathematics and physics to accounting and languages, I got my degree and found a reasonably interesting job in a large Canadian parent company with the claim to several global subsidiaries. It was rewarding to find that this time all my seemingly haphazard studies could and did blossom into a set of desirable qualifications.

Setting out into the world of working people after several years of staying home with young children can be a challenge for anyone. I faced additional difficulties.

Spending several hours a day with "real Canadians" revealed numerous differences between us; my knowledge of the language suddenly appeared grossly inadequate. Being tongue-tied underlined my ethnicity, and made me feel awkward and left out. I saw myself as standing apart--an odd individual. Perhaps other people of diverse traditions and nationalities who began to populate Canada after the Second World War, as well as the continuously arriving immigrants who have now penetrated all aspects of life in this country, also have felt like that--then again, perhaps not. Often acutely aware of not being "with it," I did not seek solace in the knowledge of possibly similar experiences of others. I had to deal with my own specific burden--a shell around me, constructed by the unusual experiences during my childhood and adolescence--the most impressionable period of anyone's life. The shell protected my background, steadying me but sometimes upsetting my fragile equilibrium. My physical life evolved quickly in Canada, but my emotional accomodation was lagging behind.

Nevertheless, leaving the house every morning to go to work was a source of satisfaction for me. I was no longer the one staying behind when Ted left for the office, and the kids ran off to high school just down the road from our house.

"Someone is willing to pay me for my work." I felt good participating in the morning rush, as I drove to the large complex downtown. That part of the daily routine was not always enjoyable--it depended on the weather. I remember driving on practically sheer ice one morning. Our heavy Monaco suddenly chose to slide slowly but steadily towards the nearest ditch, and would certainly have made it, if not for a friendly passerby who placed his finger on the monster's bumper and pushed it effortlessly back onto the road!

The wonderful informality among my co-workers never ceased to impress me. The manager would greet any lowly employee with a hearty: "How are you, John?" To which the other would respond in an equally "good-chum" manner: "Fine, and how are you, Mr. . .?" They might even stop for a brief conversation where funny remarks would give way to a loud outburst of real or pretended merriment.

A mixture of expected managerial accessibility and the sense of being acknowledged, which is enjoyed by this work force, has been like grease helping to smooth the rolling wheels of North American industry. In my case, most managers addressed me with cool politeness. Maybe I did not need to be acknowledged! Having never worked in Europe, I could not be sure how I would have been treated over there. (Actually, I did work a lot in Europe but only if England can be counted as Europe, which is a matter of opinion. Both Ted and I did try on different "careers" while struggling to reach that shining prize--the University Degree.)

Now that Ted and I were each employed by respectable companies, the joint income freed us from financial worries and opened up new possibilities for all of us. Nevertheless, our training in the school of "hard knocks" would never permit us to be extravagant.

A simple way for me to experience inner peace--one might even say happiness--is to throw a sweatshirt loosely around my shoulders, stick a pair of sunglasses on the end of my nose, and walk out the door.

Ted walks with me on a beautiful fall day. The sky is incredibly blue, and though trees have begun to lose their leaves, there are still enough of them on the branches to admirably display the dying green changing into gold, yellow, and auburn. Such days are rare in this climate, but as we walk in the quietness, interrupted only by sounds of insects and a screeching bird here and there, I experience a strong sensation of déja vu.

Such days were not so rare at summer's end just before school was about to begin in Poland. I can almost see my small girl's feet in funny little sandals marching along a path between the fields of rye. These paths were not evened out and hardened by machinery; they were beaten hard by the feet of generations of country people going about their business year after year, until finally the paths, bordered by strips of weeds on both sides, became as hard as cement.

The wind was hardly ever so violent; the air seldom so humid as here, and the quietness of the day was made melodious by a constant chatter of grasshoppers.

"So where are we going on holidays this winter?" Ted begins with the customary early enquiries before coming out with a proposal that will be hard to refuse.

"Me, I would like to go and look for those special hardened paths between the fields of pale yellow rye."

"Strange that you would like to go there again," says Ted. He is right. I contradict myself--I thought I would never want to go back again.

In 1981, the annual world translators' conference, in which I always participated, was held in Warsaw. Returning home, I pondered during the long flight over the Atlantic the vexations of visits to our homeland. It would be ludicrous to compare this flight with the trip to the POW camp after the fall of the Warsaw Uprising in 1944. And yet, there was also something very sad about it.

Our desire to visit relatives and locate old friends during the communist government era in Poland led us patiently to endure the calculated chicanery inflicted on us by the officials working at the airports, hotels, stores, public transit system, etc.--perhaps as punishment for staying abroad and refusing to shoulder the Soviet domination with which all these officials were burdened.

Not wanting to embarrass our hosts in their minute apartments, we stayed in hotels such as were available in small towns and villages. Only in large cities like Warsaw and Cracow did hotel accommodation come close to the comfort of a European third-class hotel. In a restaurant in one medium-sized city we visited back in the 1980s, we were offered only hot water for breakfast. Fortunately, our relatives and friends prepared delicious and copious meals. We enjoyed them voraciously, but the knowledge of the problems and expense of buying such food and preparing it made us feel guilty.

However, everyone cherished our visits. Visitors like us were, for most people there, the only contact with the free world. The familiar faces of relatives and friends, as long as they survived, and the old Lazienki Park, were the only memories of childhood left to be remembered and cherished. The school I attended and the apartment building in Warsaw where our family used to live were destroyed, gone without a trace, as though someone had deliberately intended to remove the most familiar, tangible proof of my past existence there.

Consoling myself with sips of red wine after an uninspiring in-flight dinner, I entered a state of soul-searching reverie. Just as the shores of Labrador could be spotted below through the aircraft window, the conclusion that I no longer belonged "over there" brought on a gloomy sense of bereavement. Getting rid of the tension interfering with my present life may be very sensible, and discarding the illusion that all memories are beautiful and worth remembering is quite logical, but emotions unsparingly deposited in the past will still remain on guard.

* * *

The labour union Solidarity was at the height of its ever-growing popularity in Poland, and gaining attention worldwide during that visit of mine to Poland in 1981. The communist government was forced to accommodate the union on some points, but the concessions were not granted willingly, and retractions carrying bad side effects could be expected momentarily. No one believed that the Soviet masters would permit their puppets to surrender to the will of the Polish people.

Prior to leaving for the conference, my mind harboured the not very enticing visions of a closed airport, interviews with secret police, meeting Anna, maybe incarceration. If I am considered a coward, so be it, I saw no reason for now acting "over and above" the call of duty, and my preparations for the trip were not very enthusiastic. Finally I went to see Raymond Y., the company's personnel manager, to clear the air and my head.

"You know, the situation in Poland at the moment is not very stable," was my opening statement.

"So?" Raymond was smiling broadly as usual. His eyes betrayed no trace of discouragement or worry.

"Well, I was wondering if it is wise for me to go there now."

"Tell me how you plan to travel?" Raymond asked.

"I fly to Zurich and from there to Warsaw."

Raymond continued to smile and his French accent made him appear especially friendly.

"Then go to Zurich and find out how things are going. If something goes wrong, you know, you fly back, and if not, continue to Warsaw," he emphasized his advice with a confident, inspiring tone of voice and persuasive gestures.

All of a sudden, nothing seemed simpler. I did not know him very well--he was quite new at his present position, but he was definitely a good personnel manager. His cheerful and encouraging manner had a comforting effect. It made me laugh to myself at my ridiculous apprehensions. Back home, I started to pack a great deal more enthusiastically; still, it was not entirely in jest that I said to Ted, "I am only taking the clothes I could leave behind without worrying about it . . . suppose I have to leave in a hurry; someone coming for me in a car, then having to go to catch the last available plane . . ." I was whipping up the adventure aspect. A fertile imagination can be a lot fun, though at times it can be a nuisance.

Arriving in Warsaw, as a representative of my company, armed with my professional credentials and looking forward to be of service with my knowledge of the language, I soon forgot all my misgivings and began to greedily absorb the excitement of the "unstable situation."

The weather was wonderful in early September, and crowds were gathering to watch the farmers' delegations demonstrating in the middle of the huge parade square in front of the hotel. The square itself has gone through a number of historic phases. Before the war, it was called "Marshal Pilsudski Square"; during the war it was called "Adolf Hitler Square"; now it had the impersonal sounding name of "Victory Square" --better than sharing a name with some communist. We did not know then that it would be ploughed over from end to end to prevent further demonstrations, after the coup d'état in December that same year.

"Victoria" was the best hotel in Warsaw at the time, and the conference was held there. The lobby was impressively huge and impersonal. Generous lighting, multiplied by its reflection in bronze-framed mirrors, belied the austerity witnessed all over the rest of the country. But then, the hotel was designed to house only foreigners or party bosses of the highest echelon, and boasted of an obscene contrast with the reality outside. The price of over $100US per day for accommodation was beyond the wildest dreams of an ordinary native.

Mindful of the long hours of sitting around and suffering from lack of exercise, I was soon making a beeline for the swimming pool. It was nice enough, as could be expected, but, inexplicably, the second-floor galleries surrounding the pool were full of people, some of them with children, all looking down on the swimmers below.

"Oh, they just like to come here on Sundays; they enjoy seeing a real swimming pool," explained the bellhop.

"Will I ever stop being shocked by what I find in my motherland?" a grumbling noise escaped impulsively from my lips.

"Excuse me, Miss?" the bellhop half-expected a tip, but did not get any. The poor man had no idea how much his comment depressed me, and he stood there surprised and disappointed.

Somewhere at the back of my mind were plans to get in touch with Stan and his wife. My brother was not "on the phone." Whether out of principle, or probably because he did not try hard enough, he was not granted the privilege of having a telephone in his house. He was not cut out to live in a "so-called" socialist country, where, for the most part, only those who live aggressively by their wits and are not afraid of being dishonest do well.

"What can I do to get in touch with him?" I asked a friendly concierge.

"Send a telegram," he suggested, handing me an appropriate form. Socialists love forms.

What ensued was a series of messages, discussions with the concierge, and more telegrams, until, finally, one day, I saw my brother marching across the elegant lobby in his shabby clothes, carrying an army haversack over his shoulder. He was obviously ill at ease in those surroundings, maybe even shy. Could he really be shy?

We took a taxi to his place. It was no longer a lone cottage in a little hole of a village. He and his wife had moved into her parents' tenement house on the outskirts of Warsaw. We sat and talked. Mary prepared a nice lunch and was overjoyed to see me.

Other than briefly during my first return trip to Poland, this would be the first occasion to have quiet time together. Six years ago, he spent some time with us in Canada, but there was no time to be alone together in the midst of sightseeing trips and visits with friends. Now, trying to talk seemed odd. Here, two birds from the same nest, we were now almost strangers--strangers burdened with embarrassing family considerations and taboos. Actually, some of these meetings were like opening old wounds.

My brother, a painter, proposed we should meet at the art gallery in the vicinity of the hotel and together revisit the old paintings we had religiously admired as young children. We both used to see those relics of our very own civilization during annual school visits.

Our vice-principal, a very distinguished, middle-aged spinster, accompanied our group during one such outing a couple of years before the war. In her elegant suit with the unavoidable remains of a fox hanging over her slim shoulders, she admired a huge painting by Matejko of the Battle of Grunwald. The painting was of gigantic proportions. A triumphant portrayal of one of the most glorious victories of the Poland and Lithuania Commonwealth over the Teutonic Knights, it showed a large section of the battlefield with life-sized figures of the Grand Master of the Teutonic Knights, the Polish king, and the Grand Duke of Lithuania, as well as the knights and their squires. It must have been well hidden during the German occupation, otherwise it would have promptly found its way to a big furnace.

The painting, in the heroic portrait style of a large number of works typically seen on the walls of the Louvre, is nothing short of impressive and worthy of sincere admiration, but its memory brings a smile to my face for a different reason--I always see the elegant, nearsighted little lady standing about a foot and the half away from the monster painting, inspecting its surface though her *lorgnon*!

The art gallery, Zacheta, though heavily damaged, survived the Uprising of 1944 and has been brought back to its former splendour. I enjoyed standing in front of it, waiting with anticipation for my brother to arrive on this sunny day. He did not come. There was probably another breakdown in communications. It would have been our last meeting. Three years later, I flew to Warsaw for his funeral.

Solidarity and Lech Walesa made it possible for Poland to try and become a European country again. Even though *Solidarnosc* and the breakup of the Soviet empire brought new hope, everyone knew that the real change would have to be realized by a long stretch of patient, hard work. Polish society was faced with the unenviable task of undergoing a painful metamorphosis. Its economy ruined by years of war, hostile Soviet interference, and the corruption of the communist government, now faced the rigours of a free market system. When the Canadian government initiated a program of aid for the countries freshly freed from Soviet oppression, Ted and I, both now retired, volunteered to help. For six weeks in 1991, Ted, offering his experience and expertise, worked with the management and staff of a factory in Inowroclaw. Ted also volunteered to work in India. Later, we returned to Poland to work together in a factory in Wolomin.

On that first trip, we arrived toward the end of August. Surrounded by suitcases, we were left to wilt away in the somewhat enlarged Warsaw Airport hall, the remains of energy inexorably seeping out from our bodies after a sleepless night on the plane. Incredulous that no one had yet shown up to meet us, we anxiously looked for some sign of welcome in the rapidly emptying arrival lounge.

"I'm going to look outside," decided Ted. As usual he could not sit still and wait for something to happen.

I agreed reluctantly. The prospect of sitting alone like an abandoned victim was not very appealing. Fortunately, apparently following local custom, nobody was showing any interest in me. People were obviously anxious to depart, and they did so in smaller and larger groups.

"Good for you to laugh," I thought, seeing them talking and disappearing behind the doors leading to the street.

Finally, when I was almost ready to start booking a passage back to Canada, Ted re-appeared, walking very fast.

"She is there," he announced rather ambiguously, and since he grabbed the two larger suitcases, it seemed logical that I should accompany him with the two smaller ones.

Out in the street, a medium-sized car was conspicuously standing in a No Parking zone. In addition to a large "No Parking" sign, there was a policeman engaged in a heated discussion with a youngish, attractive woman, most likely the driver of the car.

"But Officer--" As we approached wearily with our load, Ted and I came within earshot of the conversation. "Officer, I'm only stopping for a second to get these people, and I'm gone; how could I look for a place to park, when they are waiting for me inside." She was not ready to accept the ticket for illegally parking, and the policeman was somehow not quite ready to give it to her, although he was decidedly on the point of writing it.

"Lady," he protested, and he must have repeated the protest many times already because he had his little speech down pat, "You see this big sign--"

The situation did not alter much as Ted and I deposited our burden and stood by, resignedly listening to the refrain of the debate. And then, something happened. The two weary travellers were probably not astute enough to notice what was transpiring, but the lady smiled, and the policeman departed. It was heavenly to be suddenly noticed.

"I am the local representative, Barbara Numan." She turned to us, extending a manicured hand. It was mentioned during the rather meticulous briefing back in Canada that someone would be appointed to take care of us on arrival. The scene from a Fellini movie, just played out in front of us, was not part of the plan.

After we loaded the baggage and ourselves into the car, Barbara sped off at a fast pace--nobody in Warsaw drives slowly--then announced proudly that she had managed to out-talk the policeman, thus saving herself the expense of a ticket. If she expected to be congratulated on her success, she was sure to be disappointed, for we were too weary to take notice, and seeing no particular reason for rejoicing, took the easy way out by remaining silent.

For me, born and raised in Warsaw, the drive from the airport to downtown never fails to be fascinating and impressive--everything changes continuously. The Soviet-style grotesquely wide avenues are still there, however. It is sad to think that they will probably never disappear.

Barbara Numan informed us that a car would arrive tomorrow to take us to Inowroclaw. The medium-sized city, situated about 200 km northwest of Warsaw, used to be and still is a famous spa, with health-promoting springs, perennially attracting crowds of vacationers and cure seekers.

The next day, the drive from Warsaw during what was an unusually hot, for Poland, August day, was trying, to say the least. The car was driven by a professional chauffeur, Ben, who was dressed in what could be considered his summer uniform; he also sported a very impressive cap. He obviously knew his job well and cared for the vehicle over and above the call of duty--the car's white body was polished to an immaculate shine, and all the chromium accessories were gleaming. Nevertheless, no amount of devoted care can erase the ravages of time.

Like an elderly human, the poor car was feeling its age--its clutch would connect only under the skilful foot of Ben, and, as Ted found out later, only occasionally when someone else was in the driver's seat. It was able to steadily chug along but only at a speed that would allow arrival at our destination in just over seven hours. Needless to say, there was no air conditioning, so all the windows were rolled down as far as possible, and the wind, as well as occasionally dust, played havoc with the passengers' hair and blocked their throats and ears. We sat in almost hostile silence, steeling ourselves with a resolve to persevere in this arduous journey, no matter what.

The manager of the factory, a gracious lady almost too old-fashioned for her age, introduced a little cheer as she announced her intention to treat us to lunch.

"Will you stop at the Mazowsze Inn, please, Ben," she turned to the chauffeur. She was sitting beside him, so the guests could occupy the back seats, which were supposedly more comfortable.

"Yes, Ma'am," he answered. They were both refreshingly gentle, bringing an aura of bourgeois politeness into this post-communist country.

Fortified by tasty pork chops and sauerkraut--very Polish--and a shot of strong vodka, we continued on our way. Grateful for a chance to remove myself for a while from the sticky car seat and to cool off, I felt a little more inclined to show interest in the countryside, towns, and villages we were obliged to pass once we left the four-lane highway that had ended abruptly a few kilometres north of Warsaw.

We were travelling slowly enough to look at the faces of people standing at bus stops, or selling and buying apples and other fruit at the roadside, or simply walking. Accustomed now to seeing hardly any people while driving on highways in Canada, Ted and I welcomed the opportunity to participate in the lives of those strangers, albeit only for fleeting moments. The young kids looked no different than kids anywhere. But the women, especially older women, were dressed much more conservatively. I was silently saying good-bye to shorts and other less dignified garments--I would have to act my age! Even a ninety-degree temperature is no excuse for a middle-aged woman to prance around showing leg above the knees.

"The trouble is," I was saying to Ted when we were alone in our apartment unpacking, "there are so many people everywhere in Europe, you never have a chance to go unobserved."

The apartment made available for us to rent in US dollars was an exact copy of millions of such apartments built all over the country after the war.

Even the furniture had to be of certain dimensions and style to fit into the available space. The result was perfectly compatible with the socialist philosophy: suppress individuality, give everyone exactly the same, so as hopefully to eliminate envy (read: ambition) and initiative (not to mention good taste).

Visiting different apartments was invariably seeing the same place; only the people changed. Some lucky inhabitants had one more room or an extra square metre or two added to the total area of their dwelling. The visitors found some of the local customs baffling, but nothing more so than the habit of describing apartments in terms of surface area only. The conversation would go something like this:

"Did you know Alex got his new apartment?"

"Oh, yes? How is it?"

The answer would be: four or five or whatever square metres, and that was totally mystifying to Ted and me. This lone fact would apparently give the inquirer sufficient information about the apartment.

There was always a small entrance hall, a rather elongated living room with one large window on the narrow wall, and another, smaller, room serving an infinite variety of purposes, depending on the number and circumstances of the occupants. The minuscule kitchen and an even smaller bathroom were both masterpieces of efficient utilization of space. Not that it had anything to do with personal comfort.

Everything was there, but accessibility or appropriate size was not considered very important in the general design for living according to Marx and Lenin.

Consequently, some of the fixtures in the bathroom, such as the toilet seat, might present a major challenge for many people. Indeed, gaining access to this apparatus for personal use seemed to require careful manoeuvring between a small water heater in front and an also small, but hefty, out of proportion to its efficiency, washing machine on the side.

"Maybe that's why the Socialist Republic always seemed to encourage food shortages," continued Ted.

"They didn't want people to be terribly comfortable."

"That's for sure," agreed Ted. "Remember China, where the guide in Suzhou proudly showed us the apartment blocks, and informed us that elevators are never installed in apartment blocks which have fewer than seven floors."

"That's why we have never seen any fat Chinese."

However humble, we felt good about the place where we could finally relax.

"Well, I am very tired," said Ted, when we were just about ready for bed.

"You know," he continued, "I just realized that there's no bedroom! There are no bedrooms in socialist apartments."

"When in Rome . . ." Though aching to lie down and sleep, we had to go through the same motions millions of families happening to live in such apartments have to perform before lying down for the night.

We manipulated the sofa in the living room until it disclosed its interior. Unfortunately, the bed was, considering our age and the fact that it was slightly over forty years after our honeymoon, only big enough for one person.

Another sofa in the smaller room turned out to be a hide-a-bed arrangement as well--just the spot for tired Ted. The single bed was firmly ensconced between the wall and an imposing mahogany wardrobe with full-length mirror. Ted could make himself perfectly comfortable without any fear of falling off. Indeed, the bed could be entered or exited only by taking one short step directly from the door.

"I feel very cosy here!" he shouted and was soon sound asleep.

I went to bed but sleep would not come. The ghosts of the past were clamouring in my head. Every time I had come to this country full of people, and, more amazingly, small children, bubbling away in perfect Polish, a persistent feeling of malaise had conspired to spoil the joy of being received by welcoming relatives and friends. If they thought about being victimized by "outrageous fortune," as they surely did, nobody said who was to blame. Most people in Poland after sixty years of oppression were still afraid to voice their opinions openly.

Political discussions in an intimate circle of relatives were often interrupted by the host's going to the door or window to see if someone outside could be listening. Not that everyone blamed the Soviets only.

I remember, back in the POW camp, one musically gifted girl played a mouth organ, rescued from burning Warsaw, and we sang at the top of our voices to the whiny tune of "Swanee River":

> ". . . England will sell you for dollars,
>
> They'll decide your lot in Quebec;
>
> The dollar rules the world
>
> Your sacrifice and valour mean nothing . . ."

TWENTY
Closure

The cherished, precious memories have been recorded clearly by my eyes and ears but those overcharged with negative emotions bring confusion, as though they are trying to hide.

We arrive at our apartment in the vicinity of Orlando. The American drive and energy is reflected in the year-to-year changes taking place around this city. New high-rise apartment buildings are arranged in masterpieces of landscaping, enveloped in lush palms and exotic shrubs. Last year's sandy field, overgrown by wild, weedy bushes, is transformed into a network of boulevards and lustily flourishing exotic, tropical vegetation.

The apartment is spacious and furnished tastefully with bamboo-framed, colourfully upholstered easy chairs and couches. The vast windows are overhung with transparent drapes to keep out any excess of the most desirable local commodity and the power driving the whole enterprise of the peninsula--the sunshine.

The following week, Ted summarizes our plans to drive through the Everglades: "Tomorrow morning we'll be going to the other side of the peninsula."

"And we'll visit the L.'s," I insist over Ted's waning protest against driving as far as that.

"Okay, okay." The discussion ends on an indefinite note, but I am hopeful.

The drive through the Everglades appeals to avid nature lovers, especially alligator lovers. You cannot exactly feast your eyes on the scenery. I lost interest after half an hour.

The landscape is a blur of nondescript vegetation with the underlying marsh occasionally forming pools of water. A large variety of water birds that make their home here is advertised, but on this particular day they are not willing to present themselves for inspection.

"Look, alligators!" Ted is much more observant than I.

"Where? Where?" There is a small clearing off the road and a few cars are already parked there.

My eyes follow Ted's finger eagerly, but see nothing.

"Let's stop for a minute," Ted says obligingly.

We gingerly step closer to the clearing, where time seems to stand still with the people, apparently Indians, sitting motionless; the humid air is barely moving at all. Prompted by quiet instructions from Ted, I finally see an alligator, or, rather, two bulging eyes stuck on a small fragment of head just visible above water. There is no movement from either men or beast, as if they respected each other's peace in some mysterious communion of spirits.

"I don't think it will move during the next several hours," Ted whispers in my ear after a while. "Let's go."

The L.'s place is not as far as we anticipated. Again, impressive landscaping, huge windows, and a patio embellish the exterior of the one-storey residence with its colourful upholstery inside and out. Barbara L. brings out drinks and snacks.

Everything is in green, pink and orange. The patio furniture comes to life with people reclining on deliciously comfortable chairs; the table blossoms with different shades of drinks, salads, and other goodies.

Guests are arriving, as slamming car doors are heard from the back of the house. Hearty greetings and laughter grow in volume as the newly arrived approach the patio with their hosts. And then, the voice, the lusty, low voice, stops me in the middle of a word.

"Could it be Anna? It cannot be Anna, again," I feel I am getting emotional.

It has been some time since our meeting in the cemetery in Warsaw, but not that long. She could still be around. If I went to look now, I would recognize her husband--short and balding. I stray to the side of the garden away from the others.

But Barbara spots me first.

"Oh, Irena, do you remember . . ."

I am looking and trying not to see the smiling short, balding man, and next to him . . .

"Irena, how are you? Long time no see." The cooing voice is hers but it is not Anna.

I am looking at a woman of about my age, slightly overweight. She has a charming smile, and sparkling eyes behind a pair of glasses. I cannot place her at all. It might be one of my classmates I have not had a chance to see for well over fifty years.

"Have I aged so much during the past few years?" she says and continues her indulgent smile. "You don't recognize me, right?"

I protest that it is I who have aged so much that my memory is failing. Funny how that voice could affect me, even though issued from a different person's throat.

"But where did we see each other a few years ago?" I am racking my brains for an answer, until Barbara takes pity on me.

"It's Tamara, Silly!" They all laugh.

"Yes, of course!" I try to salvage my reputation as a person of normal intelligence. "Of course, we met at--"

"In Warsaw, at the fiftieth anniversary of the Warsaw Uprising at the military cemetery, remember?" It all comes back to me now. Walking in the cemetery, the woman with a lusty voice, her face partly obscured by a large hat . . .

Tamara continues to show her charming, nice lady smile. Her voice no longer upsets me.

* * *

"It was nice to see the L.'s again," I began, on our way back to Orlando. There is no point in telling him about my confusion on seeing Tamara Leniak. She remains just the same--self-possessed, articulate. She said she still plays the piano, but only the easier pieces.

The drive back is not very interesting. We are returning by a different, efficiently dull, superhighway. Not until the next day after supper is the time ripe for reminiscing.

"You know," I begin slowly, "I had a really funny experience; I mean Tamara--I thought she was someone else."

"Who?"

"Anna. I thought I had met her in Warsaw in 1994, and she really gave me a start then."

Ted does not understand.

"Well, to tell you the truth, I am not sure she is still alive! She is one of my 'ghosts from the past.'"

Ted laughs at stories with "ghostly" elements; he suspects that generally, people who claim to have had such experiences are abusing alcohol. But since he is willing to listen quietly, I explain that the story has its origin in the tragic past.

"The very last time I was home during the Uprising," I continue, gathering my thoughts as I go along, "I went to get my mother out of our apartment. Heavy fighting was going on around the power station."

"Wait," Ted suddenly interrupts me, "I think you told me this story once before."

"Listen, there is more . . .

"When I found Mother in the cellar, she was not alone; the person beside my mother was not a ghost, as I would be willing to accept--no, it was Anna, of all people! She was sitting close to Mother, the two obviously finding solace in shared misery. I could hardly speak, not that there was anything much to say. I embraced my mother.

"'Mama, I've come to take you with me, so we can be together.' I must have said something to that effect.

"Anna remained silent, only her eyes shone feverishly in the semi-darkness of the crowded, stuffy cellar. It was hard to think clearly, but to justify to myself what I was about to do, I called to mind all the reasons why I ought not to feel sorry for Anna . . . It cost a lot of effort to maintain a determined frame of mind, explaining that I had permission to bring only one person with me. Anna still said nothing, when, with explosions outside getting closer, Mother and I departed hurriedly, leaving her in that dark cellar."

* * *

Some time after the incident at L.'s, I found out that Anna had died in 1979. I wonder if someone played Schubert's *Serenade* for her.

* * *

Evenings after dinner, when we are alone at home, Ted and I watch the news on TV and read the papers.

Announcements about some individual or group taking action in the pursuit of justice are frequently to be seen in the press or on TV. Smokers sue the tobacco companies; Holocaust survivors sue the Swiss banks; First Nations sue the government; and most recently, the African Americans propose to sue the descendants of slave owners in the States.

It is only fair that people want to be compensated for their losses.

Reading a story about yet another newly proposed court action, I am reminded of the millions of people who looked for justice in 1945. They seldom found it. Life for those liberated from wartime oppression did not bring easy solutions to their problems or generous compensation for their losses. Answers to the questions, "What to do now?" and "Where to do it?" were stifled by inactivity and indefinite waiting. The first glow of the excitement of being free faded away, and useful energy was wasted in the futility of merely existing in the camps.

The liberated had to be satisfied with charity--the food rations, the ridiculous quasi-army clothes. Uncertain thoughts of the future were drawing a blank. A vast majority never received any compensation.

"What about us?" I ask half seriously, putting down a newspaper. "Shall we sue?"

"We don't have a good lawyer," says Ted with a smile.

1994: Polish-Canadian veterans of the Warsaw Uprising celebrating the fiftieth anniversary of the event with the minister of defence; Irena is standing to the left of the minister.

Epilogue

I wake up in total darkness. It must be very late or very early. It takes a few seconds to realize I am at home in bed. I have been dreaming about crowds of people watching a spectacle, illuminated by artificial explosions, and a clever imitation of fire erupting from the windows of the seventeen-storey Prudential Building, the only "skyscraper" in pre-war Warsaw; the building that has become the symbol of the fight for freedom through the endless decades of oppression.

My dream is yet another remembrance of mine in this year of 2004 --the Sixtieth Anniversary of the Warsaw Uprising. My daughter Marta and I spent ten days in Warsaw, remembering and paying homage to the quarter of a million people, civilians and insurgent fighters, who perished during the battle in 1944. It was good to visit with friends once again, who, like me, survived against minuscule odds. The once pretty young girls are now well past the age of maturity; some are walking with canes. Their hair is mostly grey and their faces wrinkled. Some I found downright irritating: perhaps due to their senile narrow vision of the world, or perhaps due to my senile reduced tolerance!

But our old veteran egos expanded, joyfully feeding on the festive outpourings of praise, uplifted by the carefree melodies of the old Resistance songs and the glorifying sounds of classical music. We accepted the usual Polish pathos as appropriate for the occasion, and tolerated the laudatory speeches generously sprinkled with clichés coming out of the mouths of foreign politicians--Germany's Schroeder, British Deputy Prime Minister Prescott, and Colin Powell from the United States.

Sincere or false, the foreign dignitaries have been finally obliged to pay attention to what has been happening in Warsaw, Poland. They neglected us badly in those crucial days in 1944, when, our weapons silenced by lack of ammunition, we were forced to capitulate.

Now, the triumphant fanfares, the beautiful flowers all over the city, and the crowds of people overflow the venues of festivities. People march down the streets in a jubilant parade of pride and emotion; the sight of the Girl Guides and the Boy Scouts participating and helping out the veterans during the celebrations fills us with new hope and joy. All this comes after sixty years. Why so late? Finally, after six decades, the question, "Was it necessary?" is no longer asked.

Truly a colossal price was paid, in the young lives of the insurgents and the lives of civilians; yet the tragedy did not happen in vain. It is now being recognized as a source of strength for the society under Soviet domination, as well as an inspiration for the new generations of free Poles. In the year 2004, the smiling faces of people proclaim the excitement of a happy and promising future.

While the support and friendship promised by Poland's neighbours and allies should be highly valued in diplomatic circles, the necessity of working for self-reliance hopefully will not be forgotten in the fervour of the new European scenario. Besides, like the Americans, the Poles also have a hymn that calls on God's blessing for their country. That, too, should not be forgotten.

About the Author

Irena Szpak was born in Warsaw, Poland. She spent eleven years attending the same private school for girls-- the final five years under very difficult wartime conditions. As one of the gifted students, Irena received supplementary instruction in foreign languages and math.

Irena joined the clandestine Girl Guides in 1942. After the fall of the Warsaw Uprising in 1944, she spent the rest of the war in German POW camps. In 1945, she completed her secondary education in a specially organized school in Germany.

The following year, Irena passed a competitive exam and obtained a scholarship to study at the London University in England. She married her high school sweetheart, and in time had three children. She gave her education a break to look after their children, while her husband worked full time on his engineering degree. She obtained her BA degree as an external student at the University of London (England) a few years after the family settled in Ontario, Canada.

With credits in maths, physics, and foreign languages, Irena worked for eighteen years as a technical translator in Alcan Labs in Kingston, translating documents from German, French, Russian, Japanese, and, of course, Polish. She represented her company at International Federation of Translators (FIT) congresses at different times in Vienna, Warsaw, and, finally, in New York, where she presented a paper on "Scientific and Technical Translation." After early retirement, Irena and her husband participated in the early nineties in the program (CESO) designed to help, among others, India, as well as the nations freed from Soviet domination. They spent the longest periods of time in Poland helping selected factories to adjust their operations to a market economy.

The then President of Poland, Lech Walesa, awarded Irena the Medal of Resistance and the Warsaw Uprising Cross. Irena resides with her husband in Kingston where she keeps busy with various projects and, never one to avoid a challenge, she still plays tennis and takes piano lessons.

To order more copies of

TRAINS:

A Journey
of Remembrances

by Irena M. Szpak

Contact:
**GENERAL STORE
PUBLISHING HOUSE**
499 O'Brien Road, Box 415
Renfrew, Ontario Canada K7V 4A6
Telephone: 1-800-465-6072
Fax: (613) 432-7184
www.gsph.com

VISA and MASTERCARD accepted.